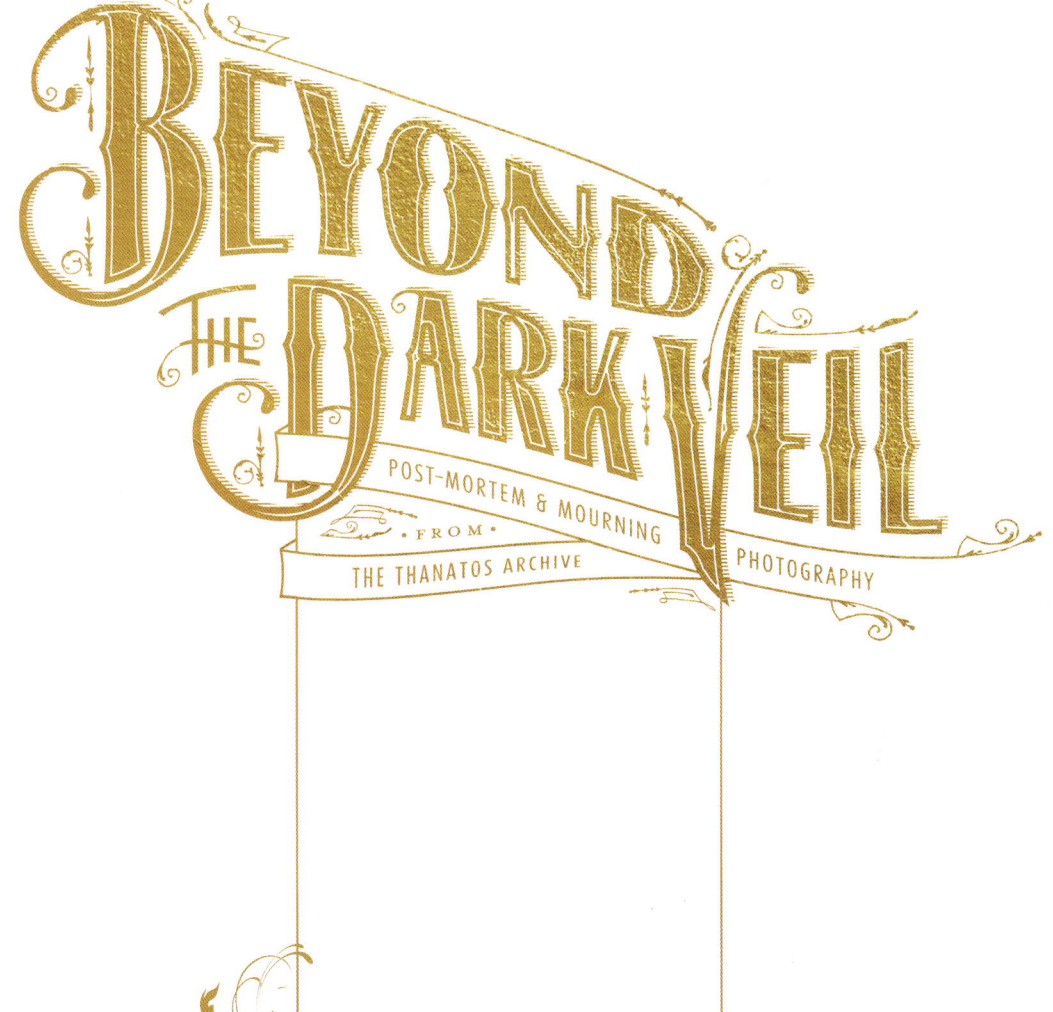

BEYOND THE DARK VEIL

POST-MORTEM & MOURNING PHOTOGRAPHY

FROM

THE THANATOS ARCHIVE

· PUBLISHED BY ·

GRAND CENTRAL PRESS & LAST GASP

PUBLISHED IN CONJUNCTION WITH THE EXHIBITION

BEYOND THE DARK VEIL:

POST-MORTEM & MOURNING PHOTOGRAPHY
FROM THE THANATOS ARCHIVE
November 2 – Decemeber 12, 2013

PUBLISHED BY

CALIFORNIA STATE UNIVERISTY, FULLERTON
NICHOLAS & LEE BEGOVICH GALLERY,
GRAND CENTRAL PRESS, AND LAST GASP
Tenth U.S. Edition 2025,

NICHOLAS & LEE BEGOVICH GALLERY
CALIFORNIA STATE UNIVERSITY, FULLERTON
800 North State College Blvd.
Fullerton, California 92831

LAST GASP
777 Florida Street
San Francisco California 94110

PRINTED BY
PROLONG PRESS LTD, CHINA

ISBN: 978-0-86719-796-9

BEYOND

THE

DARK VEIL

POST-MORTEM & MOURNING PHOTOGRAPHY
FROM THE THANATOS ARCHIVE

PLATES

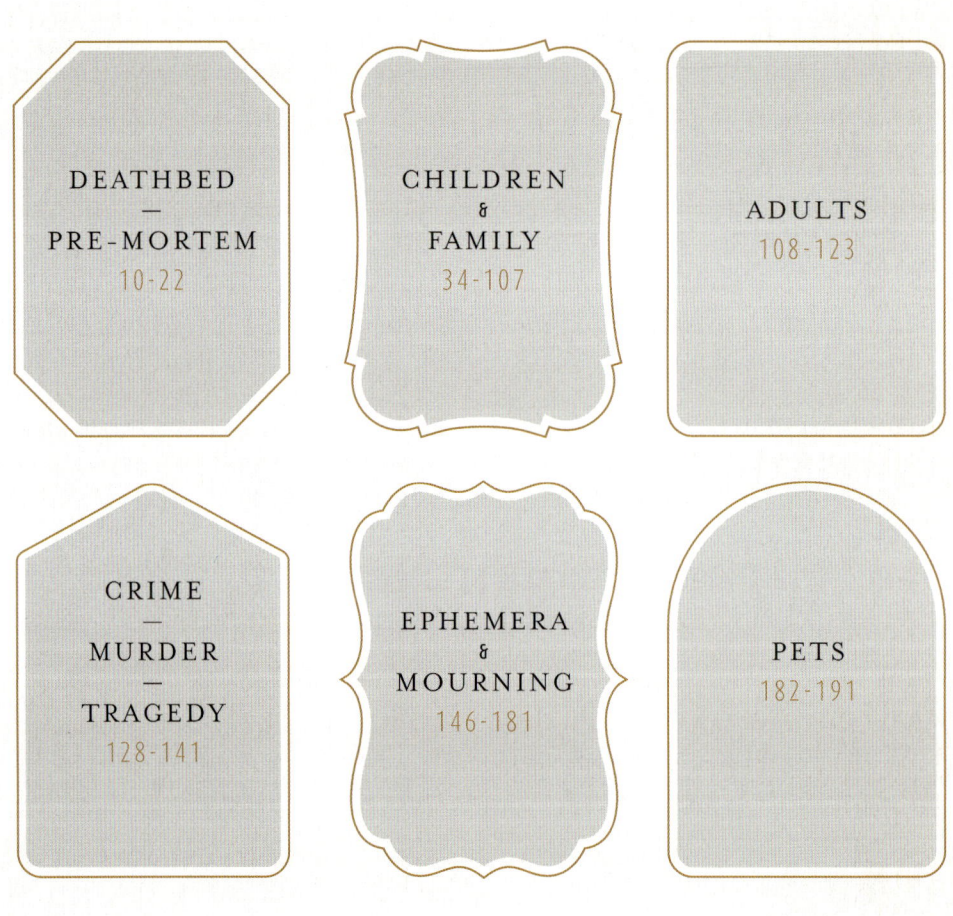

TABLE *of* CONTENTS

REMEMBERING DEATH

MARION PECK

Perhaps our first reaction to these pictures is one of shock. We are startled by the strange practice the people of the 1800s had of photographing their deceased loved ones. Today, though post-mortem photography still exists, it is not a common thing to do.

When we look a little longer and deeper, we begin to feel the heartbreaking poignancy of these images. Looking into the eyes of a grieving mother, or seeing on the face of a child the ravages of the disease it suffered from, our hearts begin to ache. We feel the terrible presence of death, but not in the way we are used to. There is an intimacy, a loving quality in these photographs that we do not associate with images of death, and so they look "shocking" to us.

The Victorians knew death much more deeply and intimately than we do now. Death was present, a reality, not the abstraction it is to us today. Rather than shutting it away, people of that period acknowledged their relationship to death

with beauty. They honored their love for the deceased through painting, sculpture, jewelry, clothing, and photography.

In contrast, when death comes close to us in the modern world, we don't really know how to act. Somebody dies, and the body is whisked away as quickly as possible. Grieving is awkward. Mostly people really don't know what to say or do. It's just hoped that we can "get back to normal" as soon as possible. Instead of funerals, we have "celebrations of life." We all just want to think positively, be healthy, get to work, do something productive. Modern capitalist society expects manic optimism from us. Death becomes an indignity, an embarrassment to be ignored as much as possible, almost an obscenity. Each of us must deal with it silently, privately, because speaking about our loss is not really acceptable.

Yet images of death surround us. It is presented to us mainly in the cold, dispassionate light of the news media, where it is blandly reported over and over again, the repetition only causing it to become more distant and unreal. Occasionally, some extraordinarily awful news story will break through our shell, and for a moment or two we will be flooded by scorching waves of compassion or sickening moments of terror, but we put those feelings away as quickly as we can, and get on with our busy day.

Though the natural emotions associated with death are repressed, images of death emerge in our culture with ever increasing strength, frequency, and ferocity, repeating endlessly and ever more graphically in television shows, video games, and the movies. Our horror movies need always to be more appalling, our video games more violent, our Halloween decorations (which have exploded in popularity) more disgustingly grotesque, to penetrate the numbness of our denial.

Perhaps the price we pay for our casual dismissal of death is the feeling of emptiness and meaninglessness that permeates our lives, a sense of malaise or depression. Our ideas about death are, by necessity, interwoven with our ideas and feelings about the significance and meaning of our lives and our place in the cosmos. When we ignore and deny death, we become hollow, less alive. Acknowledging and honoring death makes us slow down; it makes us reflect and deepen. It shuts up the chatter we cram into our heads to escape the silence. And maybe what we need more than anything else is some silence, some stillness, some deepening.

In a sense, these photographs are like ghosts. They are the shadows of people who once lived actively and breathed in a present moment, who saw the blue sky above their heads and might have felt the same passions, joys, and sorrows in their hearts that we feel in our own. If we can quiet ourselves enough to spend some time with these ghosts, contemplating, listening to them, we may learn from their great wisdom. It is the wisdom of the ancestors, of those who came before. What we are, so once were they. What they are, so we shall be.

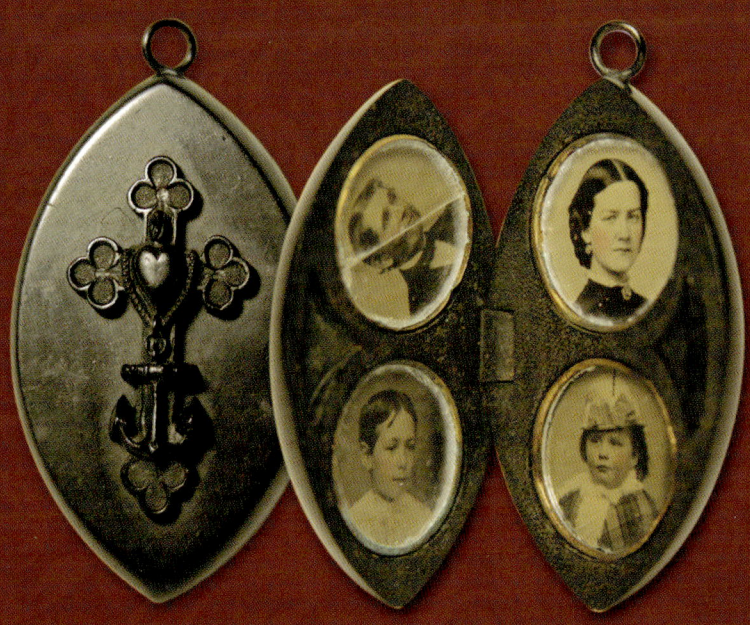

Memorial Pendant   circa 1870 • vulcanite/tintype • 2" x 1.25"

A small vulcanite pendant with four miniature tintypes inside.
The cross, anchor and heart on this piece represent faith, hope and charity.
These symbols were found frequently in nineteenth-century cemetery art, funeral flowers, and mourning jewelry.

MEMORY KEEPERS:

Photography as a Form of Remembrance

Louis Daguerre's introduction of the daguerreotype and photographic process in 1839 must have seemed nothing short of miraculous to the early Victorians. Photographs were small wonders to cherish, display, reflect upon, and remember by. They were, in a way, memory keepers.

The tradition of memorial portraiture existed long before the invention of the daguerreotype. Painted portraits and, in particular, deathbed scenes were expensive—luxury items commissioned by the wealthy. In the 1850s and 1860s, as photography studios became more widespread, and newer, less costly formats were introduced, the number of photographs being produced grew exponentially; the 1860s and 70s represented the height of the post-mortem photography genre.

As these photographs show, death was not hidden away, but prepared for, both mentally and spiritually, and celebrated through religious ceremony, mourning rituals, elaborate floral funeral displays and through the funerals themselves. They served as a vital part of a healthy grieving process, providing a tangible way to keep the memory of a departed loved one alive and close at hand in times of need, displayed in parlors and in family photo albums, side by side with photos of the living.

Beyond the Dark Veil features more than 180 photographs and related ephemera, carefully selected from the collection of The Thanatos Archive, documenting the practice of nineteenth-century post-mortem and memorial photography and related aspects of mourning customs.

The photographs are not presented as morbid curiosities but as objects with stories to tell; images of people in death that are possibly the only remaining testament to their lives and moments in time, now long past. They give us a rare glimpse into a bygone era. While a few of the people in these photographs are identified, most of them will remain nameless to us forever, the details of their lives and deaths something we can only speculate upon through clues revealed in these lasting images of them. Memories of the lost live on through their likenesses, the sum of their lives encompassed and encapsulated on metal, glass, and paper—captured shadows continuing to tell the story of their fleeting substance to all who are willing to listen.

JACQUELINE ANN BUNGE, Exhibition Curator
JACK MORD, Owner and Operator, The Thanatos Archive

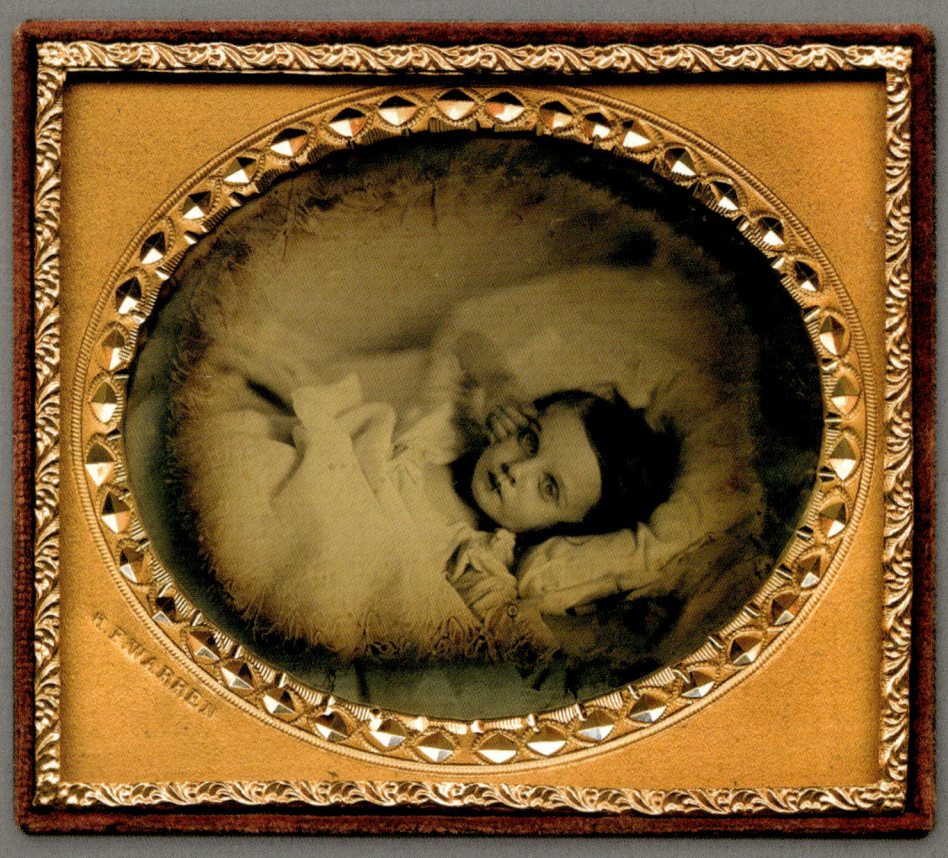

Waiting for Death   circa 1856 • sixth-plate daguerreotype • 3.75″ x 3.25″

Portrait of a dying child, photographed in Waltham, Massachusetts, by Henry F. Warren.

DEATHBED

—

PRE-MORTEM

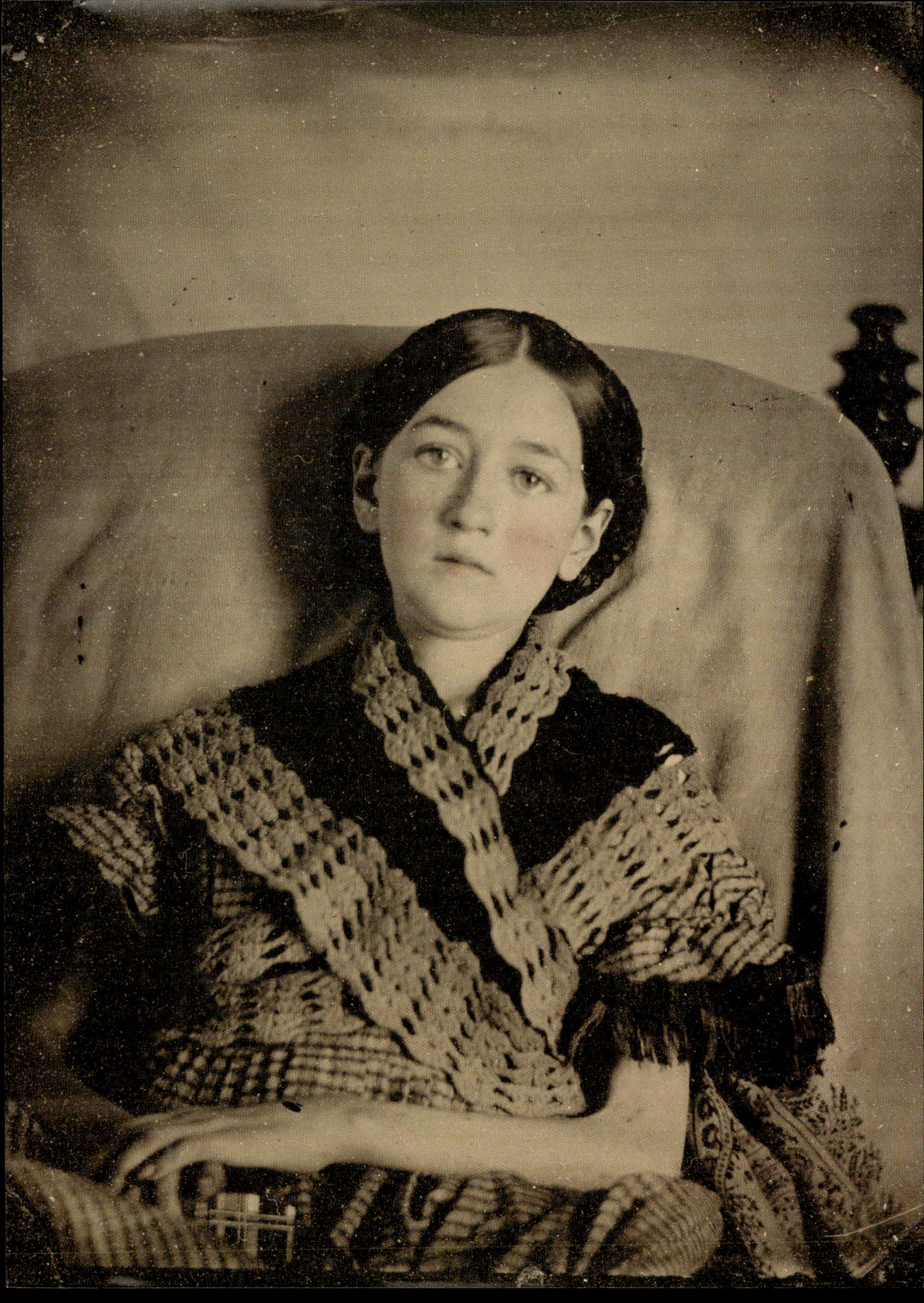

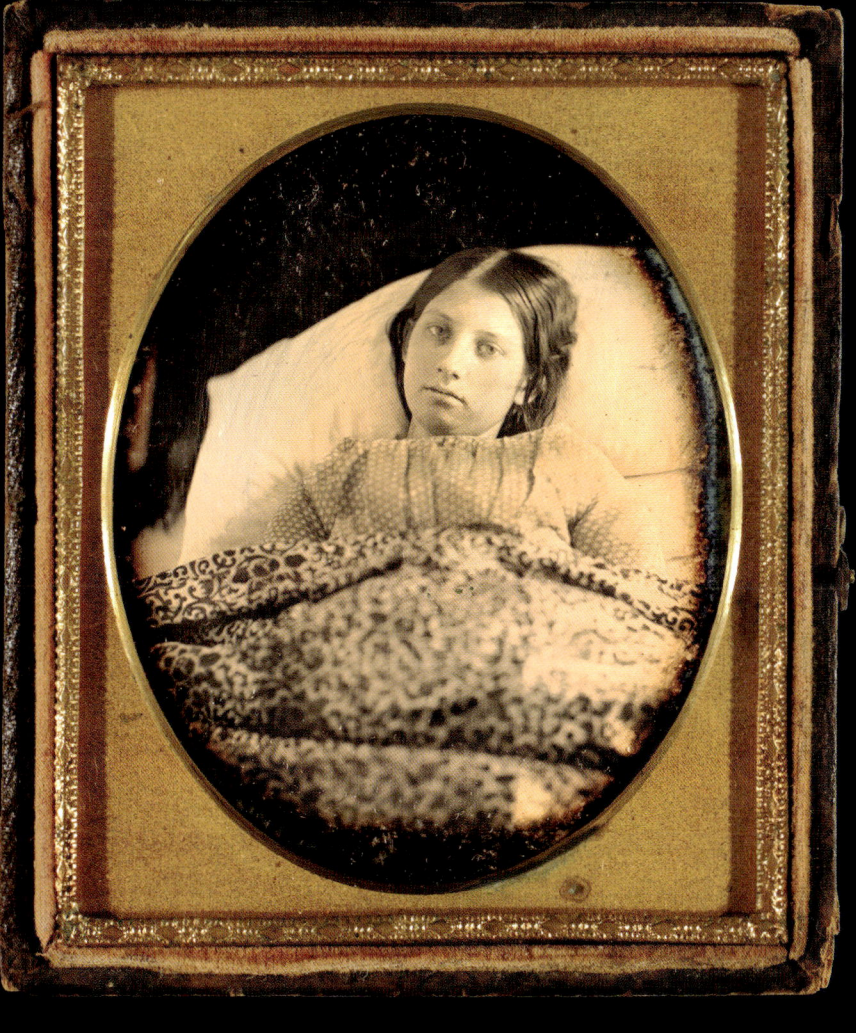

Girl in Shawl circa 1860 • sixth-plate ambrotype • 3.75" x 3.25"

A very frail little girl poses for the camera. Her arms are extremely thin,
likely the effects of a wasting disease, such as tuberculosis, for which there was no vaccination at the time.

- - - - - - - - - - - - - - - -

Young Girl on Deathbed circa 1850 • sixth-plate daguerreotype • 3.75" x 3.25"

A portrait of a dying girl. She stares back at the camera,
her face seeming to show a tired resignation and an acceptance of her fate.

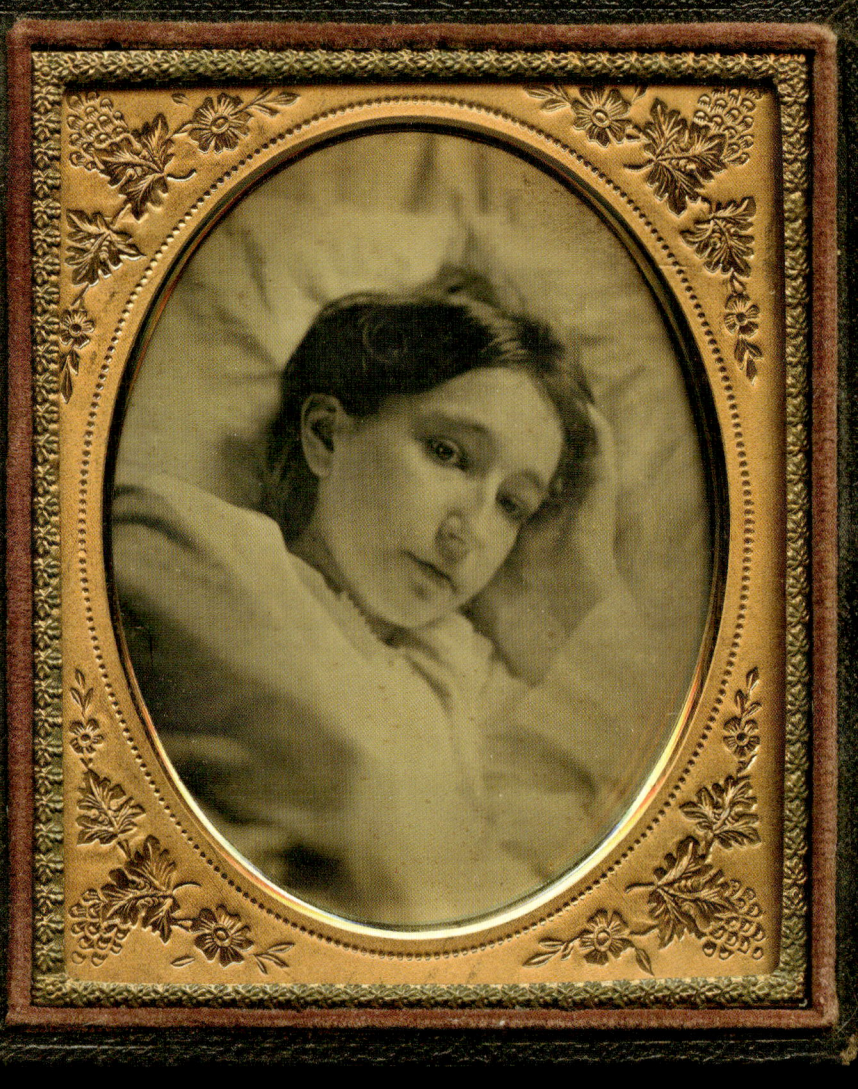

Waiting   circa 1855 • sixth-plate daguerreotype • 3.75" x 3.25"

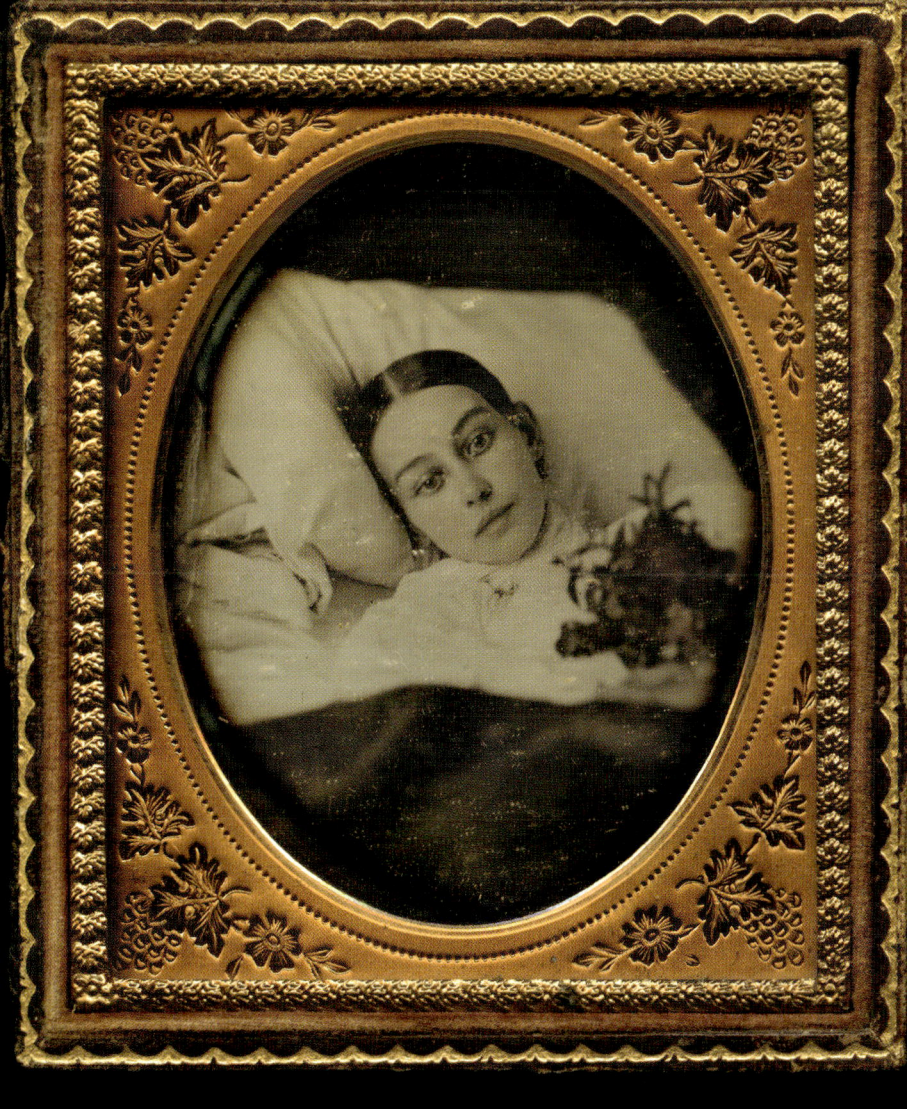

Beautiful Girl on Deathbed circa 1855 • sixth-plate daguerreotype • 3.75" x 3.25"

A beautiful young girl on her deathbed. Although her eyes are open and appear to be looking at the camera,
the flowers indicate that she was most likely deceased when this portrait was taken.

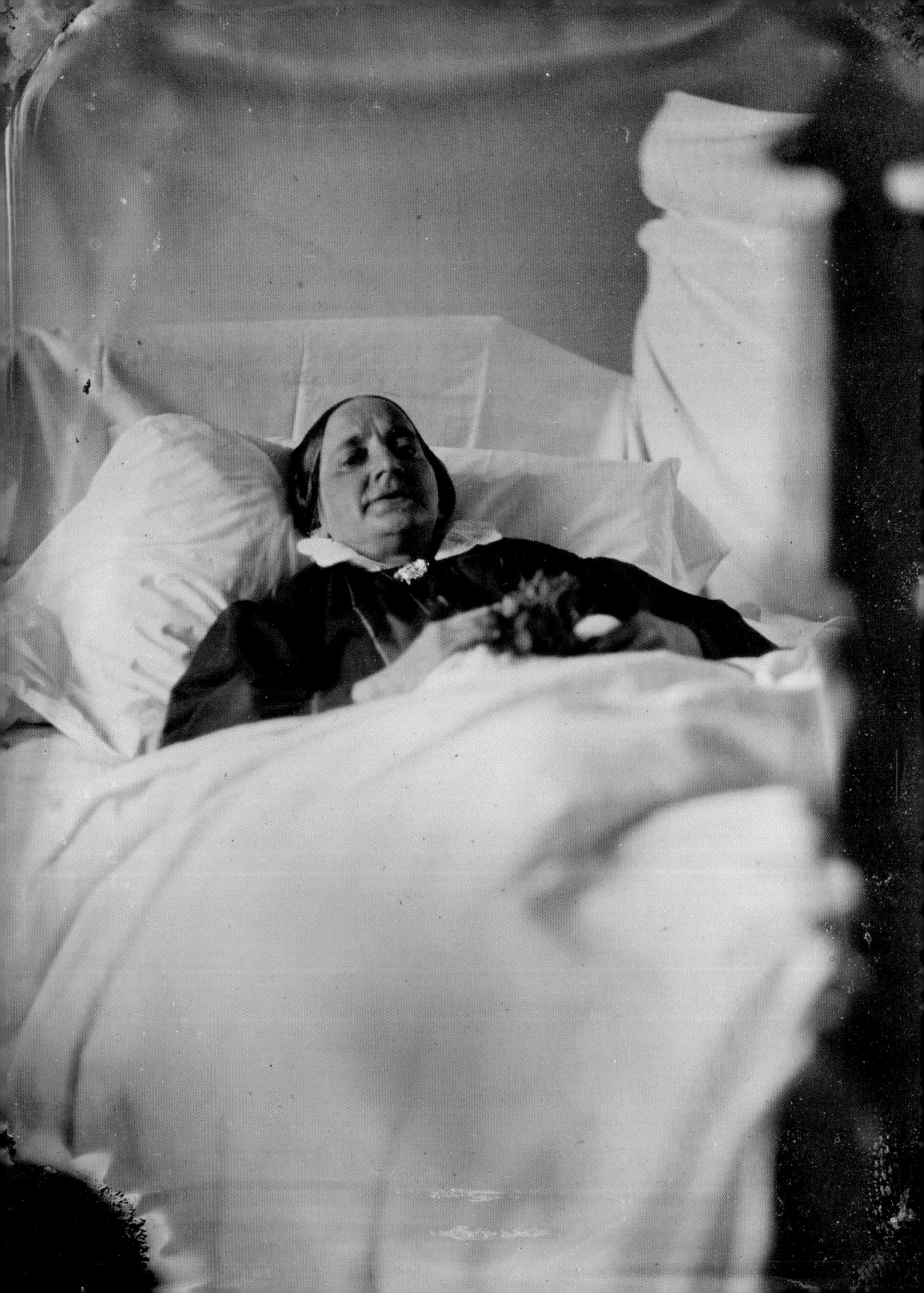

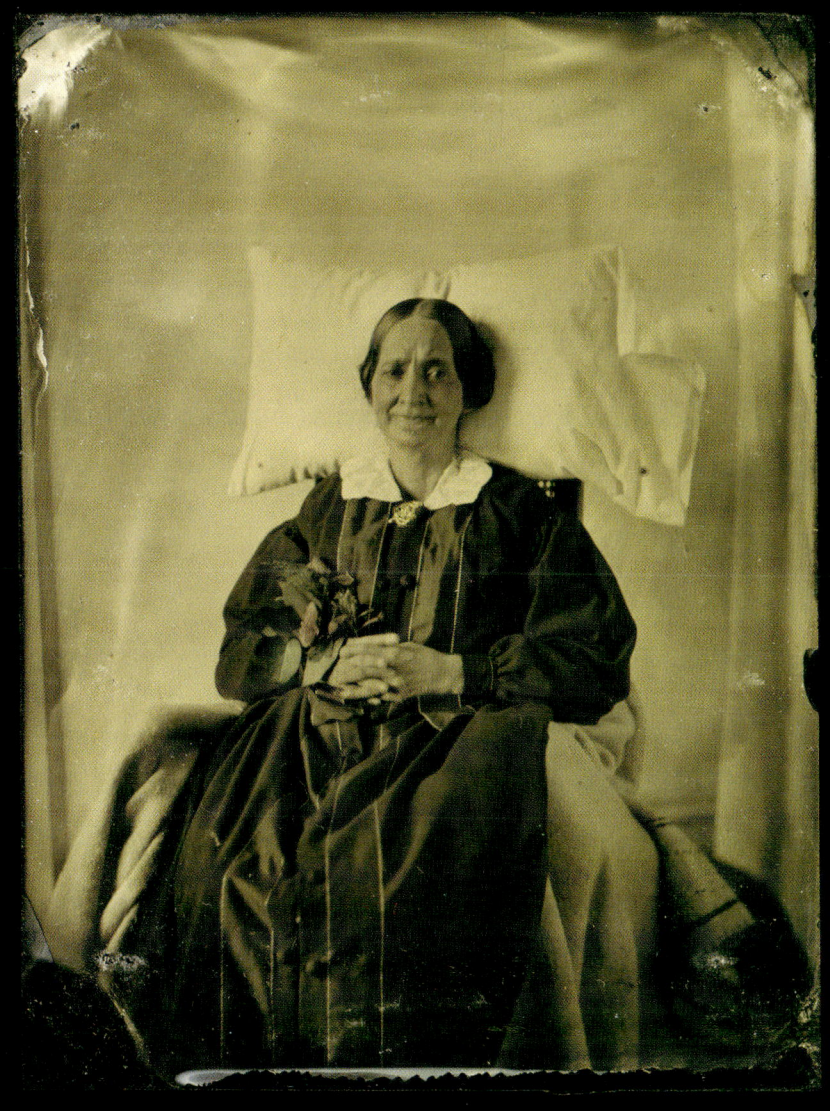

A Brave Face circa 1860 • quarter-plate ambrotypes • 4.75" x 3.75" each

A dying woman, pain evident on her face, is photographed in bed; finding the strength to sit for a final photo.

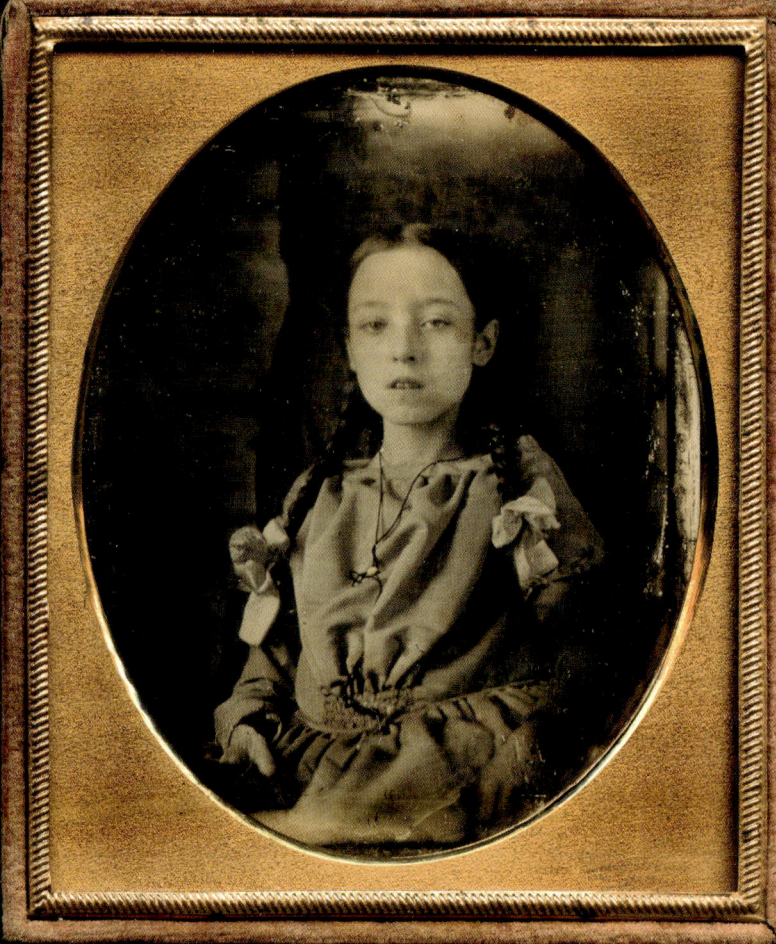

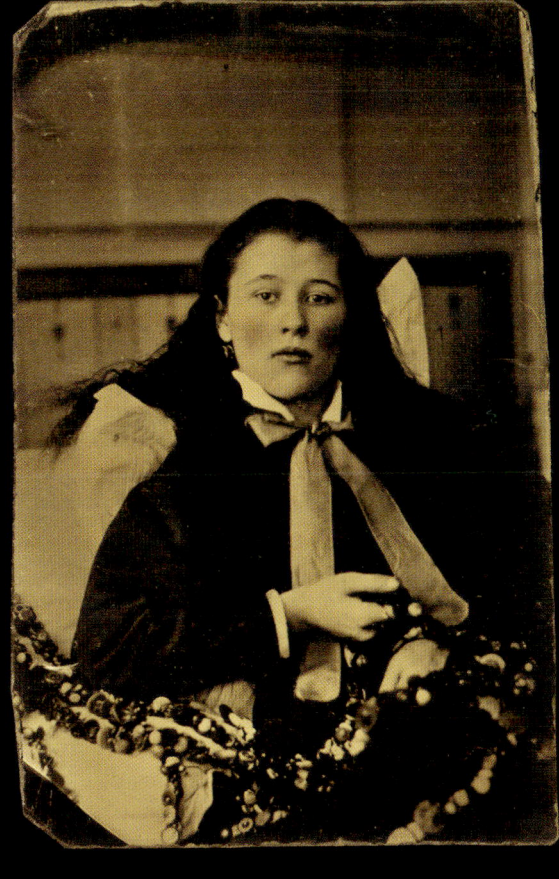

TTON, BUTTON. HO'S GOT THE BUTTON?

R FALLS, IOWA. November 22.
notice that the "charm string"
nia is raging with the great violence
of Iowa just now. How this button
bout we can't imagine, but for some
our merchants, clerks, young men,
and all, old and young, have been
by these sprightly, bright eyed
minines, with "please give me a
r my charm string?" until these
des, like spare change, have gone
n we can say Jack Robinson.
as been a good locality for 'charm
e rather "reckon," judging from the
anner in which bachelor buttons
thrown aside of late. When this
nia will end we are in a quandary to
predict that with these little
busy bodies, the real "charm string"
t yet arrived.

The Charm String   circa 1868 • tintype • 4" x 2.5"

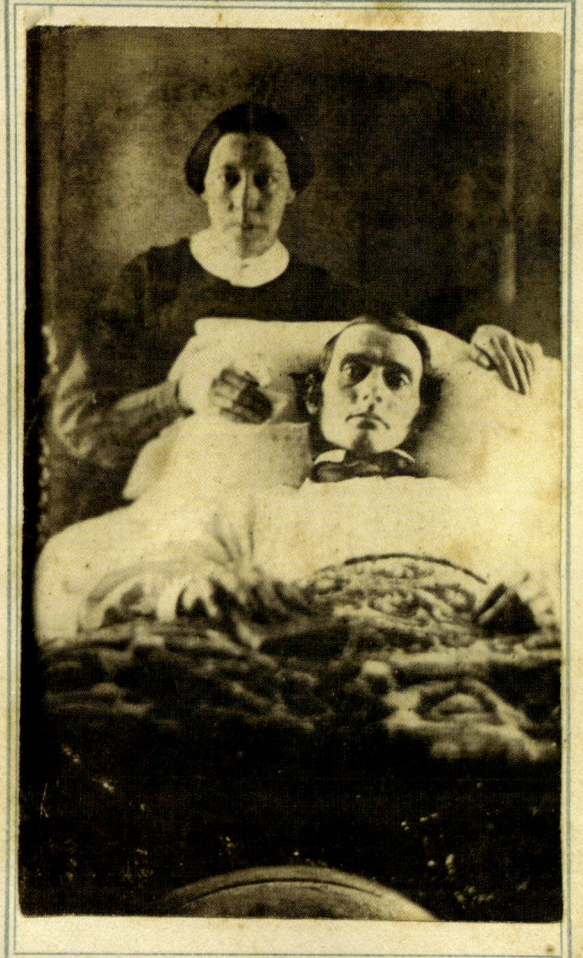

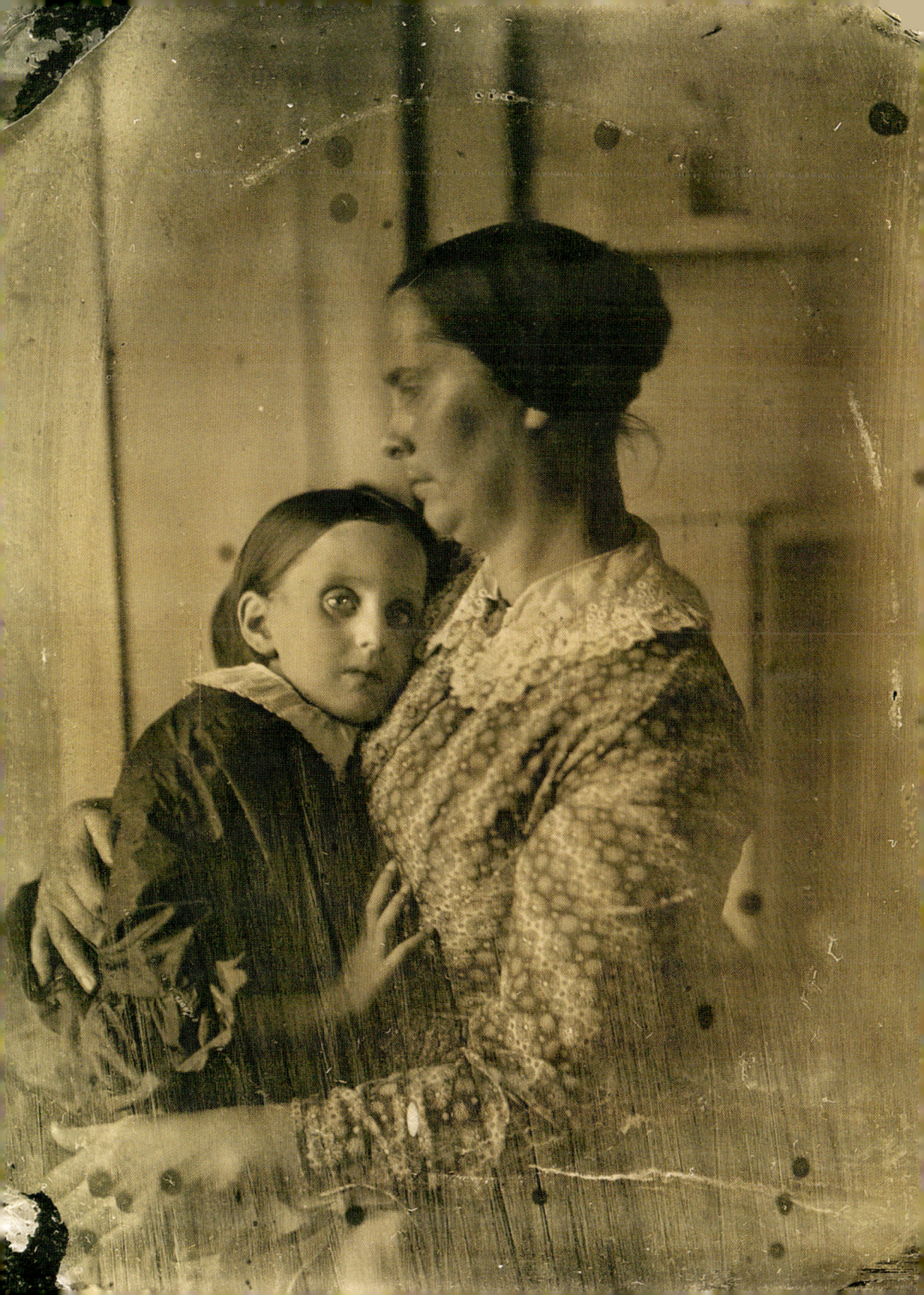

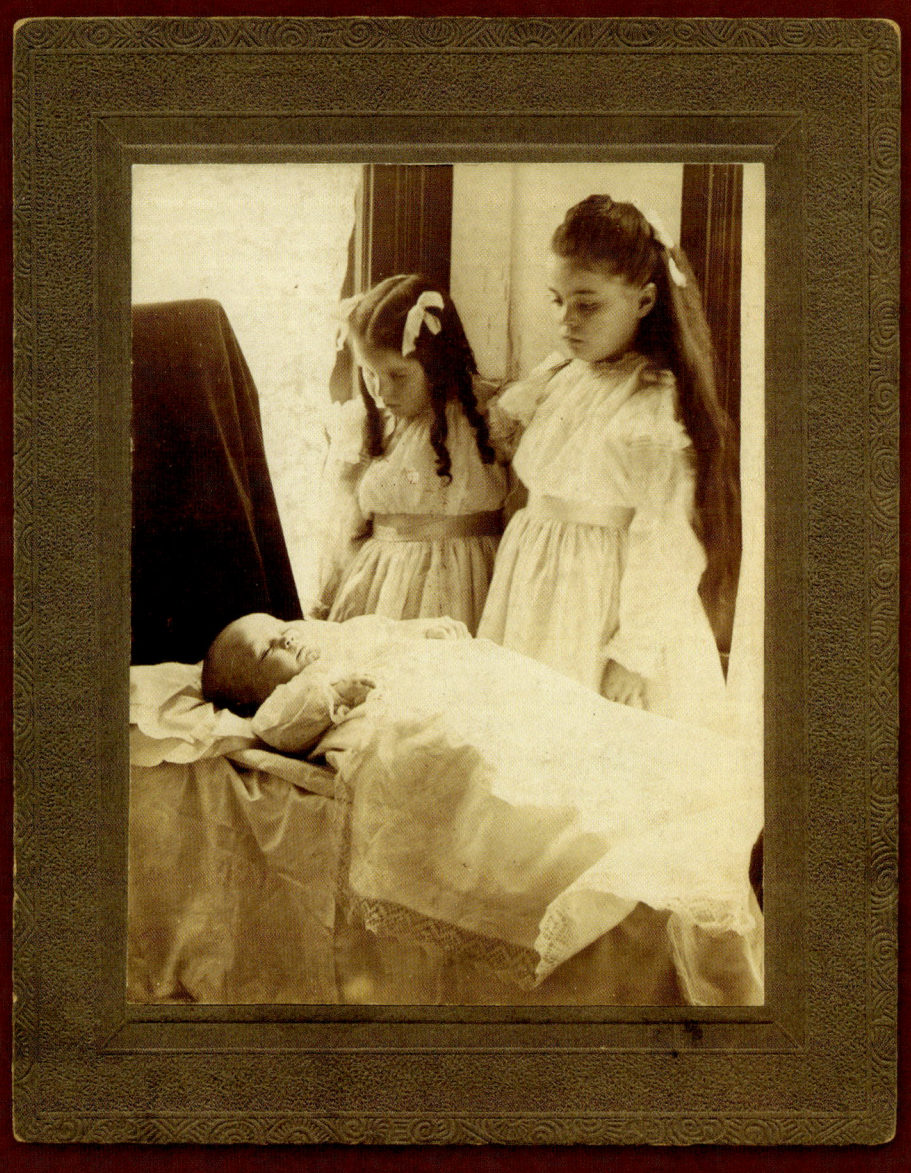

The Baby   circa 1900 • gelatin silver print • 7" x 5"
Two little girls view the body of their infant sibling.

THE SOUL & ITS SUBSTITUTES

JOE SMOKE

What are you now that I once was?
What I am now, you soon will be.

— EIGHTEENTH-CENTURY GRAVESTONE INSCRIPTION

Several months ago I enjoyed a television program that showed how nuclear magnetic resonance images can illustrate where and when analytic versus creative thinking occurs in the brain. The day after the program aired, I encountered an image of the world's first replacement ear, created by a 3-D printer that stacked cells, hydrogel, and electronic nanoparticles. These imaging developments emerge from a long sweep of advancement in visual portraiture and human science[1] from post-Enlightenment through postmodernism. The Thanatos Archive is a repository of artifacts from the same historical period, so I will use poignant examples from this collection to address social change intertwining three topic areas: story-image making, human invention, and spiritual consciousness.

---

[1] The term "human science" is used here to encompass the empirical/nature sciences, social sciences, and humanities. I believe that the only great difference between these areas is whether theories are used to explain phenomena (as in the formal sciences) or comprehend phenomena (as in the informal sciences).

I will endeavor to illustrate how and why post-mortem photography and the greater practice of photography exemplify profound shifts in scientific and philosophical attitudes.

How are visual constructions used to reconcile perseverance and loss? How have these reconciliations altered through time and technology, expressly before and after the photographic revolution? Philosophical thinkers such as Roland Barthes and Susan Sontag have highlighted photography's epistemological link to death. My wider research aspires to connect photography to the total breadth of accelerated social-scientific change between 1840 and 1990.

Mankind's passion for story originates as an ancient inclination to learn from surrogate figures, which may be performers, portraits, or other representations. Aristotle was the first to conceptualize a dual theory that humans want and need to study likenesses because they give us pleasure and aid in reconciling our securities and insecurities. Aristotle had closely considered the idealistic sculptures of his era and in doing so connected pleasure to desire, a cognitive activity in which an event or object is associated with self-possibility.[2]

Aristotle's theory is complementary to "the gaze" as described by psychoanalyst Jacques Lacan. He hypothesized a "mirror stage" in which people first encounter self-image and realize that consciousness is bound within appearance and expression. According to Lacan, we understand the world through a "gaze effect," which is an awareness of seeing/being seen and objectifying/being objectified. Our gaze assists us in developing relationships between persons/objects and linking self and other through self-regulation.[3]

Current neuroscience confirms that we process aesthetic experiences involving human content in a fashion different from the way we process aesthetic experiences without human content. Furthermore, our primary attraction to humanness extends to human-like forms (e.g., animals) and human artifacts (e.g., common tools). As per Lacan, the gaze effect can be produced and is continued through human inventions (e.g., cameras or television/computer screens).

According to studies in neuroscience, our reading of visual experiences occurs in at least two layers, mental and perceptual. Researchers describe "semantic factors playing important roles in preference-ascription when viewing human content." In layman's terms this means that when we listen to a mentor or gaze at a portrait, our brains prioritize "mental informativeness" over compositional structure as we associate with a face, connect through someone's eyes, consider body language, and hear/perceive messages.[4] Through a mix of watching, emulating, and

2 H. Stuart Hughes, *Consciousness and Society: The Reorientation of European Social Thought 1890-1930* (New York: Vintage Books, 1961/1977): 3-32. With his acute explanation of the reason that humans enjoy seeing likenesses, Aristotle reconciles the common query of why we are attracted (even excited) by images of death. The answer is simply "self-possibility." 3 Jacques Lacan, "The Split between the Eye and the Gaze "(1964), in *Book XI: The Four Fundamental Concepts of Psychoanalysis,* ed. Jacques-Alain Miller; trans. Alan Sheridan (New York: Norton, 1978). 4 D. Massaro et al., "When Art Moves the Eyes: A Behavioral and Eye-Tracking Study," PLoS ONE 7(5): e37285 (University of London, May 18, 2012) http://www.plosone.org/article/info%3Adoi%2F10.1371%2Fjournal.pone.0037285. This study outlines and tests current theories about visual analysis as a combination of visual exploration and mental inquisition. The two layers of reading a visual experience are described as "bottom-up" and "top-down," with top-down processing originating from mental processing through the viewer's context (i.e., cultural knowledge, status, decoding, and comparative possibilities) and bottom-up processing originating with perceptual composition analysis (i.e., subject identification, scale and balance of elements, significance of color/tone, etc.).

imagining, we establish a comfortable mind shift between viewing a portrait/subject (outside to in) and envisioning ourselves in their role/world (inside to out).[5]

History's earliest surviving portraits were created in Classical Greece.[6] These include sculptures of Socrates (deemed realistic because they are unflattering enough to match literary references to his unattractiveness) and painted eternity portraits of unidentified men and women (preserved on wood or ivory tablets that were inserted into mummy wrappings). Unlike later post-mortem photographs, our earliest portraits were living-representations of the departed used for memorial or funerary purposes. The coexisting gaze we find in such portraiture is co-owned. It is true relationship, although always separated by contextual space and time. Within this exchange we can embody both the "offering gaze" and the "demanding gaze." The offering gaze is our spectator's gaze, which initiates the inquiry. The complement is the subject's demand to be viewed.[7] Multidimensional comprehension incorporates each spectator's knowledge, values, and current context as

Figure 1. Under the Stars

well as the sitter's demonstration, expression, and historic context.

Like traditional portraits, post-mortem images emphasize the face as the site of communication; but the subjects are dead with eyes closed (or open yet vacant). Hence, post-mortem gaze analysis becomes more complicated by taking us deeper. We must go into the closed space of the deceased's head to imagine a demanding gaze; this becomes our interpretation or understanding of death. In this way, post-mortem photographs represent a new kind of story-image analysis, while continuing to symbolize a belief in an afterlife or continued spiritual journey facilitated by devotional exchange. Figure I (*see also page 89*), for example, depicts the lifeless bust of a young boy within luxuriously tufted bedding facing upward toward a pattern of celestial dots. He is unknown, or unidentified, to us and becomes both vessel and vision for our fairy tale. For his family this scene would be more cinematic, culminating a shared history. Their kindred experience is also triple signified in arranging, affording, and protecting the resulting memory-souvenir for future generations. When I enact a story from under this

5 Daniel J. Graham et al., "Preference for Art: similarities, statistics and selling price," Society of Photo-optical Instrumentation Engineers (SPIE Conference Series, 2010) http://people.hws.edu/graham/SPIE2010_print.pdf. **6** Scholars have not yet agreed if portrait art developed in Late Period ancient Egypt (672–332 BCE) or Qin dynasty China (221–207 BCE). Egyptian pharaohs and royals were portrayed as individuals in various forms of highly stylized god-like characters; however, it appears this treatment was limited and cultural portraiture among nobles was either rare or undeveloped. Likewise, the 8,800-figure "Terra Cotta Army" commissioned by China's first emperor, Qin Shi Huang, consists of soldiers, horses, chariots, bowmen, and archers with unique faces; however, the technique of making these characters from a handful of basic molds and the lack of literary references creates doubt that these figures are indeed portraits. **7** I use "offering and demanding gaze" as terms that are more intuitive than "indirect and direct gaze," which are concepts proposed by cinema theorists Gunther Kress and Theo van Leeuwen.

child's eyelids, I feel a journey through double darkness to a distant-but-bright next destination. For me, stars become metaphors or equivalents for his/our possibly unending narrative.

Mindful viewers of such portrait-stories will also consider how interpretation is predisposed by a photographer's compositional choices. The design strategies that are most noteworthy in post-mortem portraits are body repositioning, intimate distance, and the selection and placement of props. The best nineteenth-century photographers will have used these strategies to transmit tenderness, sympathy, hopefulness, dismay, and/or pity. In early photography the chemistry, optics, and tools of the day did not allow for true color or artificial lighting effects, so story is heavily based on framing, scale, and referencing.

Figure 2. Child with Facial Trauma

Photographs are subtly sophisticated fabrications. Slight technical differences in position, focus, aperture, and speed can change everything a viewer notices or feels. Divergent from the hand-eye arts of painting or sculpture, camerawork functions like the art of theater. The practice of living-portrait photography is an interaction governed by sociocultural behavior. Hence, the distinctive decisions that photographers make with patrons or models (or with themselves when acting alone in a space) are embedded in the result. The collaboration (or lack thereof) demonstrates the shared conduct of the players within the values of their era.

Such mutual consent is especially important in post-mortem photography, when the bereaved players would have a heightened sensitivity about the solemnity of the situation. Hence, even small permissions with the mildest visibility demonstrate artistic emphasis.

Figure 2 *(see also page 92)* is a useful example to address creative composition in post-mortem photographs, because in this instance the photo-artist was challenged to create a portrait while deemphasizing the face. Here the angle of the camera serves a dual purpose. It positions the subject's head in deeper space and mildly out of focus to reduce the detail of her fatal trauma (which also moderates the viewers' horror); and it invents an emotional axis, portraying the subject as if she is floating diagonally up and away from her fluffy white pillow into the darkness beyond.

Let us pause here to appreciate how the technology of photography brings a novel mix of rationality and artificiality to artistic portraiture. Cameras capture believable stories with recognizable syntax, yet photographic images work like time machines for conceptually transporting viewers to past scenes and dates. Stated another way, every photograph is a fact yet also an illusion. Therein lies the medium's hypnotic power. Even the most candid images with the purest documentary intentions are designed compositions that tease cognition with condensed or expanded dimensionality.

Yet the human mind wants to see photographs as mirrors and windows rather than unreal constructions. Similarly, most people prefer to understand death as a new beginning rather than a complete stop. Death and photography have a metaphoric similarity—both are transactional and transferential.

The possibility of our own passing makes death images into experiences of reconcilia- tion. From early cave paint- ings to today's immersive video games, it is psycho- logically stimulating and reconciling to experience realistic human stories, especially when they nar- rate transformation. See- ing/becoming a subject that passes from one state to anoth- er effectively builds human capac- ity for future change by visualizing/ envisioning reformation.

In the long sweep of social history, nei- ther death rites nor cultural portraiture could flourish until the Industrial Revolution fostered

a democratic milieu for equivalent public ex- pressions of both individual worth and benev- olent nature.[8] Two concrete testaments to this sociological shift were the immediate naming of infants and the personification of pets. Grave- stones from the eighteenth century demonstrate that infants were often called "babe" or "child" for at least twelve months, due to high infant mortality rates. This postponement of bequeathing names/iden- tities to infants slowed during the development of germ theory and virtu- ally ceased with advanced sanitary standards during childbirth. Comparative- ly, by the mid-nineteenth century, pets had become so common and beloved that even they were given individual names. This practice was not limit- ed to household cats and dogs but extended to smaller pets and working animals. The elaborate, custom-made brass-and-marble sarcophagus il- lustrated in figure 3 *(see also page 165)* indicates

Figure 3. Victorian Bird Sarcophagus

8 Transformative story-learning did not advance consistently between Classical Greece and the age of Enlightenment. For instance, paint- ed portraiture between the fourth and sixteenth centuries remained limited in both illusion and symbolism, until the "genre-subject" movement of the seventeenth-century Northern Baroque cultivated increasing inquisitiveness and inventiveness. Only then did the over- whelming benevolence that originally hitched portrait art to funerary art (and which kept both genres stylistically conservative, although not always modest) give way to a new openness. It is likewise noteworthy that the pure landscape was not a subject of Western art until industrialization had drawn people into urbanity; and thus a retreat into quiet contemplation or scenic beauty became a newly perceived goal expressed through social customs and photography. From the fourth century AD through the Enlightenment, vistas and scenery in Western art history are almost exclusively backdrops for human/animal stories. Meditations on the pure landscape are presented in Eastern art (particularly East Asian art) from ancient to contemporary times, as expressions of Daoism and similar philosophical traditions; but they are rare in Western art until after Sublime Aesthetics are defined (beginning in 1700) and latently expressed in nineteenth-century photo- graphs and artworks of the Barbizon School (1830-1870). Likewise, a general philosophy of sociology (i.e., social theory and nontheological history) also lacked development in the period between Classical Greece and the Industrial Revolution; during the time of industrialization, democratic civic ideals were reestablished and Positivism united with social contract theory to form Sociology as an intellectual pursuit. Berch Berberoglu, *An Introduction to Classical and Contemporary Social Theory: A Critical Perspective* (Rowman & Littlefield, 2005): 11. Thus, I hypothesize, storytelling activities like portraiture could/can not develop greatly without democratic context to support both ideological freedoms and technological innovations.

that the bird Wee-Wee was a cherished member of its family. Moreover, the companion note to Wee-Wee's casket confirms that this beloved bird was cared for dutifully and lovingly until its final breath at 7:55 on Monday, 18 June 1874.

Today, life is long and overfull of recorded memories, but when the new art-science of photography was invented, in 1839, average life expectancy for a man or woman was barely 35 years. Until that time, most family memories were spoken tales or written notes (at best). Only the wealthy class could afford to memorialize itself with visual pomp and enact its reflection as communal display via painted portraits or sculptural likenesses. When industrial innovations in health science, public safety, and workers' compensation laws began to extend life, a middle class formed, accumulated wealth, and initiated a fuller public narrative. Photography was both a practice of and an accelerating agent for this civic transformation.

Figure 4. Tombstone Carver

The invention of photography made living and memorial portraiture desirable and affordable to new classes of people. Camera images were faster and more realistic than pictures made by graphic artists, who were known to charge double if a subject was already dead. The earliest photographic images were handmade, unique objects on metal or glass plates and were most often (and best) displayed like encased jewels or hand-held books. The generally grayish tones of these daguerreotypes, ambrotypes, and tintypes still remind us that photographic images were originally heralded as "mirrors with memories."

Photography's praxis and acceptability were not achieved without considerable discomfort and disagreement. Imagine the incomprehension that people felt when photography was first practiced on them — the command to remain motionless for minutes in front of an "artificial eye," and soon thereafter the bewilderment at seeing themselves replicated in miniature. How strange that the simple diffraction of light through a curved glass onto chemically sensitive material could transmit a copy of nature. To the uninitiated it was scary magic, a first adventure with a replicant technology. Indeed, photography's exactitude stirred first-encounter fears that the apparatus would steal the soul and freeze it for other people to control (like a voodoo doll). Early photography also had to overcome a medieval worry that a person's soul had limited layers and that the camera would peel away part of a sitter's life or destiny.

Photographs printed on paper were invented almost concurrently and could be inserted in albums or affixed to documents. With the advent of paper photographs, handicraft and self-taught artisanship gave way to an industry of products with commercial values offered by tradesmen. Similarly, the provision of a coffin by a village carpenter and its implementation by a church were commercialized. During this same period, the word *casket*, a euphemism for jewelry box, generally replaced the word *coffin*.[9] Not surprisingly, the aesthetics of funerary caskets and early photographic frames followed parallel design developments (see figure 4, *see also page 175*).

With the new consumerism that emerged via the Industrial Revolution, utilitarian and decorative keepsakes (of which photographic portraits are both) became important quasi-public elements of custom and fashion. Such precious objects-with-permanence came to fulfill a complement of related class goals. They represented taste and beauty as metaphors for status and style. They represented heritage and spiritual sentiment via personalization and renewable elucidation. They represented contemporaneousness in entwining design and context. And they symbolized tangibility by stretching the inevitability of human decay into the future by investing memory into materials of great physicality. Overall, this new collecting of and conferring about souvenirs became (and continues to be) a way to balance our need to be recognized

Figure 5. Lincoln Funeral Train

and/or influential against our fear of being and/or ending as a nobody.

Of course, consumerism requires demand, which photography also created by instituting concepts such as mass marketing and celebrity. Between 1850 and 1865, "star" photographers such as Nadar and Mathew Brady worked to convert popular names into famous faces and brands. Only sixteen years after photography's invention, photographic public relations could reach larger audiences than any auditorium event, parade, or public festival; and panoplies of freshly posed personas and products came to exemplify prosperity within and between nations. In fact, the precious personal attributes of vernacular death portraits emerge as the modest cousins of public-event representations to honor famous individuals.

For example (see figure 5, *see also page 152*), a tactical living photo-portrait of Abraham Lincoln was mounted on the front of the 1865 memorial train that carried his (and his son's) body from Washington, D.C., to his home state of Illinois. Millions viewed the train along its six-state route, but far fewer got a chance to see the assassinated president's body as it lay in state during thirteen presentations over sixteen days.

---

9 Kenneth G. Wilson, *The Columbia Guide to Standard American English* (New York: Columbia University Press, 1993). Early North Americans drew a distinction between "coffins" and "caskets," using "coffin" for a tapered anthropoidal (hexagonal or octagonal) shaped burial box and "casket" for rectangular burial box, but this distinction faded as the funeral industry developed "jewel-box caskets" with carved moldings, velvet interiors, and decorative hardware.

This living-portrait was clearly intended to signify Lincoln's immortal character (rather than passing spirit) for current and future audiences. Indeed a supporting policy was introduced that prohibited photographing his dead body before, during, or after the train procession. Only one "official image" of Abraham Lincoln in his coffin was authorized, because Secretary of War Edwin M. Stanton sought to limit itinerant photographers from proliferating and profiting from casket images. One by-product of this public theater was that the science of embalming, recently perfected during the U.S. Civil War, became immediately popular through the reportedly (and repeatedly) fine embalming of Lincoln's corpse.

Science in general became a popular branch of education through photography, as people came to want challenging new data and perspectives. In this regard, the anticipated power of photography went beyond depicting "everything the eye could see" to depicting things "beyond human vision." The visible world was expanded greatly with nineteenth-century telescopes, as it continues to expand today with high-speed imaging of ultra-fast phenomena. In particular, early photomicroscopy radically

Figure 6. The Twins

altered mankind's conception of illness, which directly changed the science of medicine and indirectly adjusted mankind's piety.

This shift in post-Enlightenment piety can be noted in printed educational materials and specifically in both printed quotations regarding death and gravestone epitaphs. Death was commonly regarded by late-eighteenth-century U.S. pilgrims as a warning (to all who stray) of their own mortality.[10] However, by 1870, human-centered and humane sentiments became most common, including descriptions of death as "a cultural closure when the current and future struggles of a person's lifetime fell away and treasured last words could be uttered without earthly motives," or "a beatific moment of comfort when the mystery of human potential was laid into God's hands."[11,12] During the Industrial Revolution, people's burial headstone engravings expanded from primarily factual distinctions with phrases of spiritual wisdom to include personal poetics such as pleas, admonishments, accounts of reputation, testaments of faith, and claims to fame.

The climax of this new middle-class mindfulness, which integrated private sentimental

10 The film *Death in America* (www.deathinamerica.com) is the best overview of the cultural and philosophical evolutions of the subjects of illness and death in the last four centuries of American history. It is a 1997 collaboration between producer/director J.R. Olivero and Dr. Stanley B. Burns of the Burns Archive of historic photographs, based on Dr. Burns' prior book, *Sleeping Beauty: Memorial Photography in America* (Santa Fe, N.M.: Twelvetrees Press, 1990). **11** Phoebe Lloyd, "Posthumous Mourning Portraiture," in *A Time to Mourn, Expressions of Grief in Nineteenth Century America*, ed. Martha V. Pike and Janice Gray Armstrong (The Museums at Stony Brook, 1980): 72-82.**12** Lewis O. Saum, "Death in the Pre-Civil War America," in *Death in America*, ed. David E. Stannard (Philadelphia: University of Pennsylvania, 1974): 41-47.

realities with rational social perspective, is best visualized by a subgenre of post-mortem photography, the mourning images. These photographs depict living relatives with the dead. An excellent example is figure 6 *(see also page 42)*. It is more psychologically complex than a typical memorial image, seeming extra brave and defiant out of its historical context. It layers the topics of mourning and survival onto the principal purpose of memorial imagery in connecting the dead with transference.[13] How do you judge the demanding gaze of the mother in figure 6 as she collaborates with her photographer to express compassionate equilibrium with her body? How do you balance empty feelings for the shrouded corpse she holds in her right embrace with some connectedness to the living twin she holds with her left arm? I hope after reading this essay you will consider this image less shocking, since it is simply a frank allegory from a phase of great transition in the history of human realization.

During a recognizable second-stage of the Industrial Revolution that phased in after

Figure 7. The Weepers

1870, the syntactic elements of photography's rising influence became apparent. Most of these developments relate to the collaborative contest between photography and the printed word in reflecting private and public narratives.

Following technological advancements starting in 1875, photographic reproduction became a communication platform that expanded from printed postcards to fully illustrated newspapers. A point of no return was reached when the print media universally employed half-tone ink printing around 1890.[14]

Once photo-images could be reproduced easily alongside words, photography climaxed its redirection of human awareness via what was understood in magazines and books, wanted in stores, and expected in human relationships. Within this enormous new field of photojournalistic news, etiquette manuals and ladies' journal articles explained, for example, the respectful forms of mourning dress and address for the bereaved and sympathetic friends (who were encouraged to limit their visibility, vanity, and accessibility).[15] (See figure 7, *see also page 148*.)

---

13 The most comparable objects to mourning photographs in art history are gravestones from fifth-century Classical Greece. These stelae show low-relief portraits of the deceased shaking hands with other figures in front of a closed doorway. Most such stelae portray the deceased shaking hands with Charun or Vanth, so in these instances the handshake motif signals a welcome beyond the door to the underworld. In other stelae, these handshake figures could be portraits of the dead's living relatives. If so, these objects need to be reconsidered as key elements in the history of portraiture because their illustrated handshakes represent humanistic moments of spiritual release. **14** The Austrian post office approved use of the first "postal card," a hard paper note that could travel without an envelope, in 1869. The first newspaper fully illustrated with halftone reproductions of photographic news appeared in 1882. **15** Karen Halttunen, "Mourning the Dead: A Study in Sentimental Ritual," *Confidence Men and Painted Women: A Study of Middle-class Culture in America, 1830-1870* (New Haven: Yale Historical Publications, 1986): 124-152.

A still greater alteration in private/public rationality surfaced as photography took its place as an actualizing agent in the promotion of behaviors as beliefs, during which time multiple industrial technologies synergized sociocultural modifications and human science to spur a succession of innovations, such as anesthetic drugs, the cataloging of world languages, establishment of secular/public schools, the germ theory of disease, honeymoon rituals, idealist philosophy, locomotive trains, the personification of pets, and the writing of non-theologically framed history texts.

Finally, between 1880 and 1910, the general practice of post-mortem photography succumbed to the handheld-camera snapshot revolution, whereby baby portraits and chronological family photo albums became standard. In retrospect, the specific period during which the practice of post-mortem photography climaxed was a transitional period in which interpersonal communication and middle-class gentility originally converged.

Figure 8 (*see also page 71*) is one of the later and more powerful images in the Thanatos Archive. It is a testament to the fact the tradition of post-mortem photography receded but has never stopped. This artifact represents the effort of a poor family to memorialize their father/grandfather. Our discomfort in viewing this scene is tempered by our consideration that, most likely, no photographs were made of this

Figure 8. Mexican Family

beloved man during his life. The fact that the image was created as a postcard may underscore that his death was unexpected and his passing needed to be commemorated for distant relatives who could not afford or quickly travel to attend his burial.

By 1910, photography was fully synergized with society and science in a newly egalitarian and greatly industrial world. Photography opened a pathway for the growing influence of "visual literacy," from concept to college curriculum. Photography has long been considered entertainment without serious content, in comparison to the literary arts, history writing, and journalism; but internationally popular picture books and magazines published from 1920 to 1955 propelled new interpretations of visual multimodal (text-plus-image) literacy. Indeed, photo reproductions have contents to be "read" like a written text; yet their meanings are flexible rather than prescriptive. Photographs, like other memento objects, retain their story-holding powers, as their meanings are never overly prescribed. Hence, recycled and reintroduced object-experiences have become common/essential as every objects' livelihood gets extended further.

By the middle of the twentieth century, the visual world and human consciousness had become utterly "photo-realistic." Two photography-based technologies, cinema and television, took prominent positions by delivering longer story structures and real-time visuality. By the 1960s, everything visible had become immortalized and overexposed through the three camera arts. Philosopher and activist Guy Debord summarized, in several statements in 1967, the profound ways photography had altered human interactions: "In societies dominated by modern conditions of production, life is presented as an immense accumulation of spectacles. Everything that was directly lived has receded into a representation." "The spectacle is not a collection of images; it is a social relation between people that is mediated by images." "The spectacle cannot be understood as a mere visual excess produced by mass-media technologies. It is a worldview that has actually materialized, a view of a world that has become objective."[16]

Post-mortem photos depict the four traditional expressions of the memory-image funerary arts—historic love, status, piety, and eternal remembrance—combined as object or purpose for contemplation. In retrospect, the general practice of photography and the genre of post-mortem imagery represent a shift in human awareness that can be philosophically described as coming to embrace the artificial as progress toward the infinite. Photography's ability to make unseen things knowable has contributed to a consciousness that everything is related.

It is said that postmodernism marked the beginning of a new chapter for society. We can see that photography has progressed to digital imaging and that industrial science has pushed beyond the artificial into the synthetic. Science and art continue to collaborate on the exploration and synthesis of life's three most fundamental questions: who are we, what is everything else, and how is everything related? As a framework, this essay outlines how the postindustrial segment of this quest was synergized by chemical photography and the logical sciences. Future progress is being carried forward with new tools (e.g., genetic engineering) and a new mental collectivity (e.g., the World Wide Web). The old photographs displayed here are important transitional souvenirs from the end of the Age of Enlightenment, when "knowing was touching," to the nineteenth century, when "seeing was knowing." Digital photography, the contemporary zombie of chemical photography, is a sure sign that we have entered a new era of reinscription or reprogramming.

By the way, the new bionic ear marks the first time 3-D printing technology has successfully constructed a human organ with combined tissue and electronics. Its new owner will be able to register frequencies beyond normal human hearing, similar to a dog's range of hearing. I am fascinated to know how that owner's brain will react or develop differently because of this extra sensitivity.

16 Debord draws several connections between the new role of mass-media marketing and the historic role of religions in *The Society of the Spectacle* (Oakland, Calif.: AKPress, 2006).

The writer additionally acknowledges that Michel Foucault's book *The Order of Things: An Archeology of the Human Sciences* (New York: Vintage, 1994) and Rafael Capurro's essay "On Artificiality" (Università di Urbino Laboratory for the Culture of the Artificial, 1995; now updated and available online, 2003-2009) provided an aerial perspective for the historical and philosophical precepts of this essay.

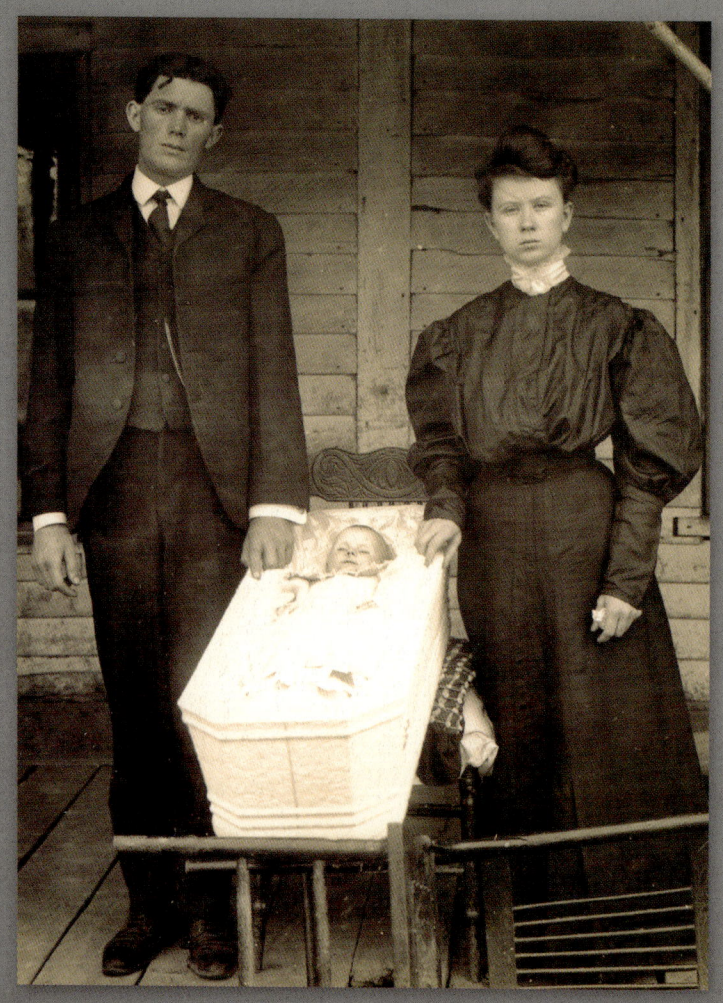

Young Parents circa 1900 • gelatin silver print • 7" x 5"

Devastated young parents pose on the family porch with their deceased infant,
whose small casket is supported on top of two chairs.

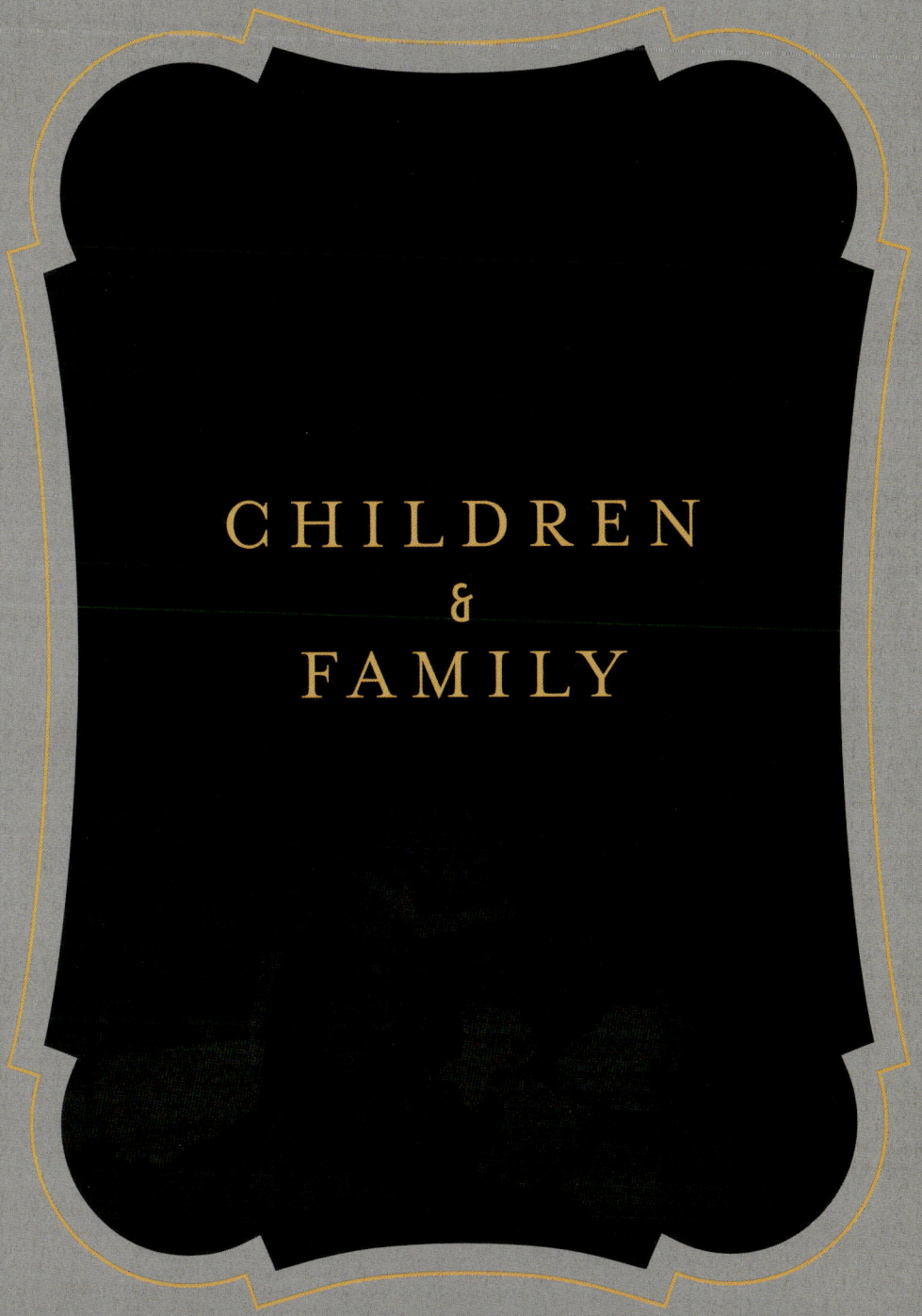

CHILDREN
&
FAMILY

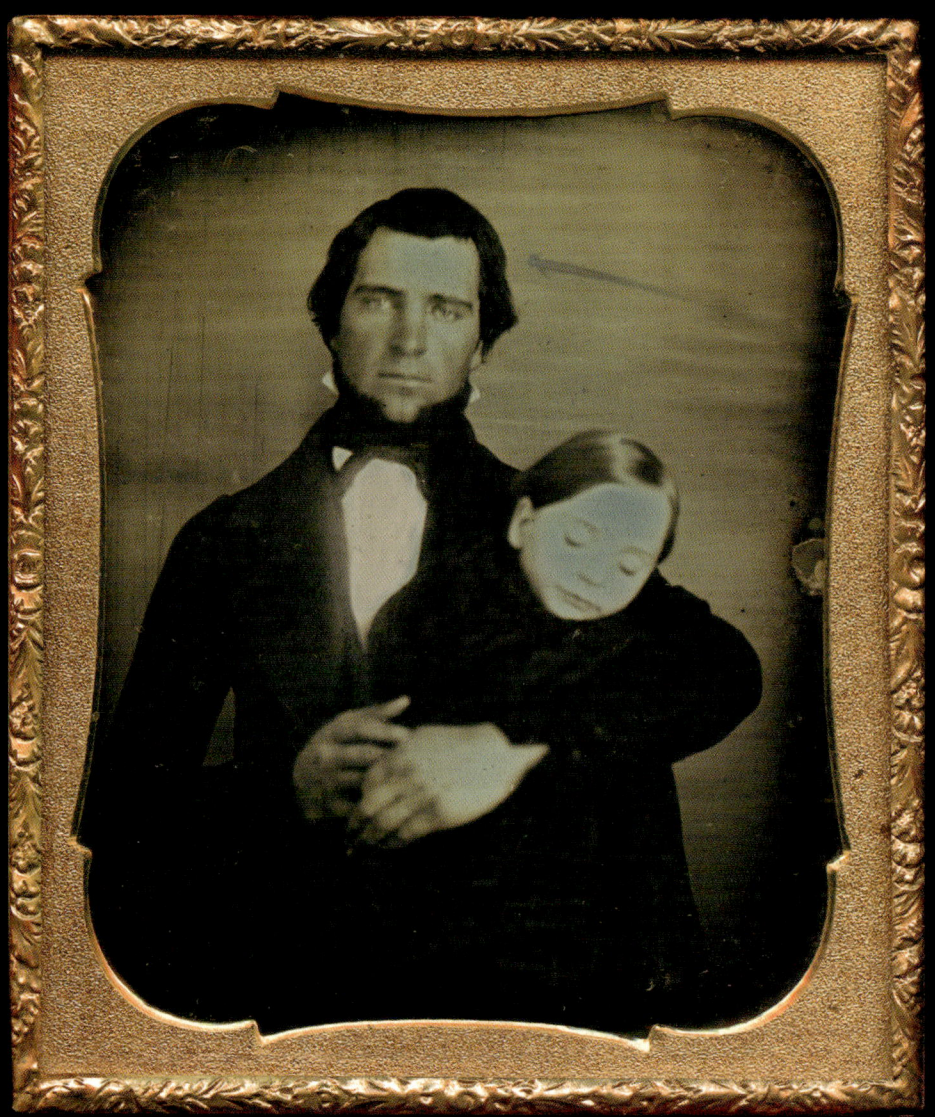

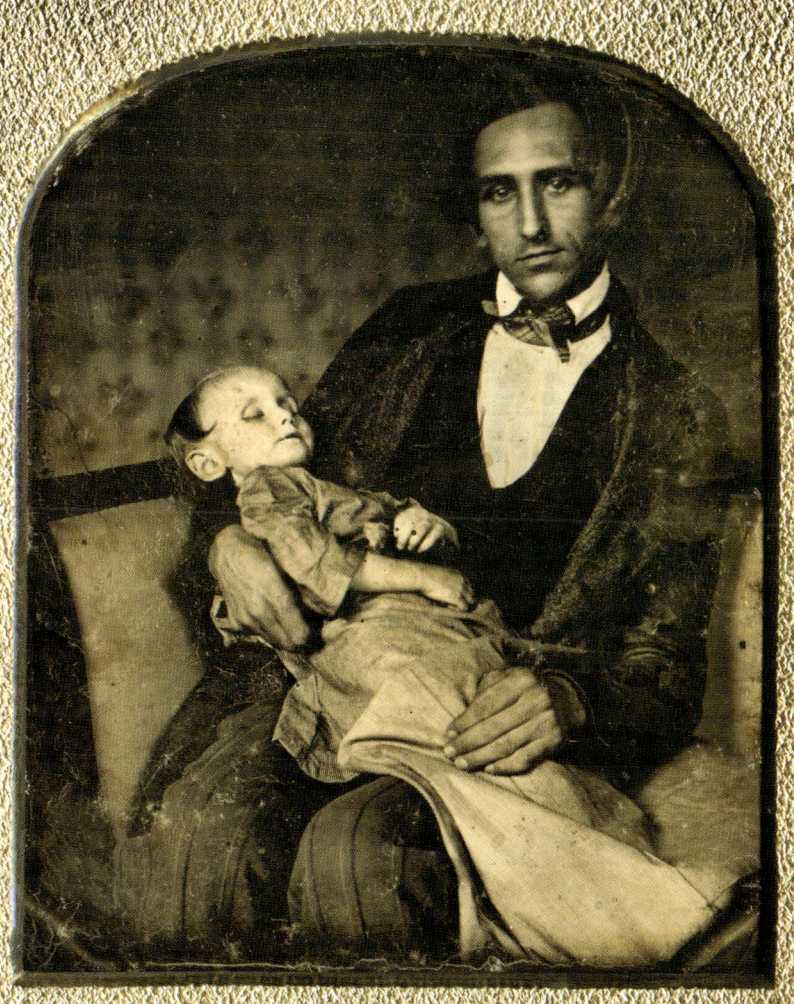

Father and Son circa 1844 • sixth-plate daguerreotype • 3.75" x 3.25"

A young father with his deceased son across his lap. The boy's waxed curl was frequently seen in early post–mortem photography of children.

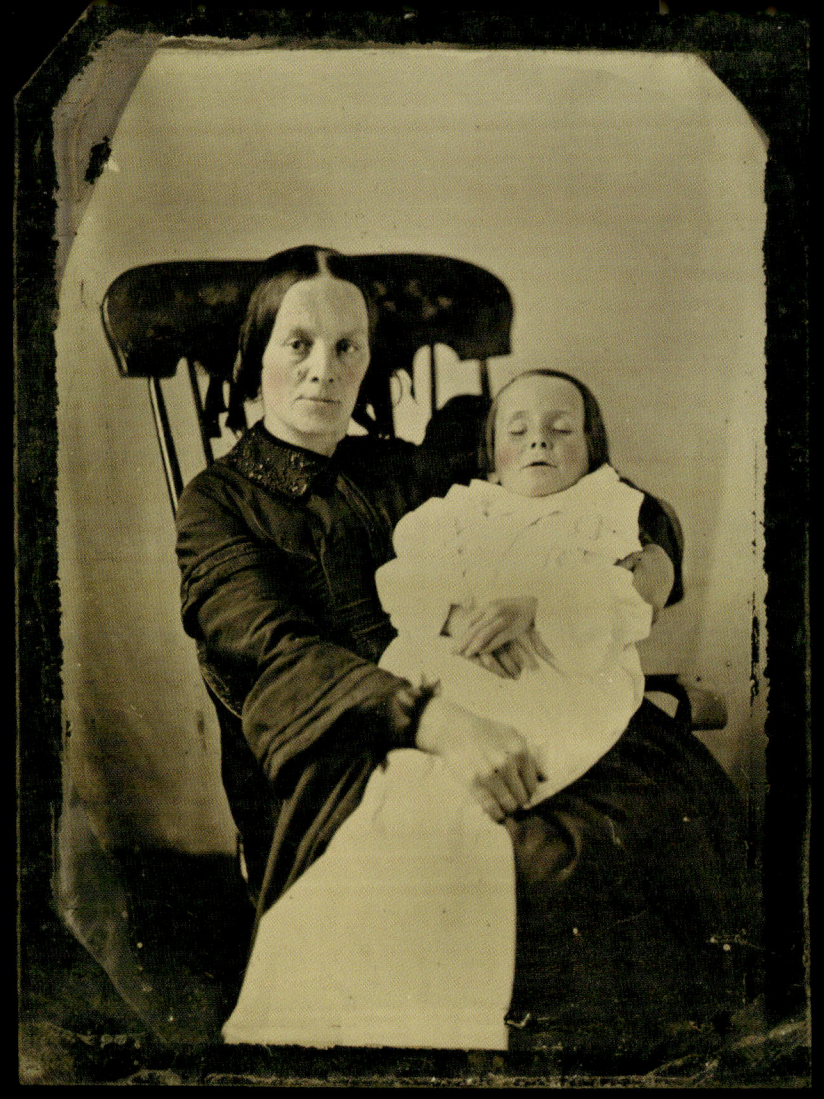

Rocking Chair   circa 1860 • quarter-plate ambrotype • 4.25" x 3.25"

Woman in a black mourning dress holds her son, who is dressed in a white burial gown.

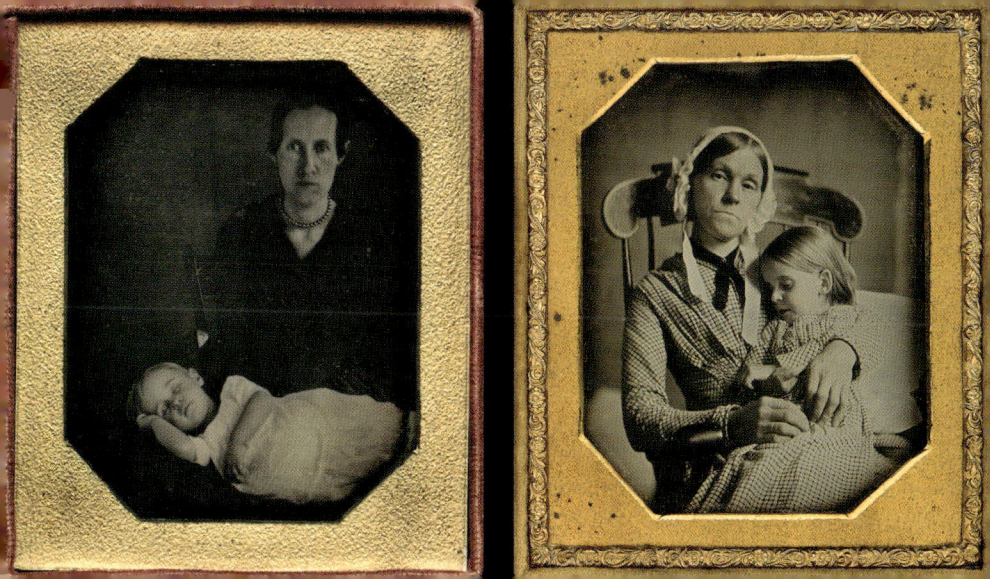

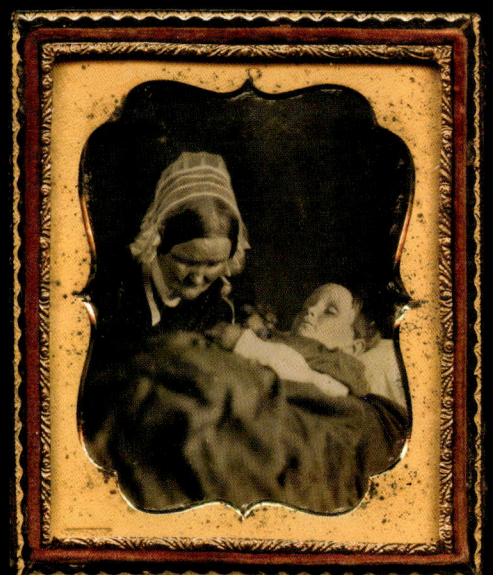 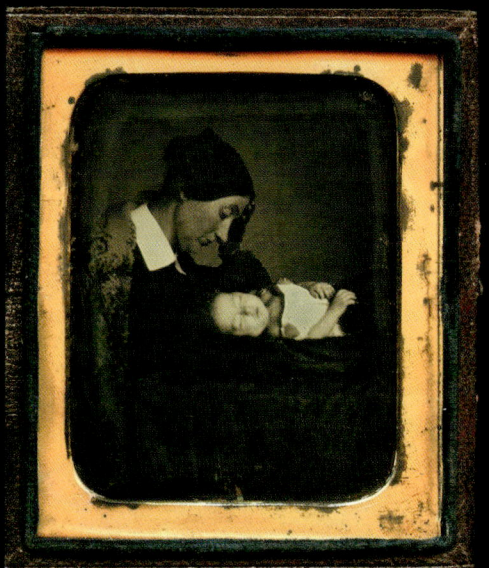

A Mother's Sorrow circa 1852 • sixth-plate daguerreotype • 3.75" x 3.25"

Woman grieves at the bedside of her deceased little boy, who holds a small bouquet of flowers.

- - - - - - - - - - - - - - - - - -

Woman Mourns Lost Child circa 1852 • sixth-plate daguerreotype • 3.75" x 3.25"

In this poignant and dramatically arranged scene, a bereaved woman,
her gloved hand placed against her forehead, gazes down at her lost child.

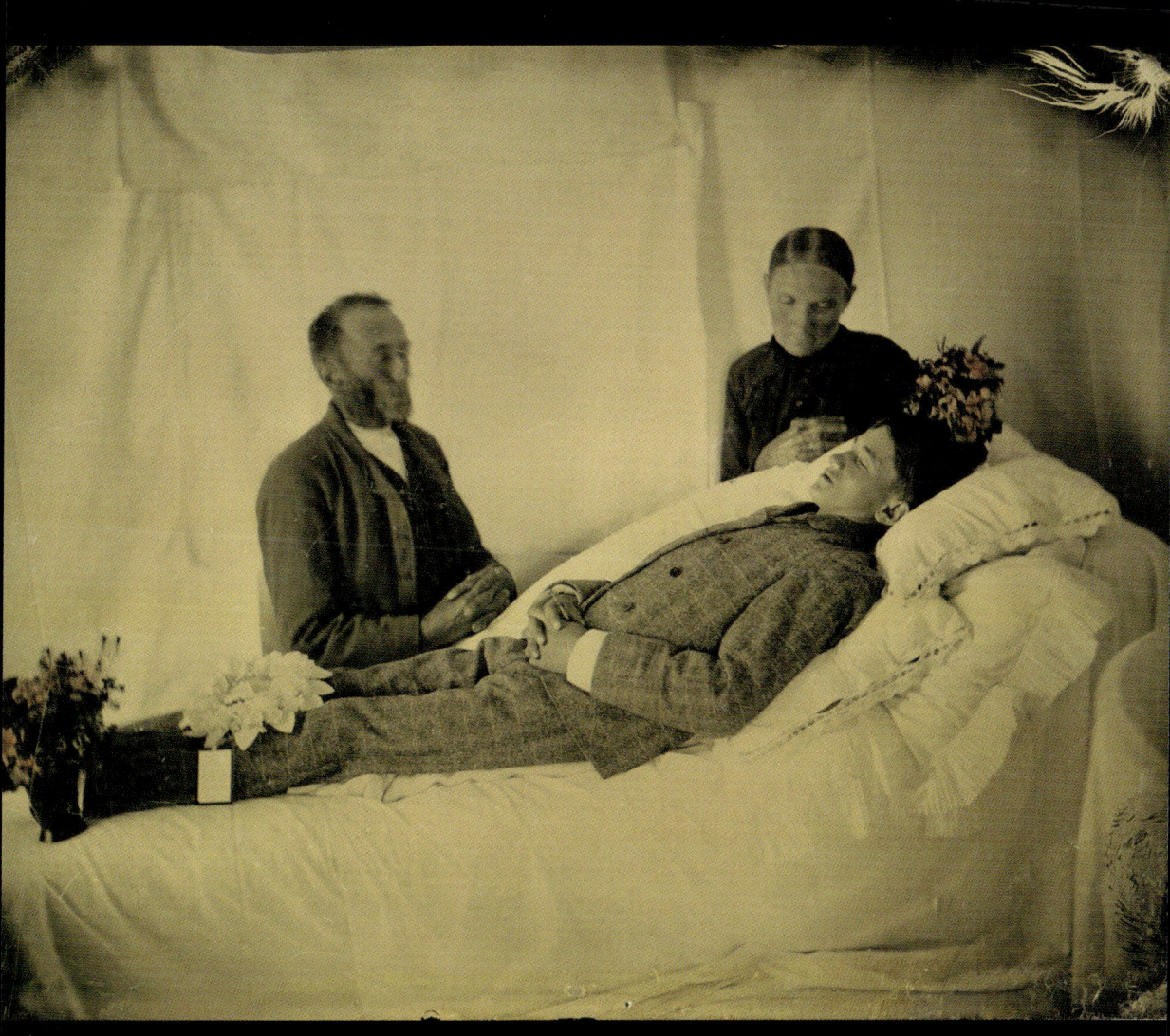

Prayer for a Son   circa 1872 • half-plate tintype, hand colored • 5" x 6"

Middle–aged couple pray at the side of their deceased teenage son.
Funeral flowers have been laid at his head and feet.

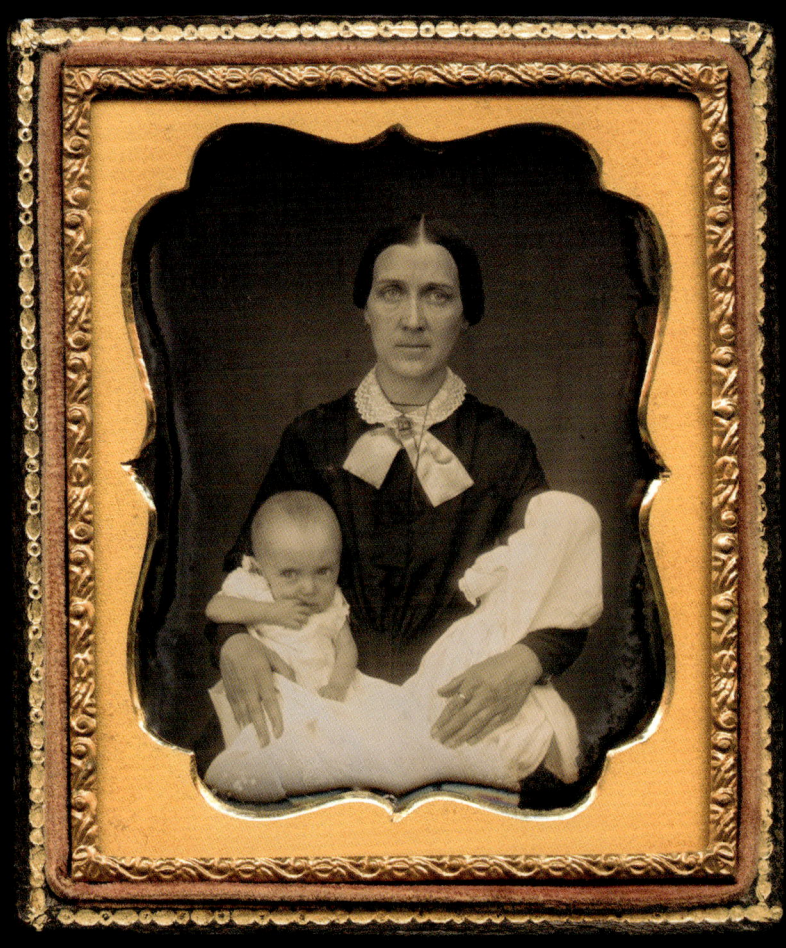

The Twins   circa 1852 • sixth-plate daguerreotype • 3.75" x 3.25"

*In this highly unusual scene, a woman holds two infants, one living and the other deceased
and completely hidden from the viewer in a shroud-like wrapping. The most probable explanation is
that this was done in order to conceal signs of advanced decomposition, injury, or illness.*

Together in Death   circa 1854 • half-plate daguerreotype • 6" x 5"

*A woman and her newborn infant. In the nineteenth century, a difficult birth,
such as breech, could often lead to death for both the mother and the child.*

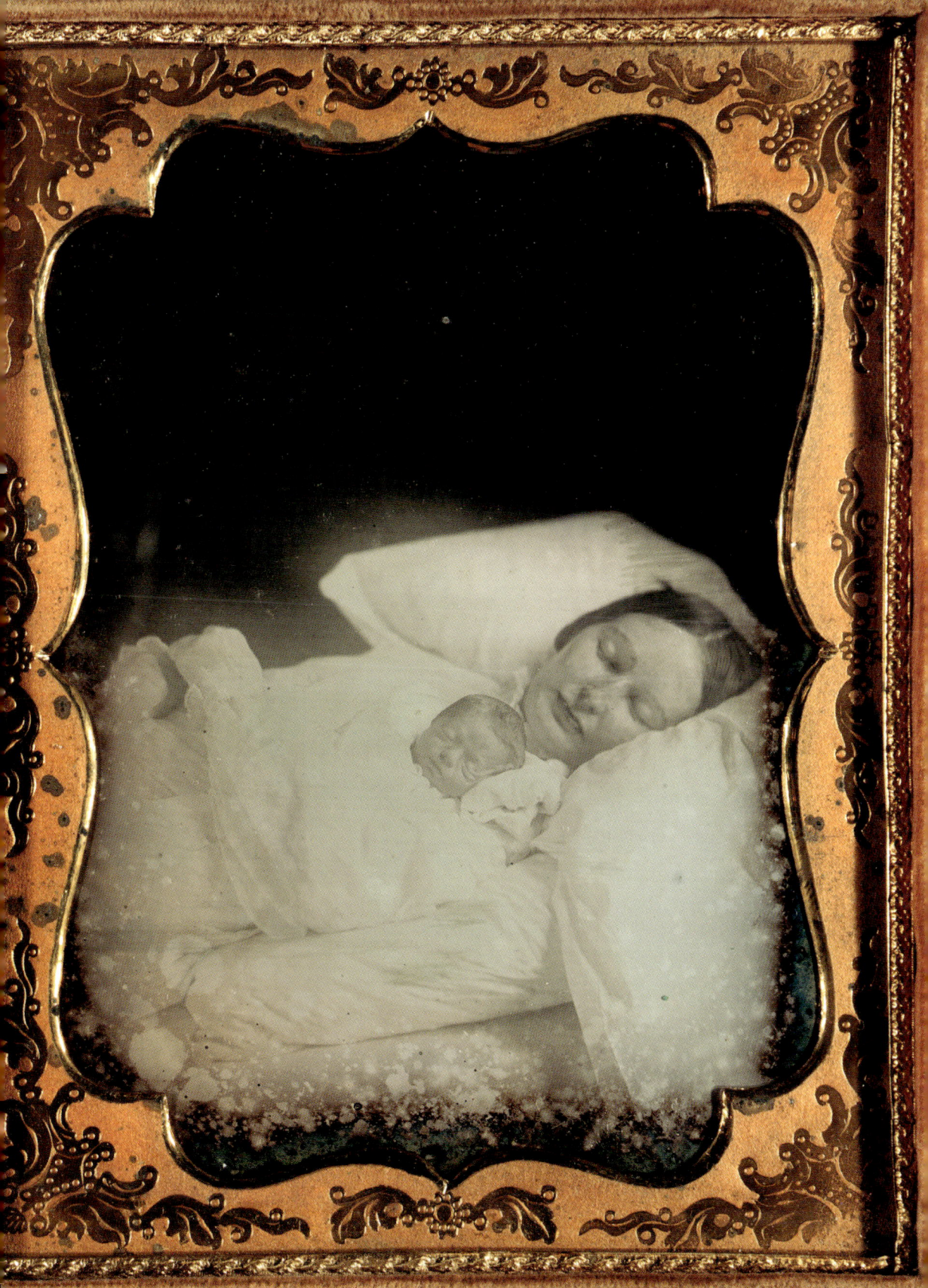

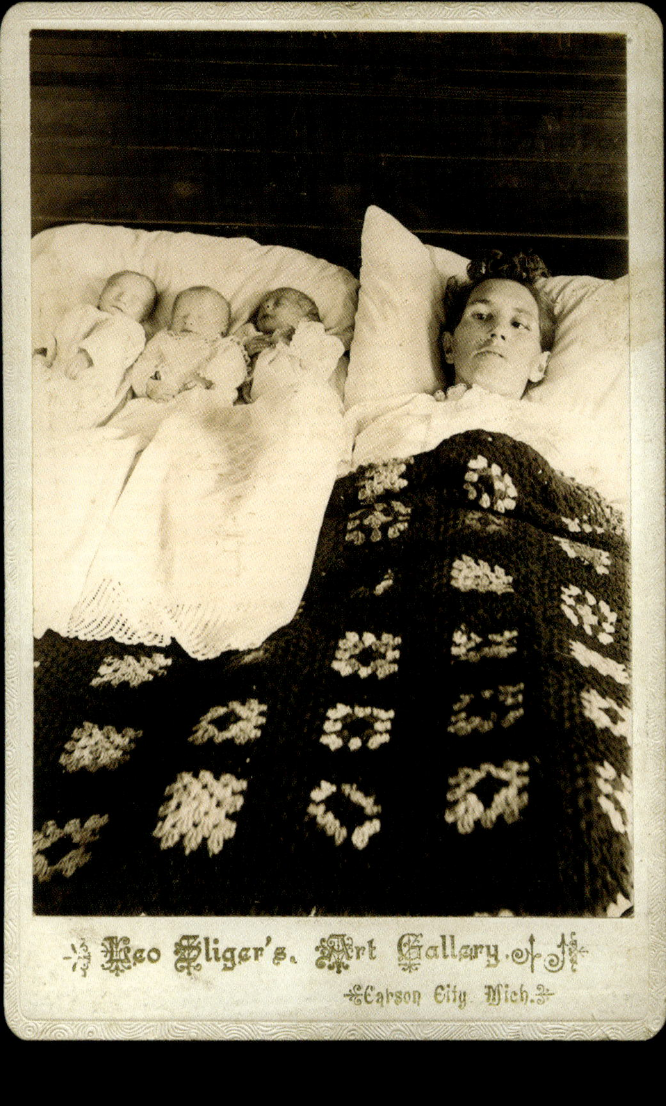

Edeth and Her Triplets   1888 • cabinet card • 6.5" x 4.25"

"The body of Edeth L. Mills, who died during childbirth on September 11, 1888.
At least two of the infants in this photo are also deceased.
baby closest to Edeth appears to have still been alive at the time this photograph was to

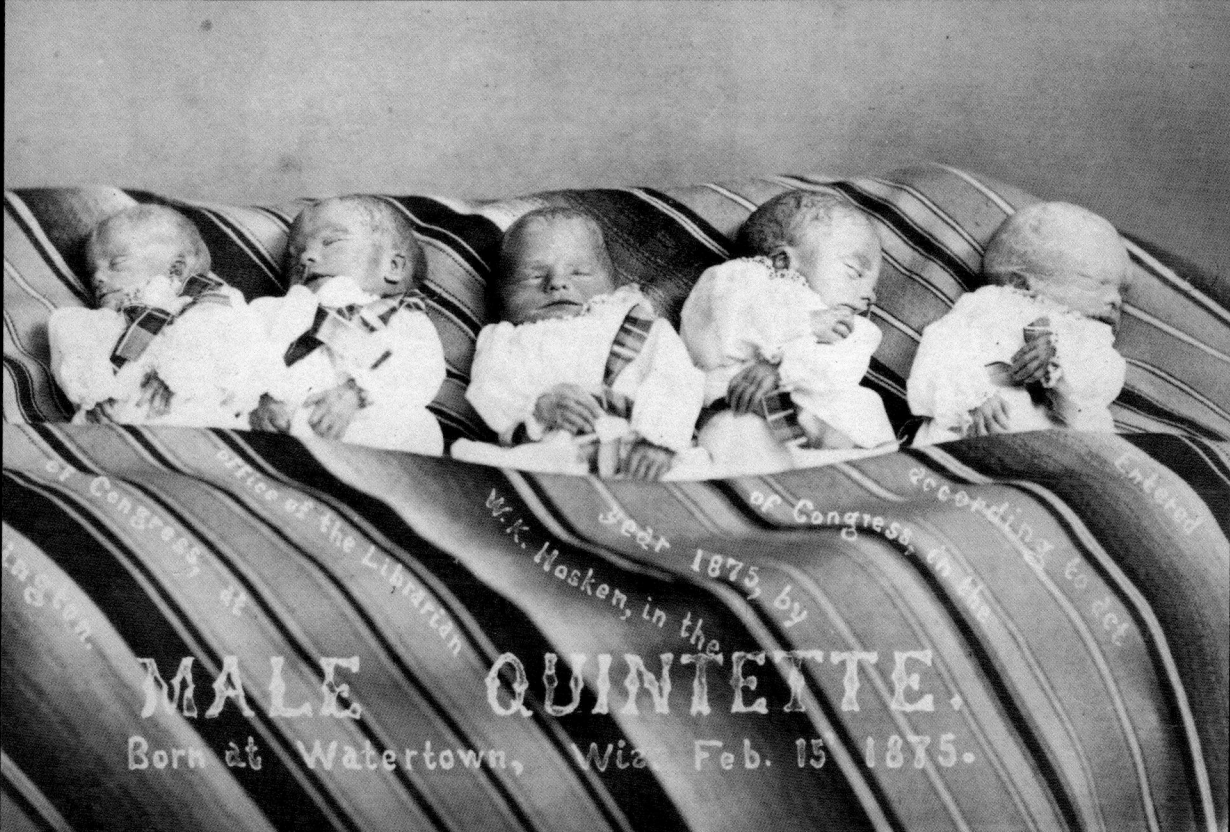

Within the image:

MALE QUINTETTE.
Born at Watertown, Wis. Feb. 15 1875.

W.K. Hasken, in the year 1875, by ... of Congress, in the ... according to act ... Entered ... office of the Librarian ... of Congress at ... ...ton.

Kanouse Quintuplets 1875 • carte de visite • 2.5" x 4"

The Kanouse boys, believed to be the first recorded quintuplets born in the United States.
Unfortunately, none of the babies lived more than a few hours. After their burial, the family, fearful of
the boys' bodies being stolen from the local cemetery, had them exhumed and reburied in a secret location.

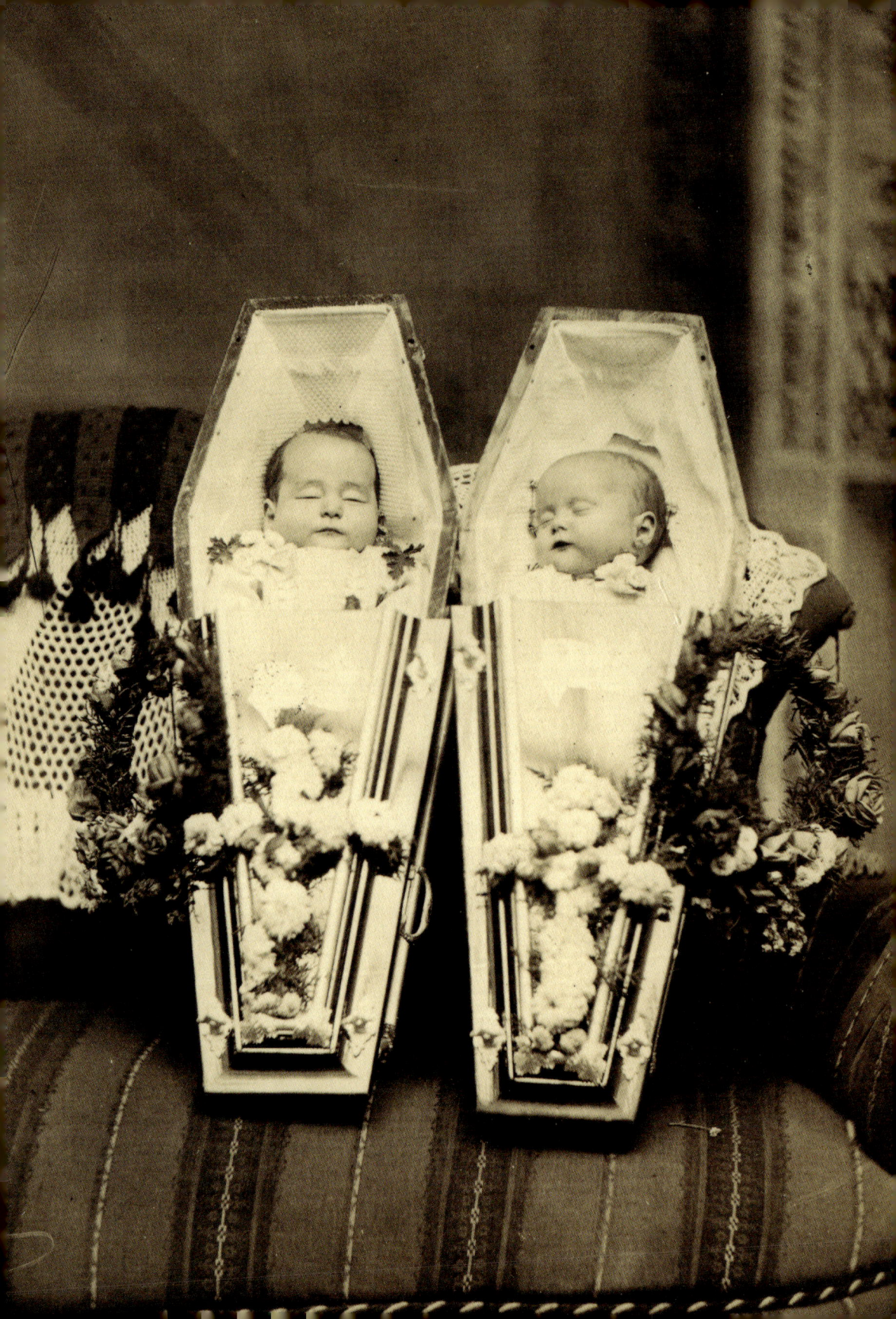

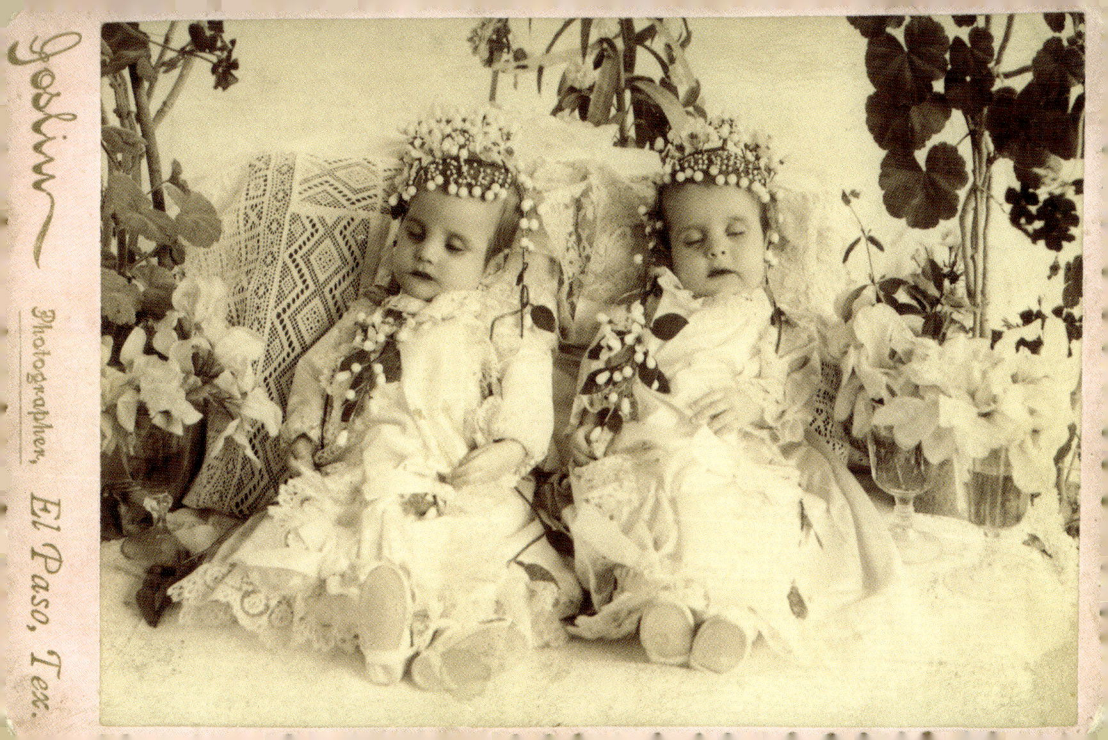
Goslin
Photographer,
El Paso, Tex.

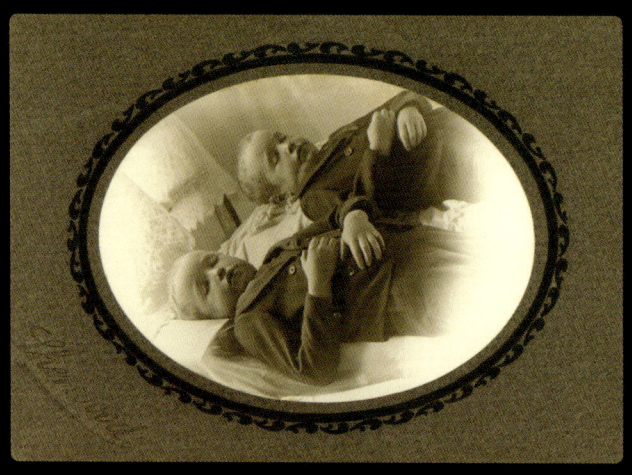

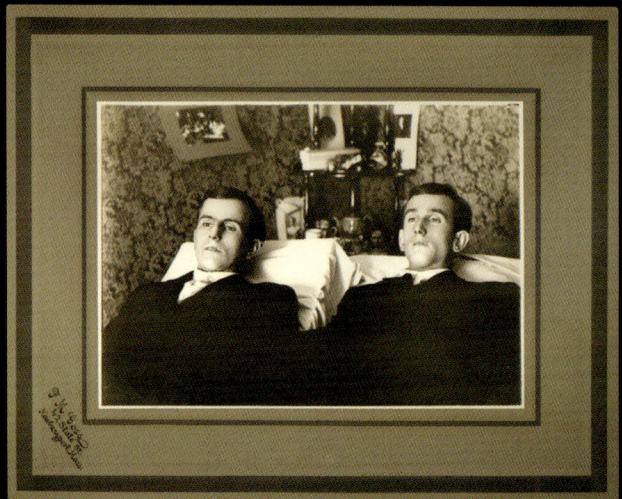

Inseparable in Life and Death circa 1902 • cabinet card • 4.25" x 6.5"

Saint Charles, Michigan: Identical twin boys, dressed in matching wool suits, are laid side by side beneath an open window.

. . . .

In the Parlor circa 1915 • gelatin silver print • 8" x 10"

Two young men on display in a parlor. Both appear to have suffered traumatic injuries to their lower faces, which were cosmetically repaired by a mortician.

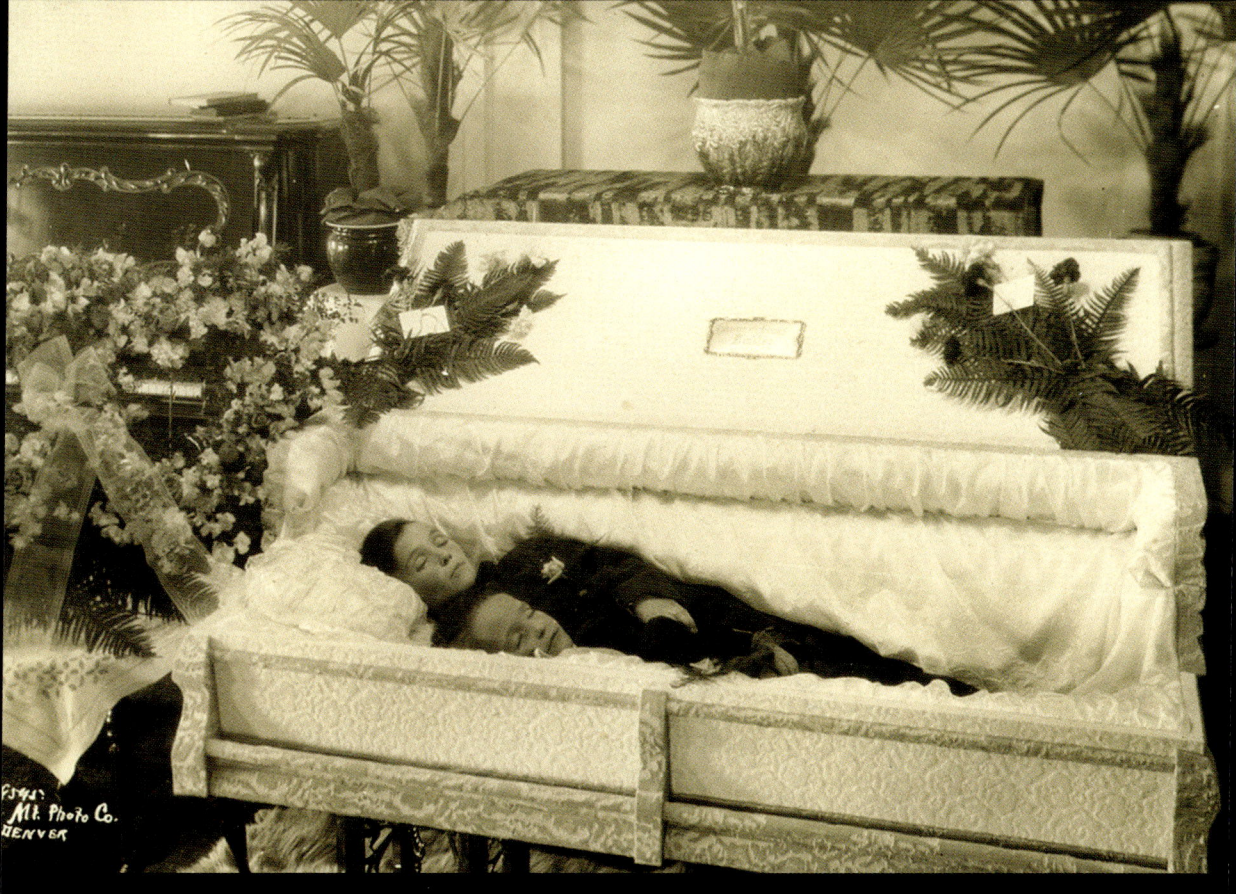

The Binkley Brothers 1923 • gelatin silver print • 10" x 8"

Edward K. Binkley (Jul. 22, 1917—Feb. 11, 1923) and Lawrence A. Binkley (Dec. 22, 1913—Feb. 12, 1923).
Records indicate the brothers died of pneumonia, and are buried in the same casket at Fairmont Cemetery in Denver,
Colorado. Their headstone has since disappeared.

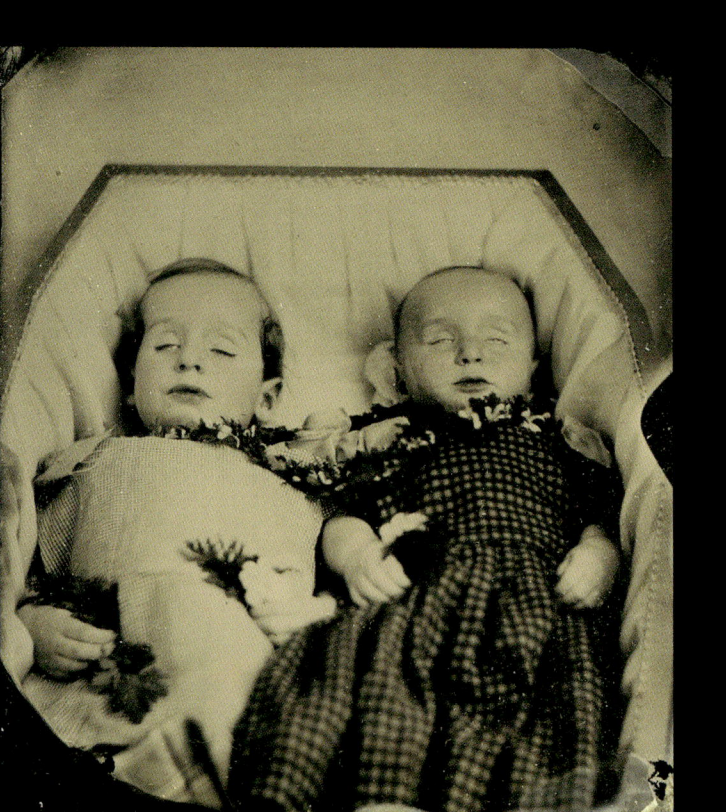

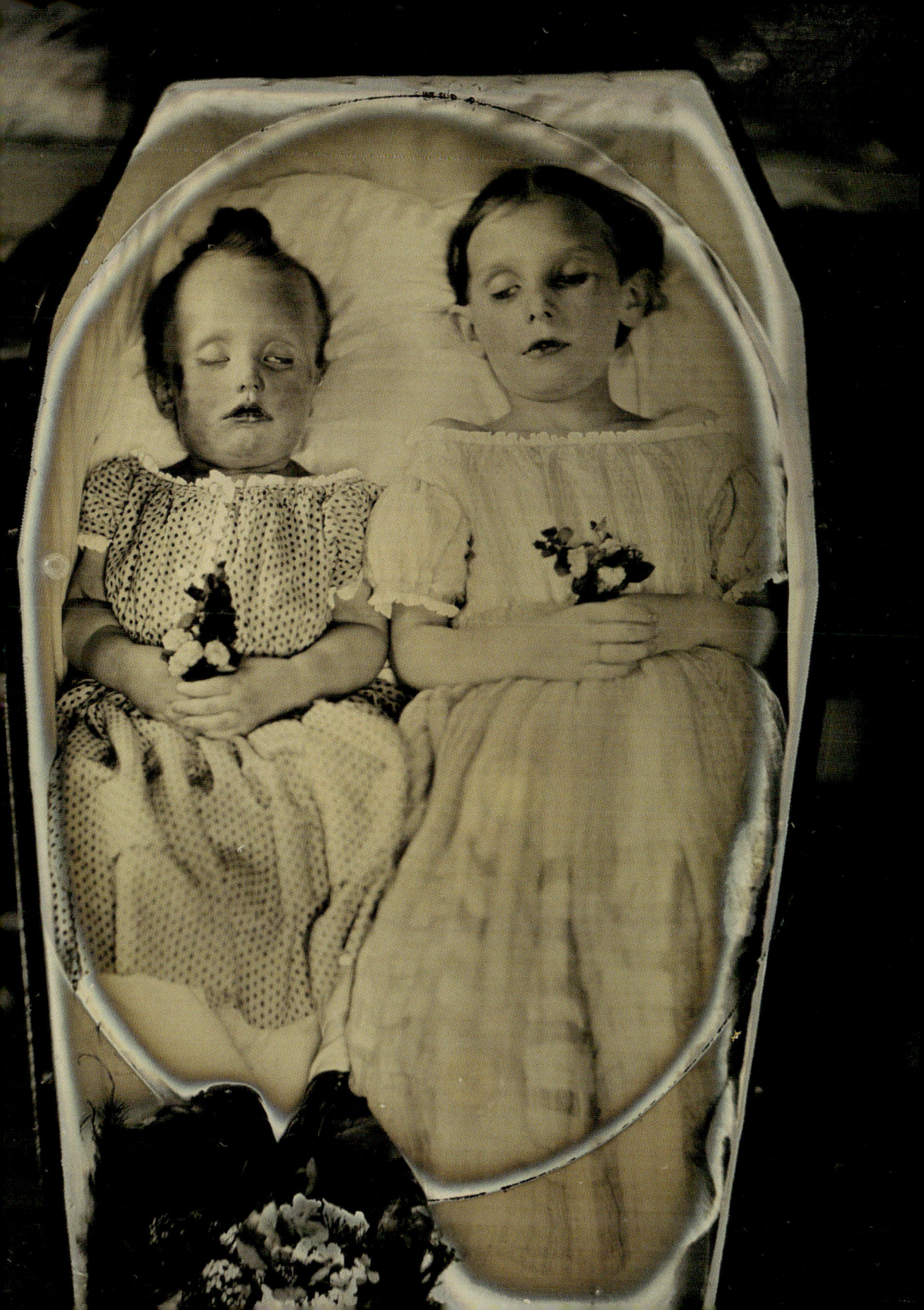

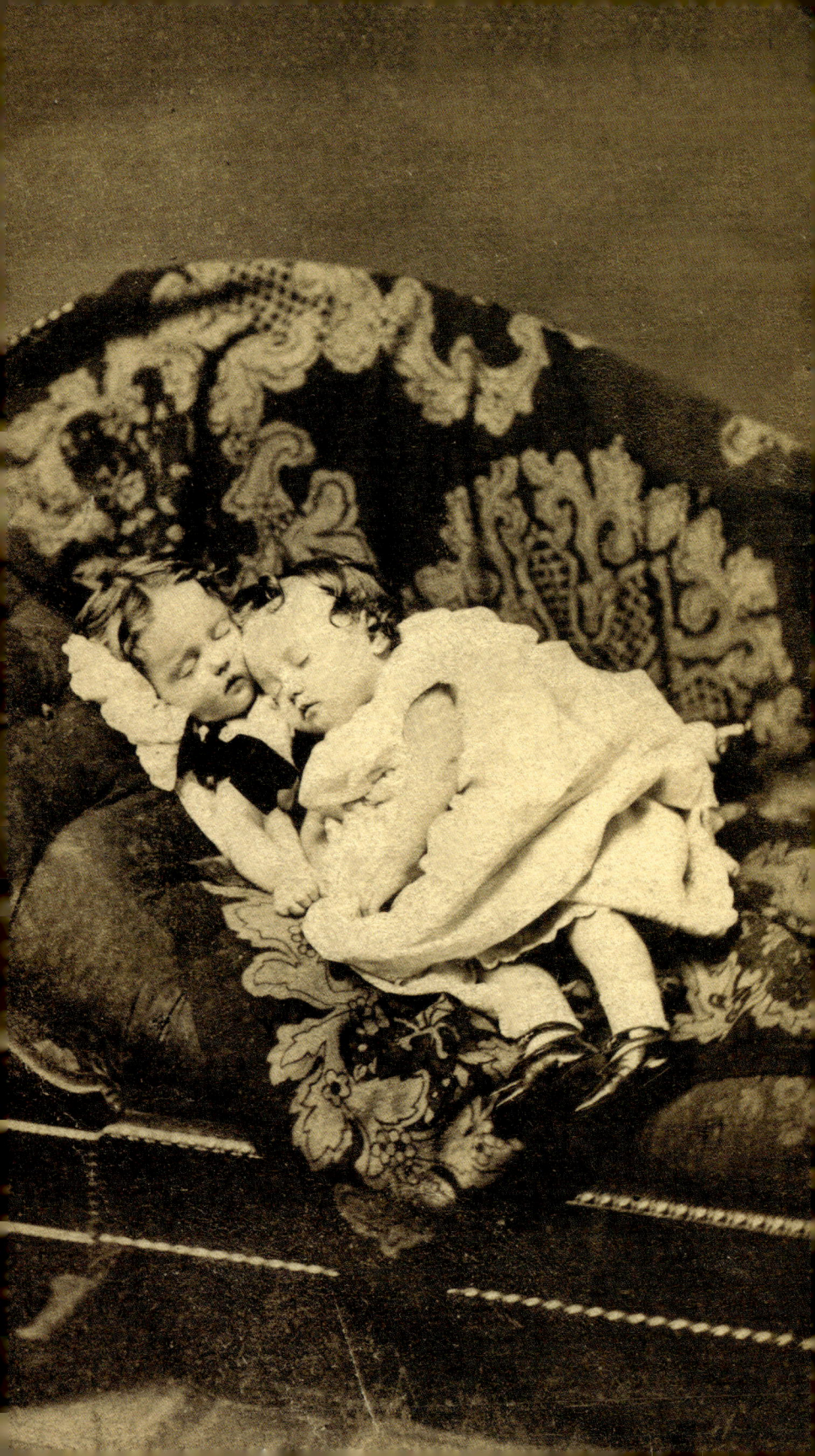

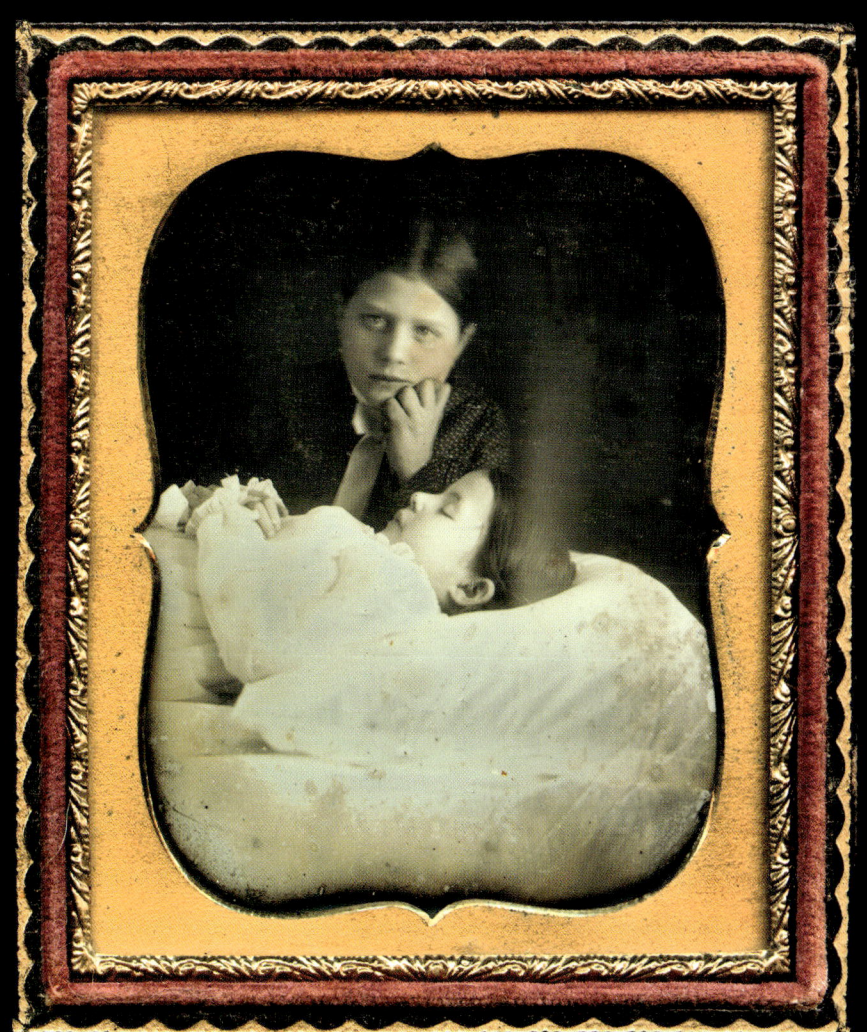

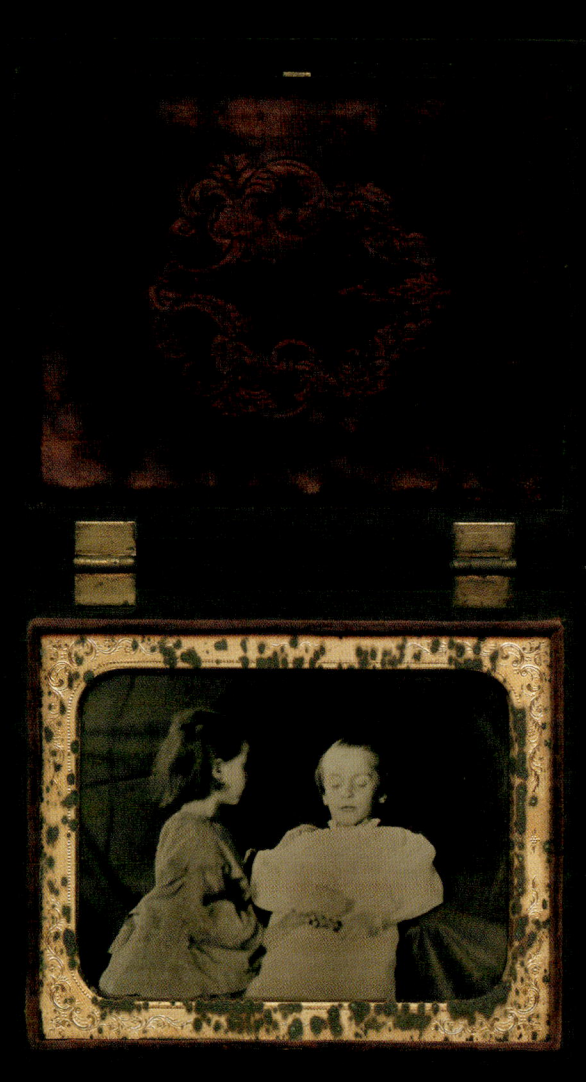

Big Brother circa 1858 • quarter-plate ambrotype • 3.75" x 4.75"

A young girl, her hands tenderly placed on the body of her older brother.

Sisters' Bond circa 1870 • cabinet card • 6.5" x 4.25"

In this early cabinet card, a young woman, likely an older sister, kneels at the side of a little girl, clasping the child's hand in her own,

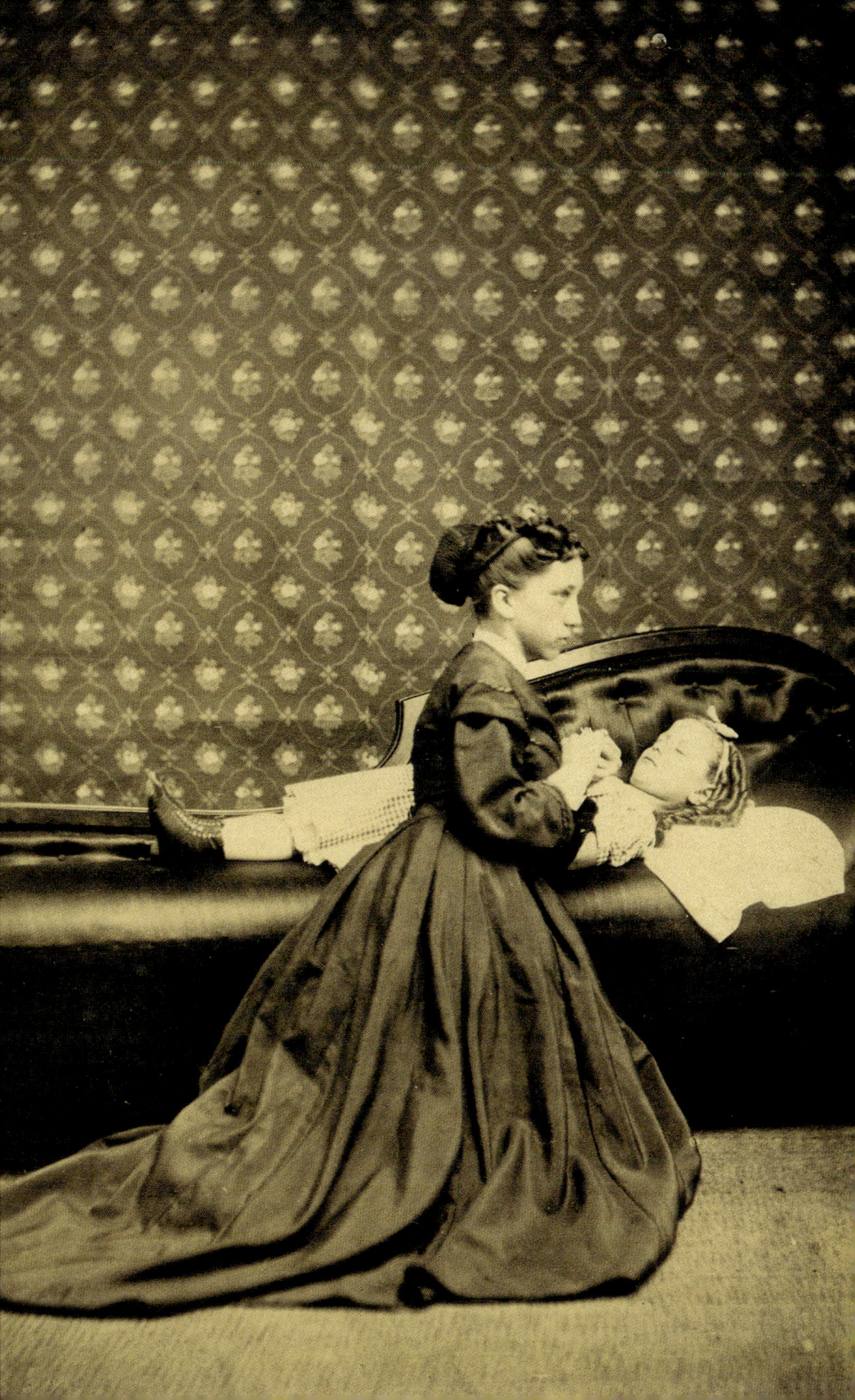

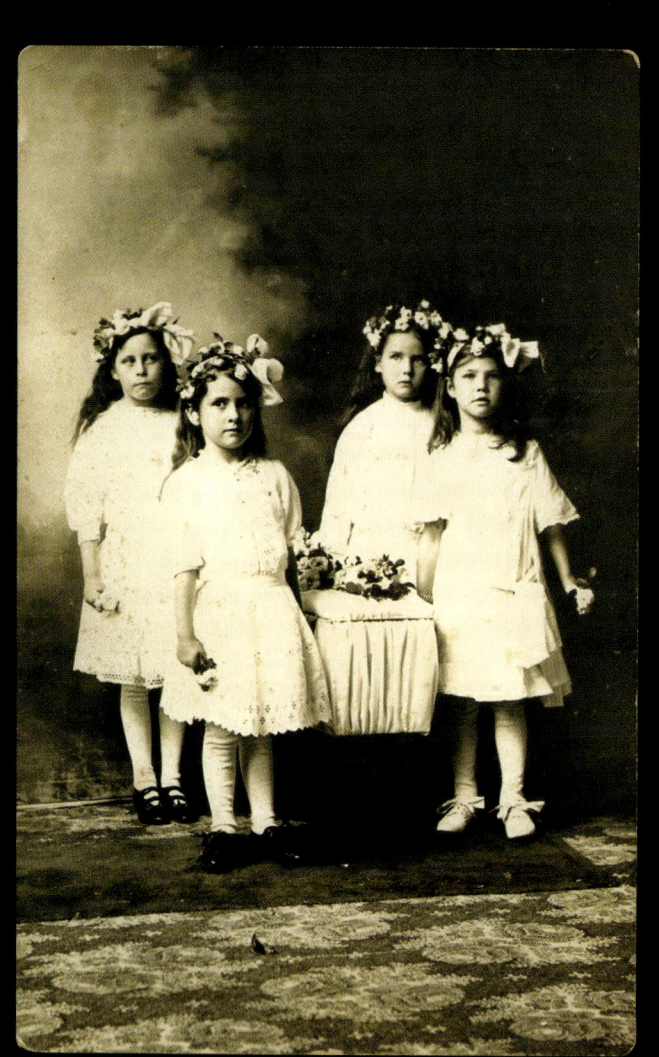

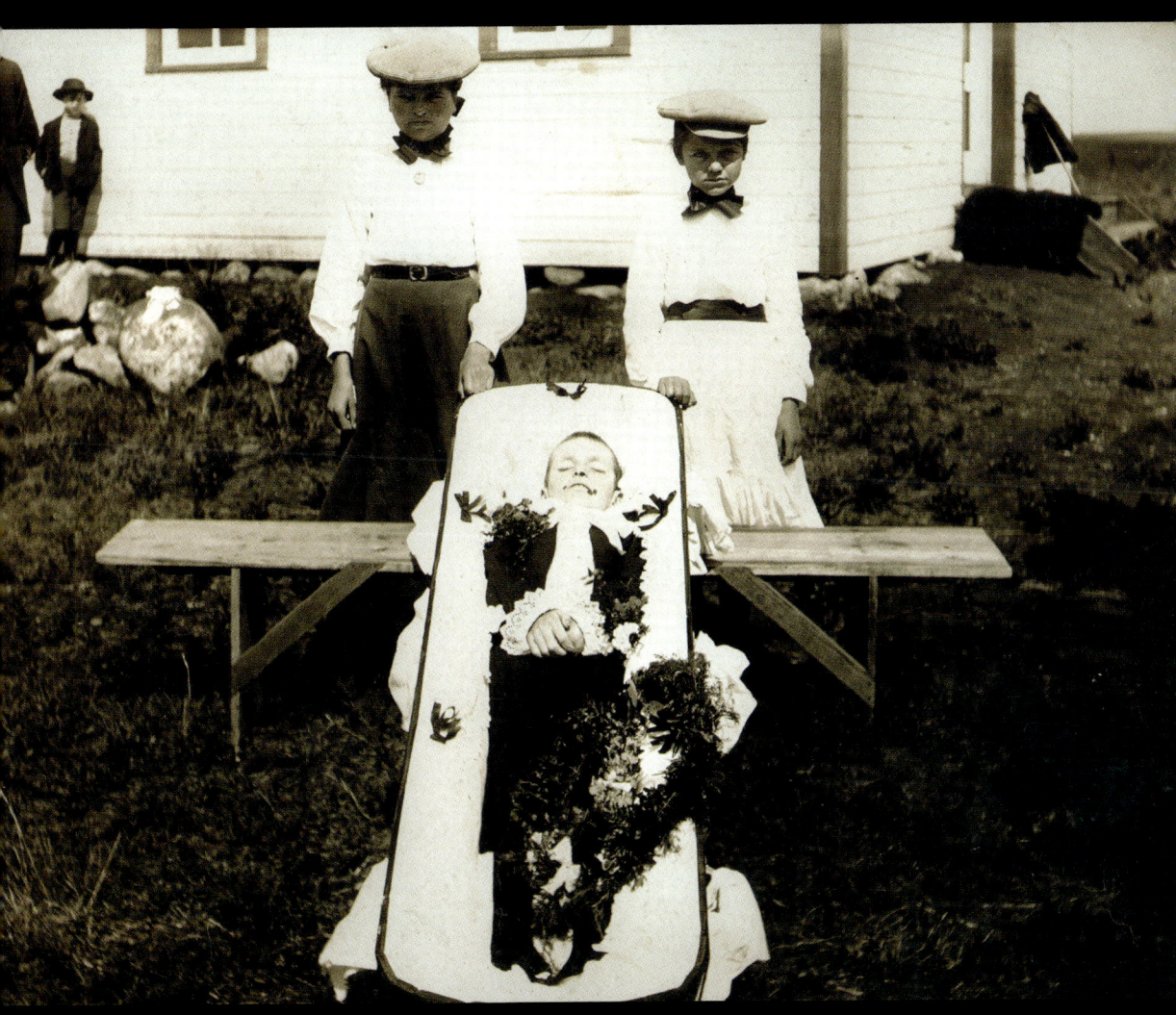

Watertown   1910 • gelatin silver print • 10" x 12"

In Watertown, Minnesota, Alma and Anna Hammarstrom pose with the body of their younger brother, Peter.
Most of Watertown's small population (less than 500 in 1910) was made up of Swedish and German immigrants.

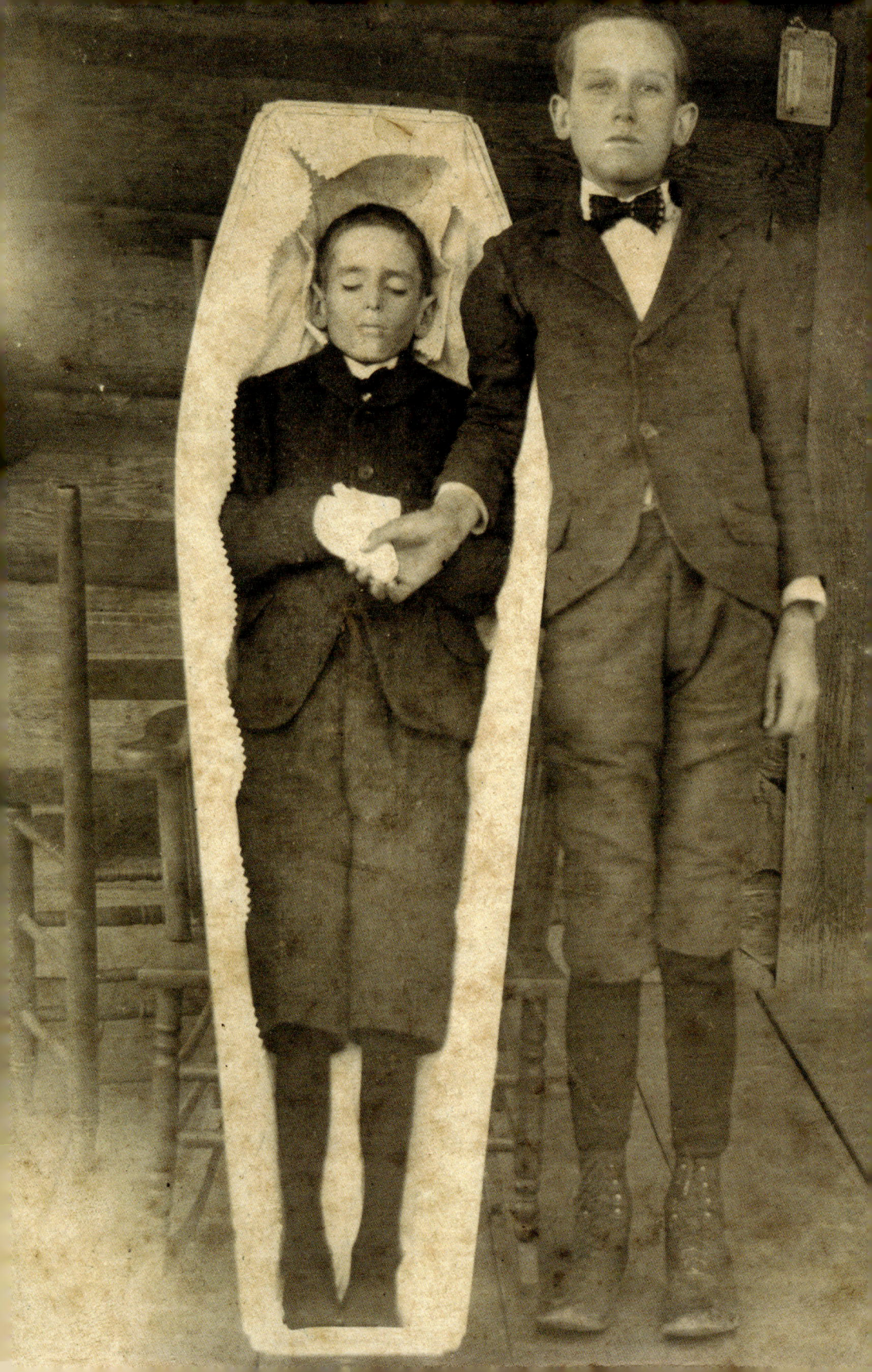

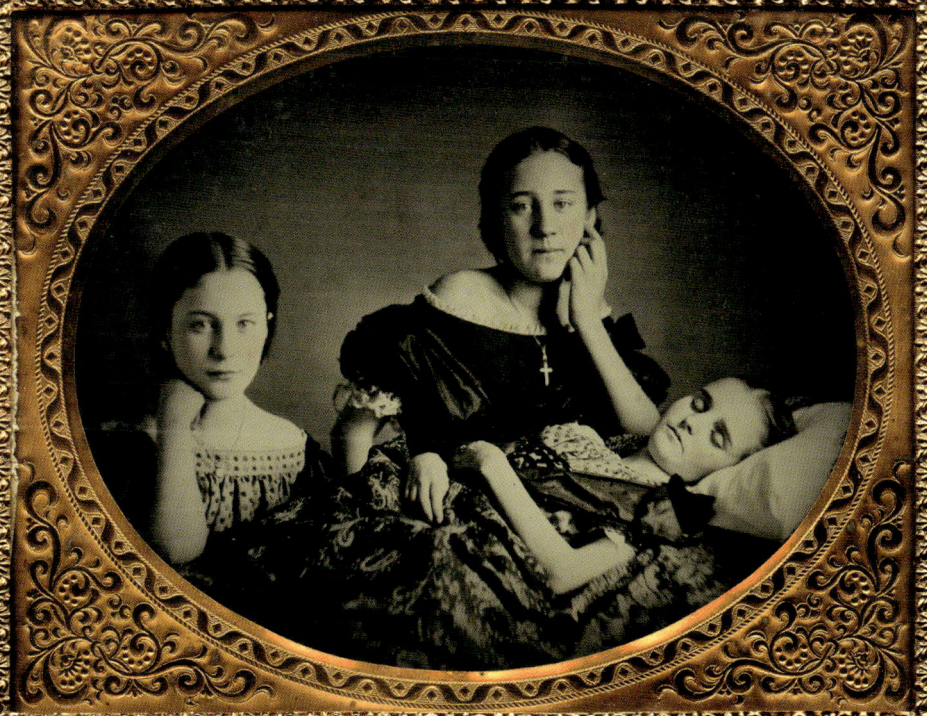

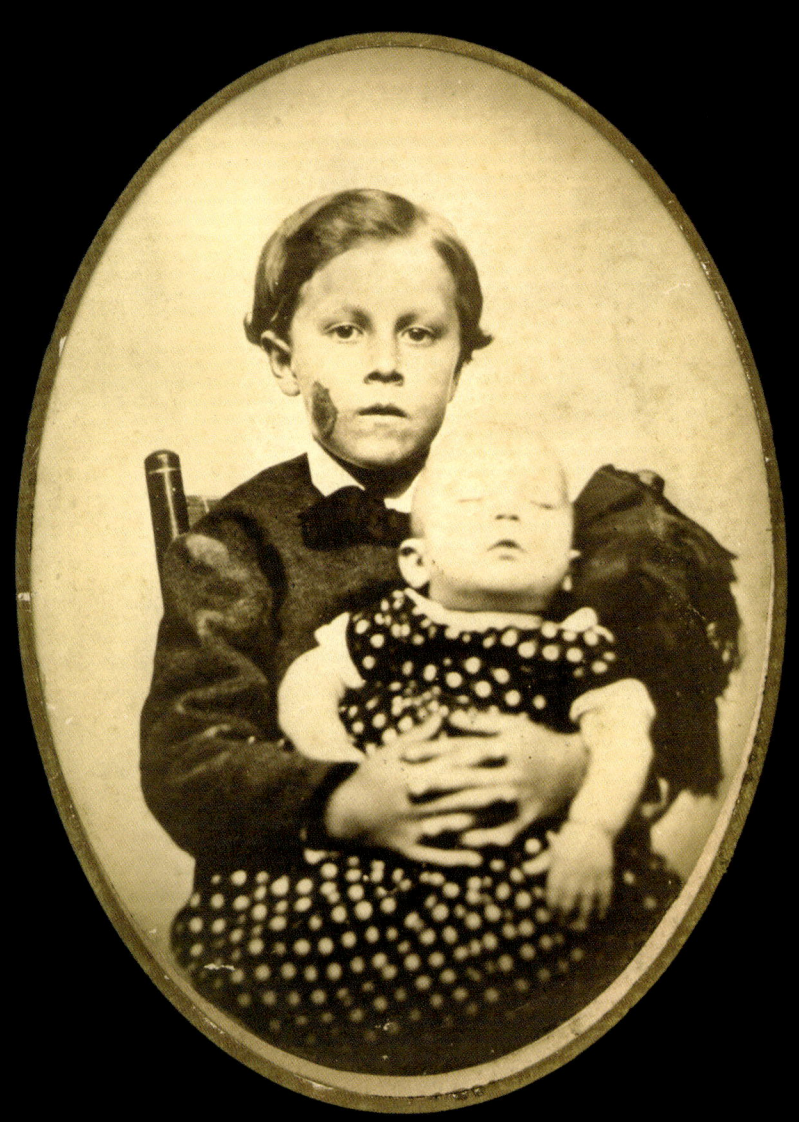

Polka Dot Dress   circa 1864 • albumen photo • 9" x 7"

A young boy holds his deceased sibling. The discoloration on the boy's face appears to be a port–wine stain birthmark.

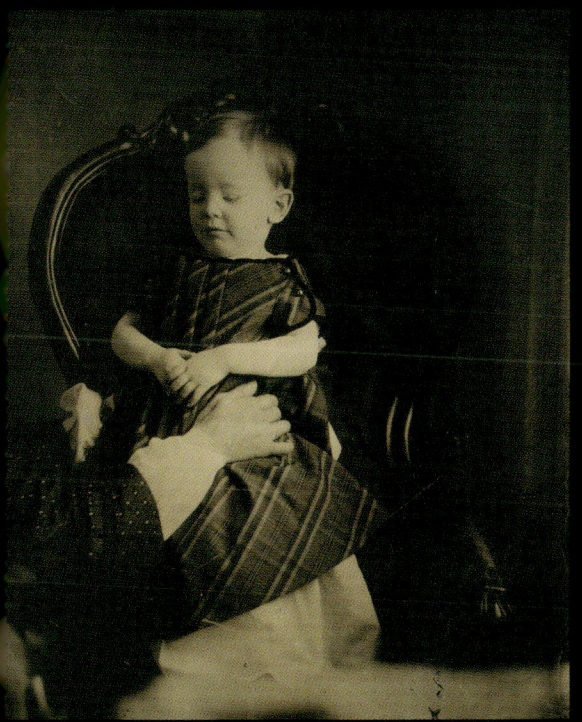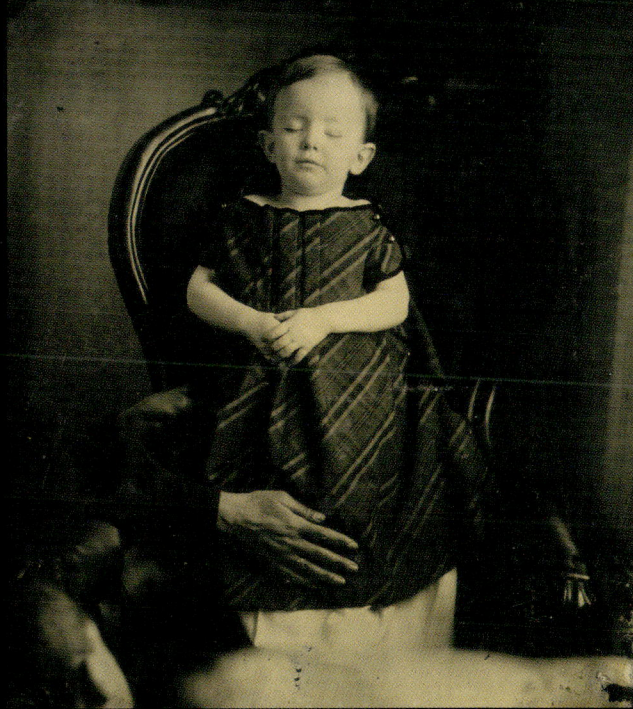

Woman with Dead Son   circa 1862 • sixth-plate tintypes • 3.75" x 2.75" each

Two views of a woman holding her dead son in a chair.
Note the head of another little boy, most likely the deceased boy's sibling, visible in the lower left of the image.

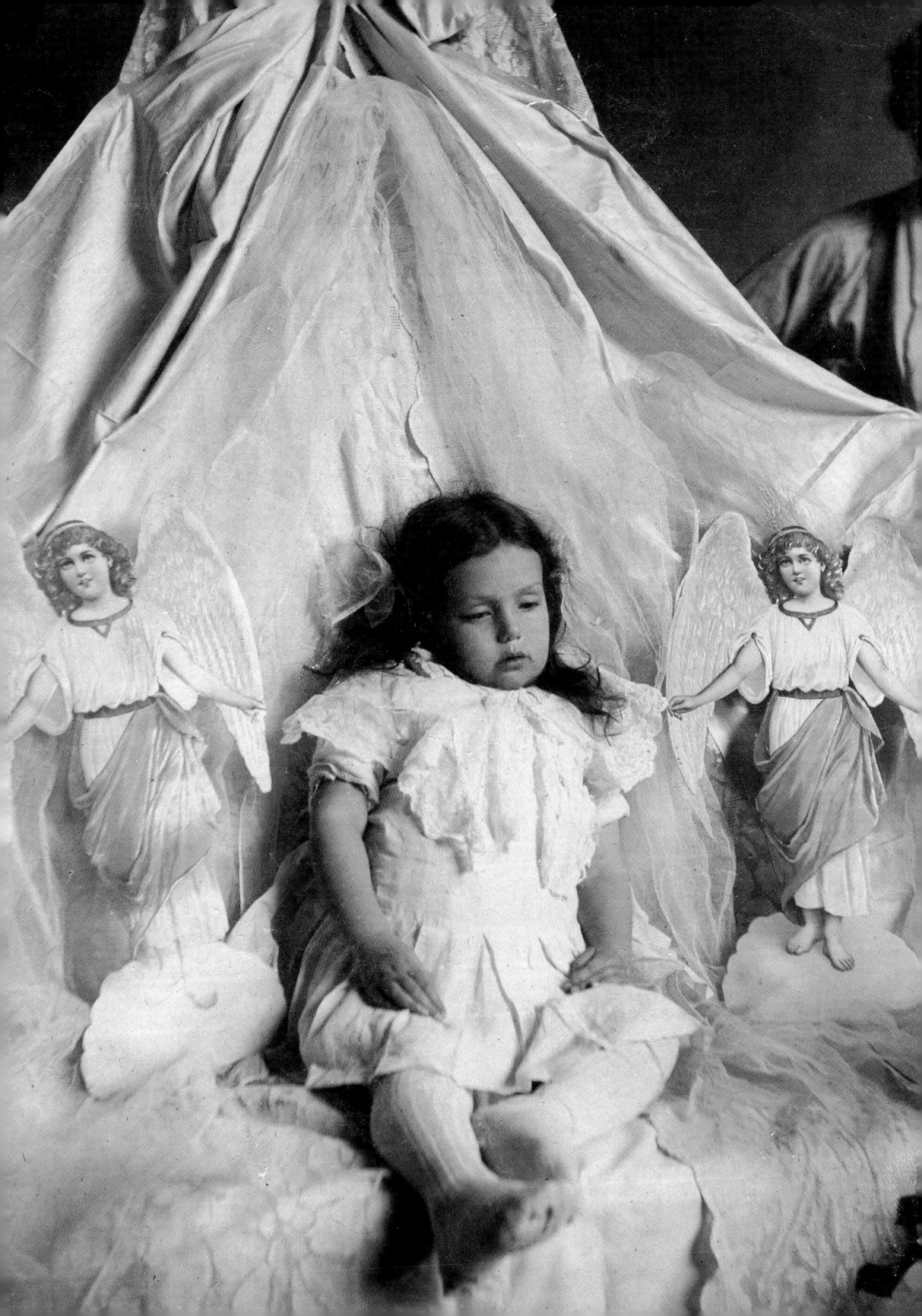

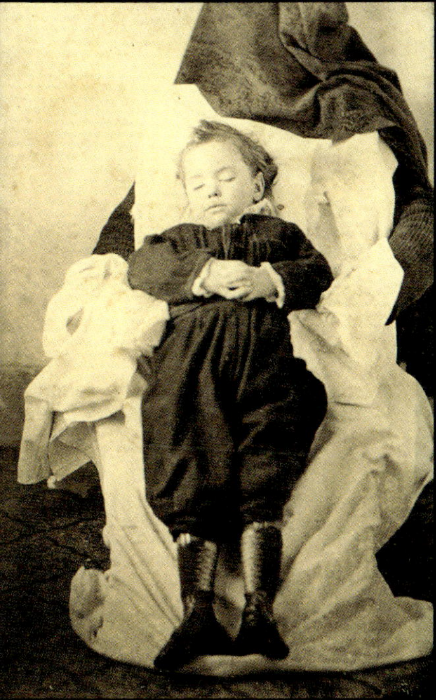

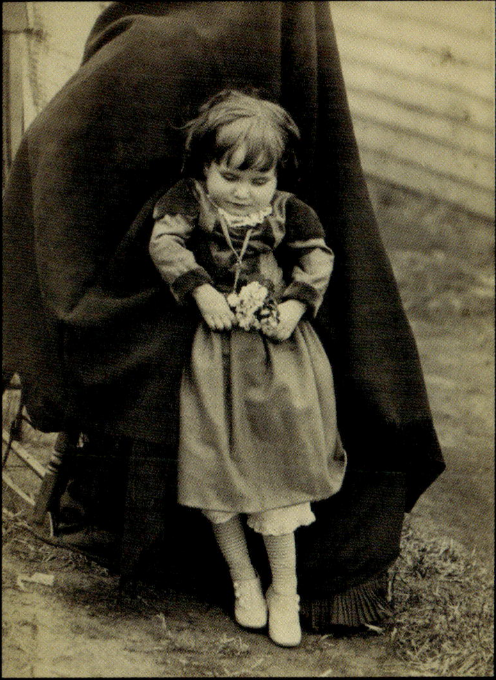

Angel Attendants   circa 1910 • gelatin silver print • 7.25" x 5.25"

Pretty little girl in stockinged feet, flanked by large lithographic angels. This is another example of a child being supported by a hidden, or shrouded, assistant; the outline of the assistant's body is vaguely apparent beneath the sheet.

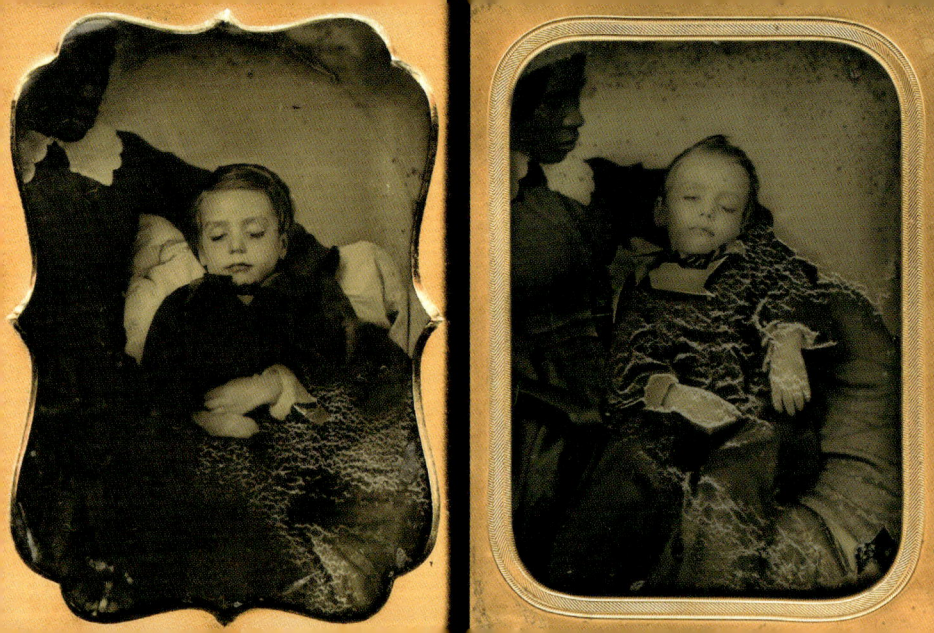

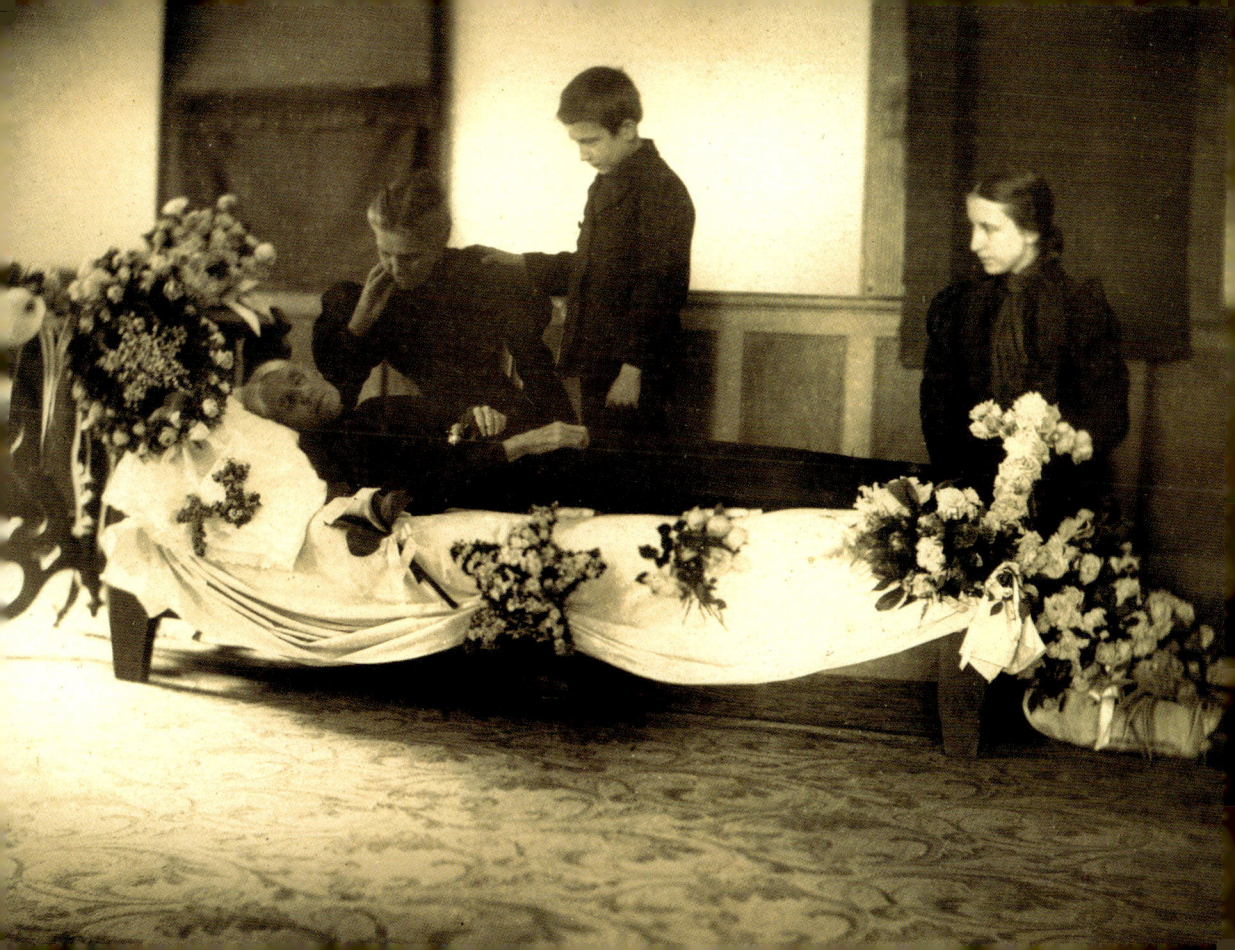

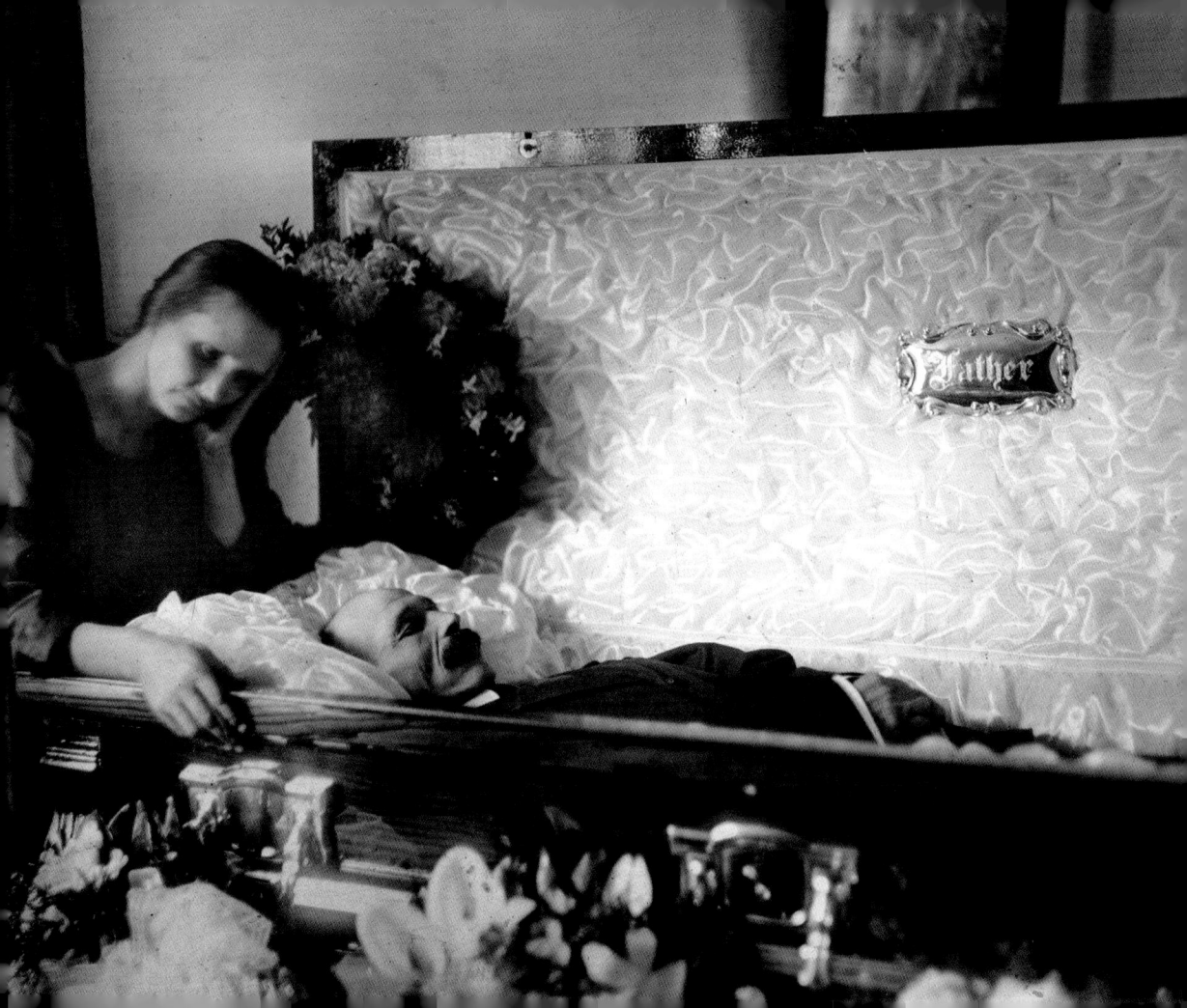

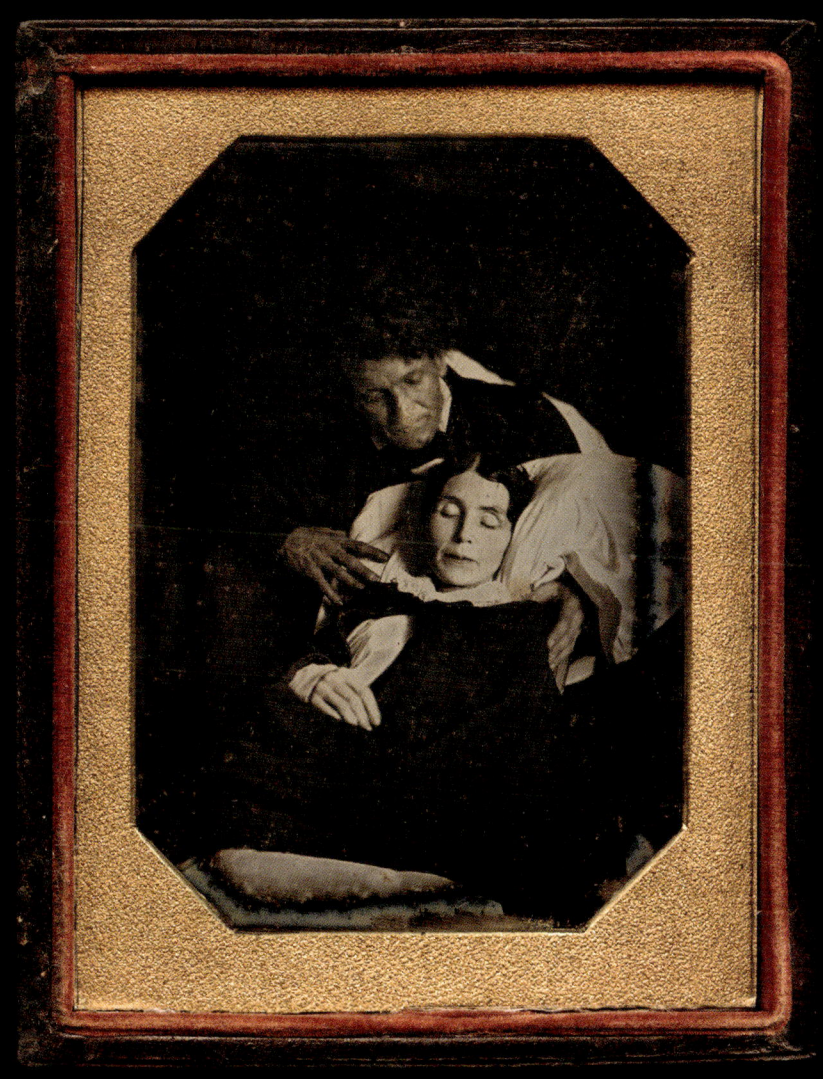

Lost Love circa 1845 • quarter-plate daguerreotype • 4.75" x 3.75"

In this affectionate scene, a man gazes down at the face of his deceased wife, whose head he supports with a pillow.

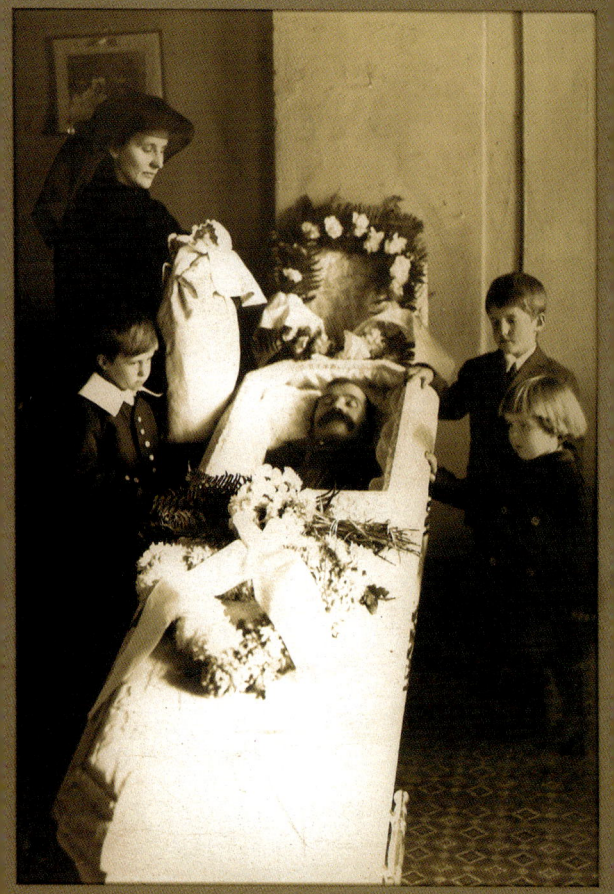

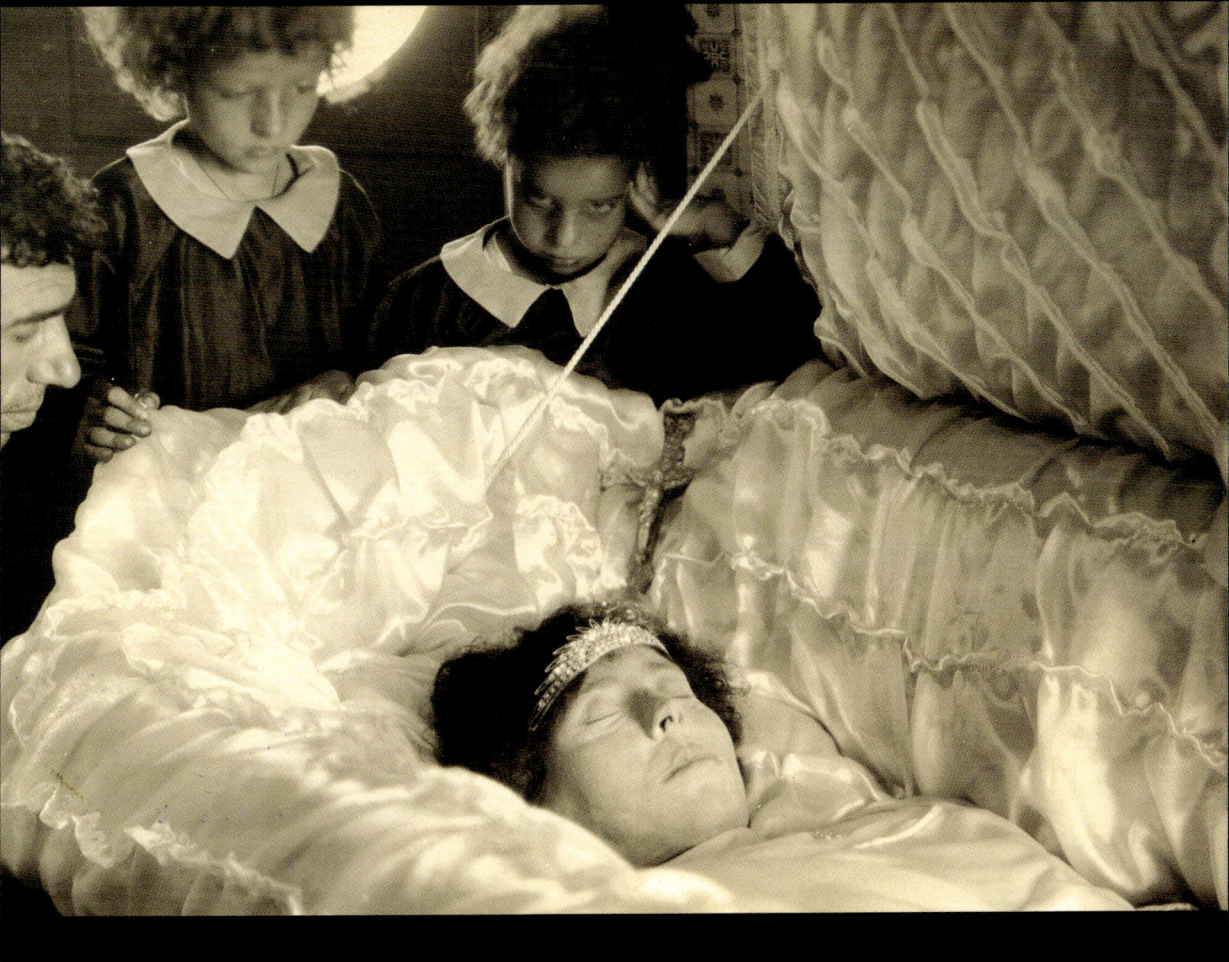

The Musca Family   1929 • gelatin silver print • 10" x 12"

Joseph Musca and daughters at Mrs. Musca's casket.

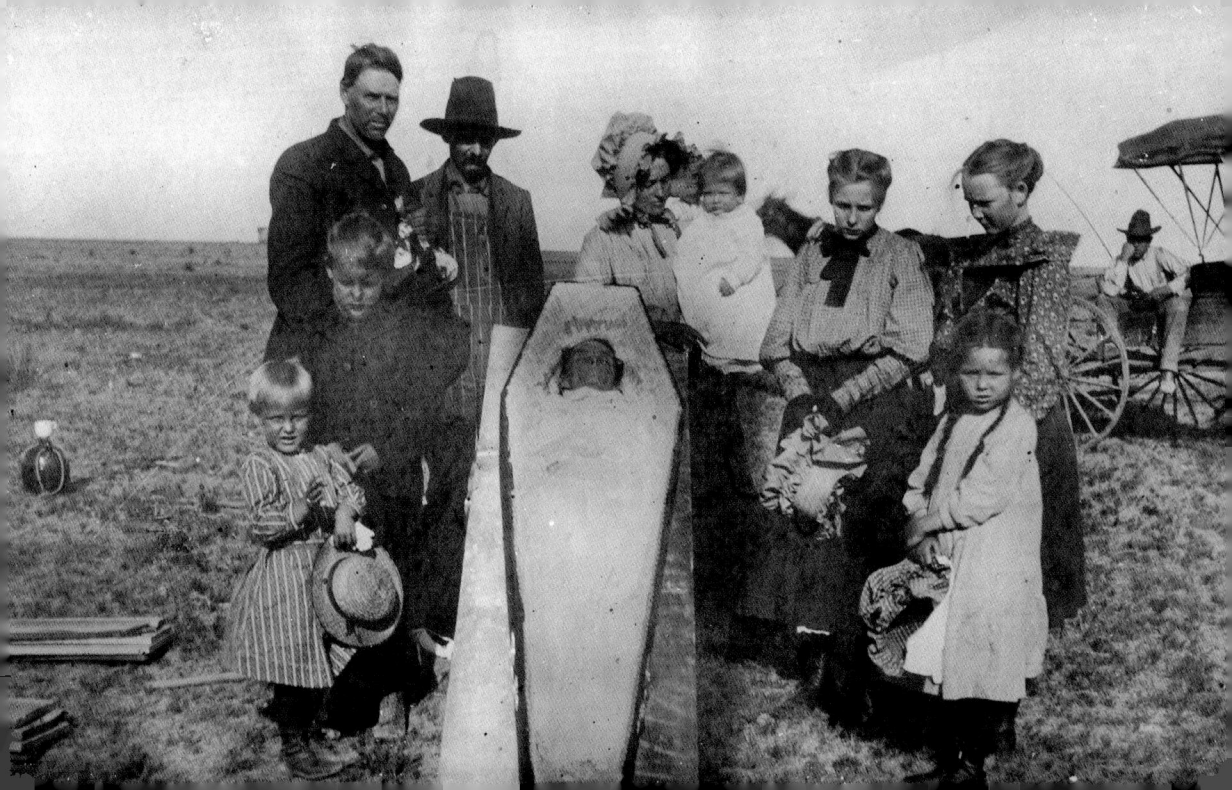

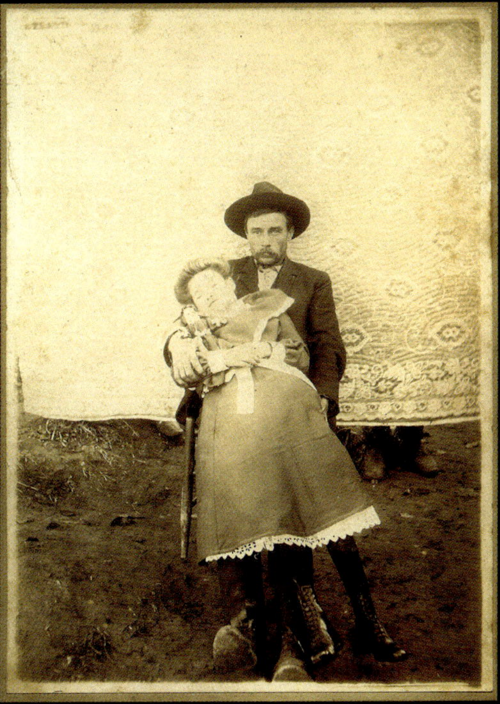

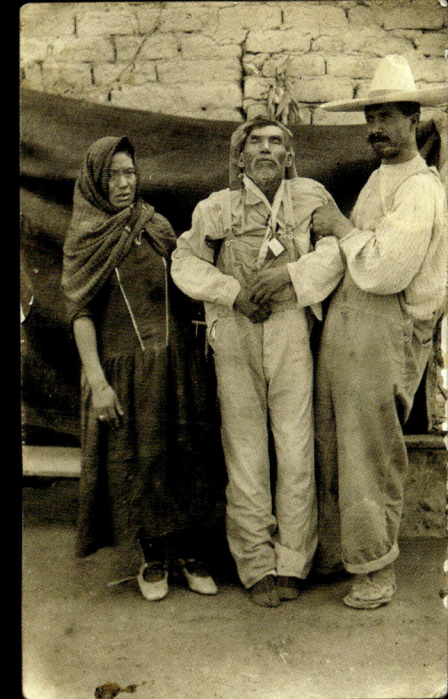

Tennessee   circa 1910 • gelatin silver print • 7" x 5"

In rural Tennessee, a forlorn man holds a teen girl or young woman across his lap.
A homemade doll has been laid on her shoulder. Taken outdoors in front of a makeshift backdrop,
the boots of the men holding it in place are clearly visible.

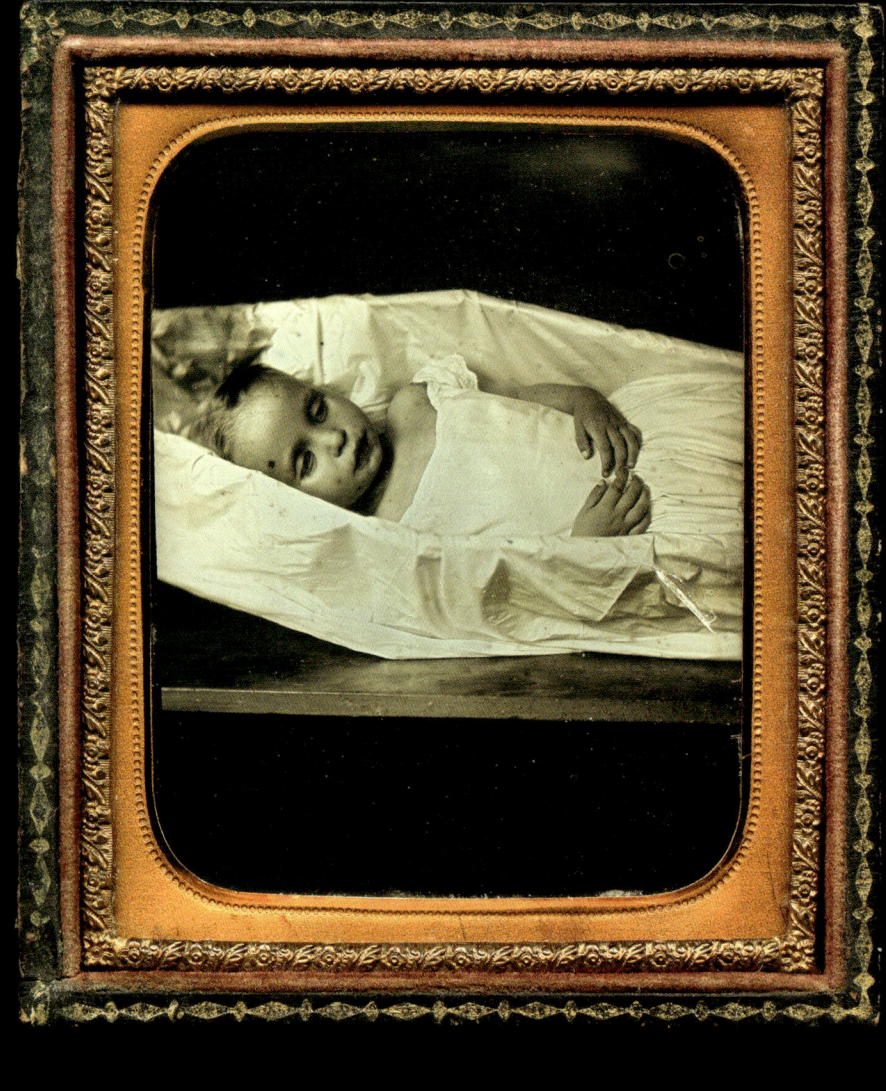

Girl in a Cloth-Covered Coffin circa 1853 • sixth-plate daguerreotype • 3.75″ x 3.25

ttle girl in a cloth-covered coffin, with signs of decomposition apparent in her hands and face, mostly around the n

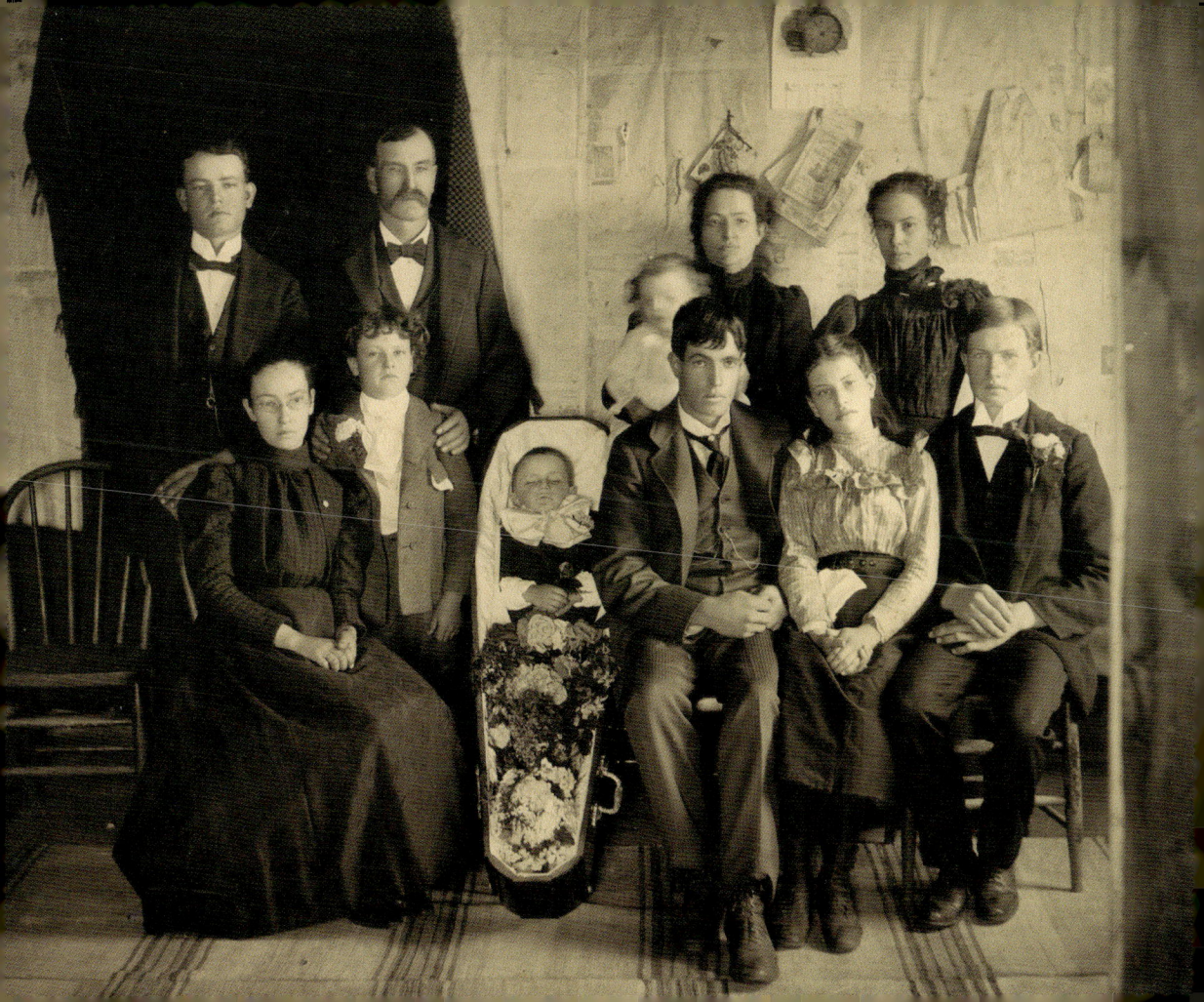

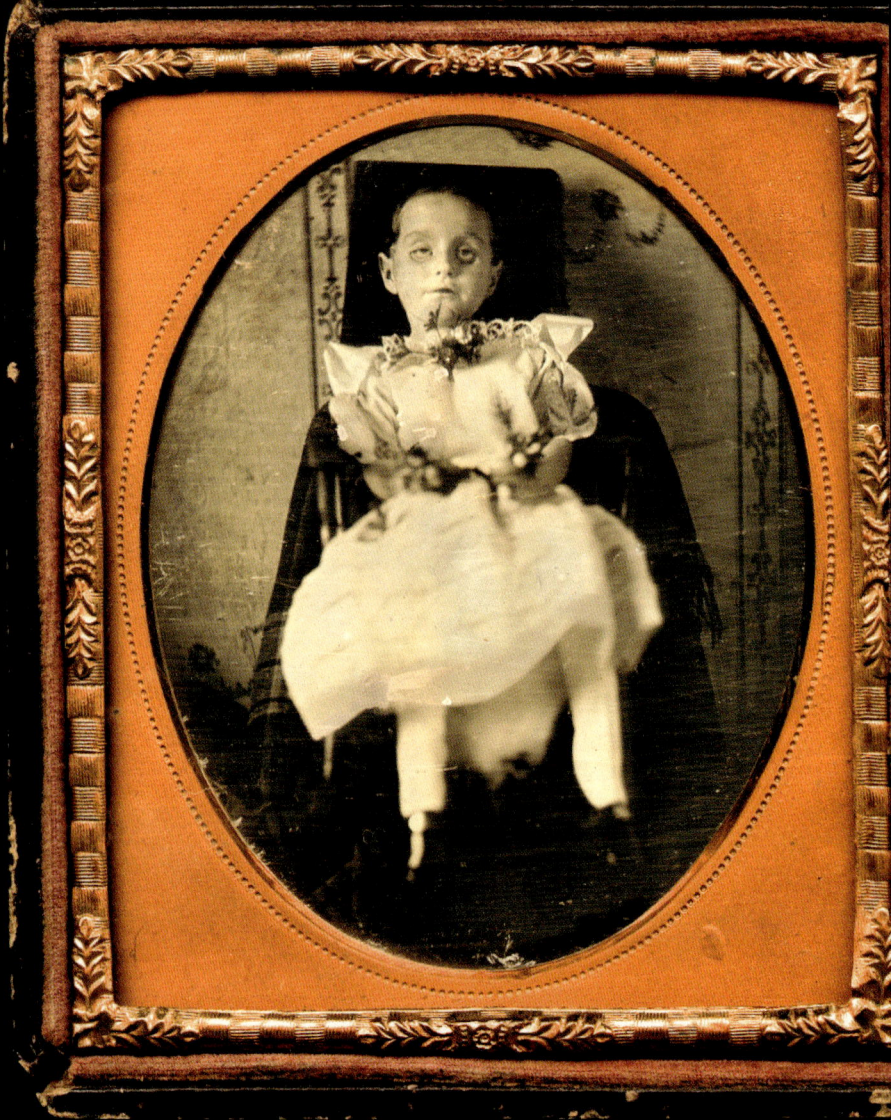

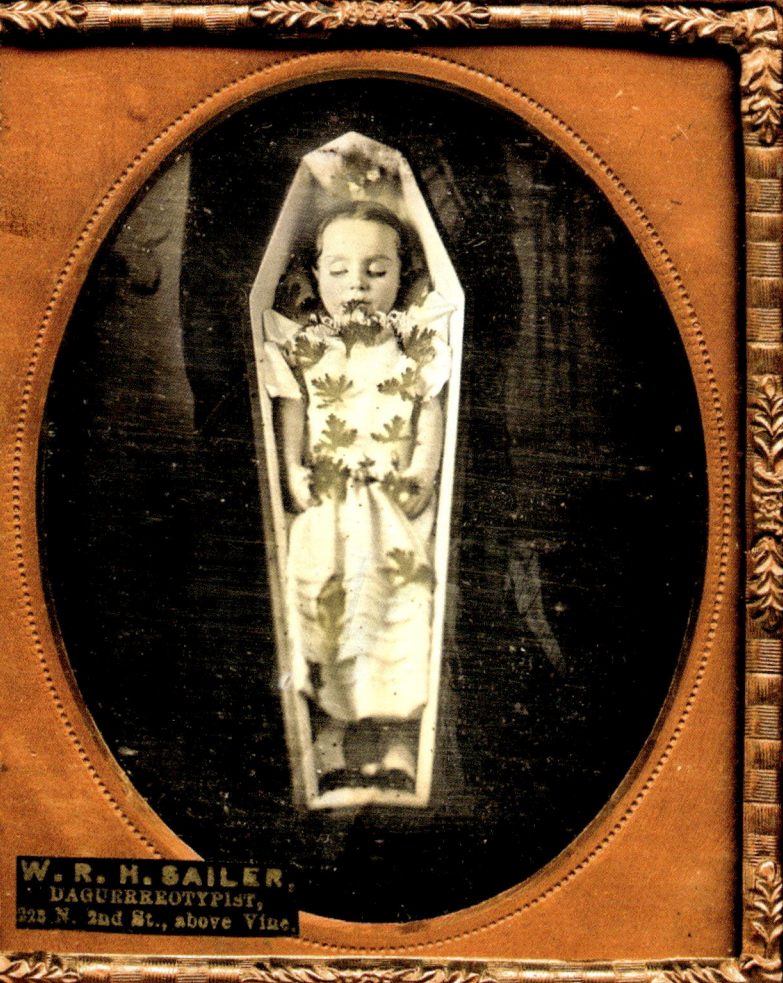

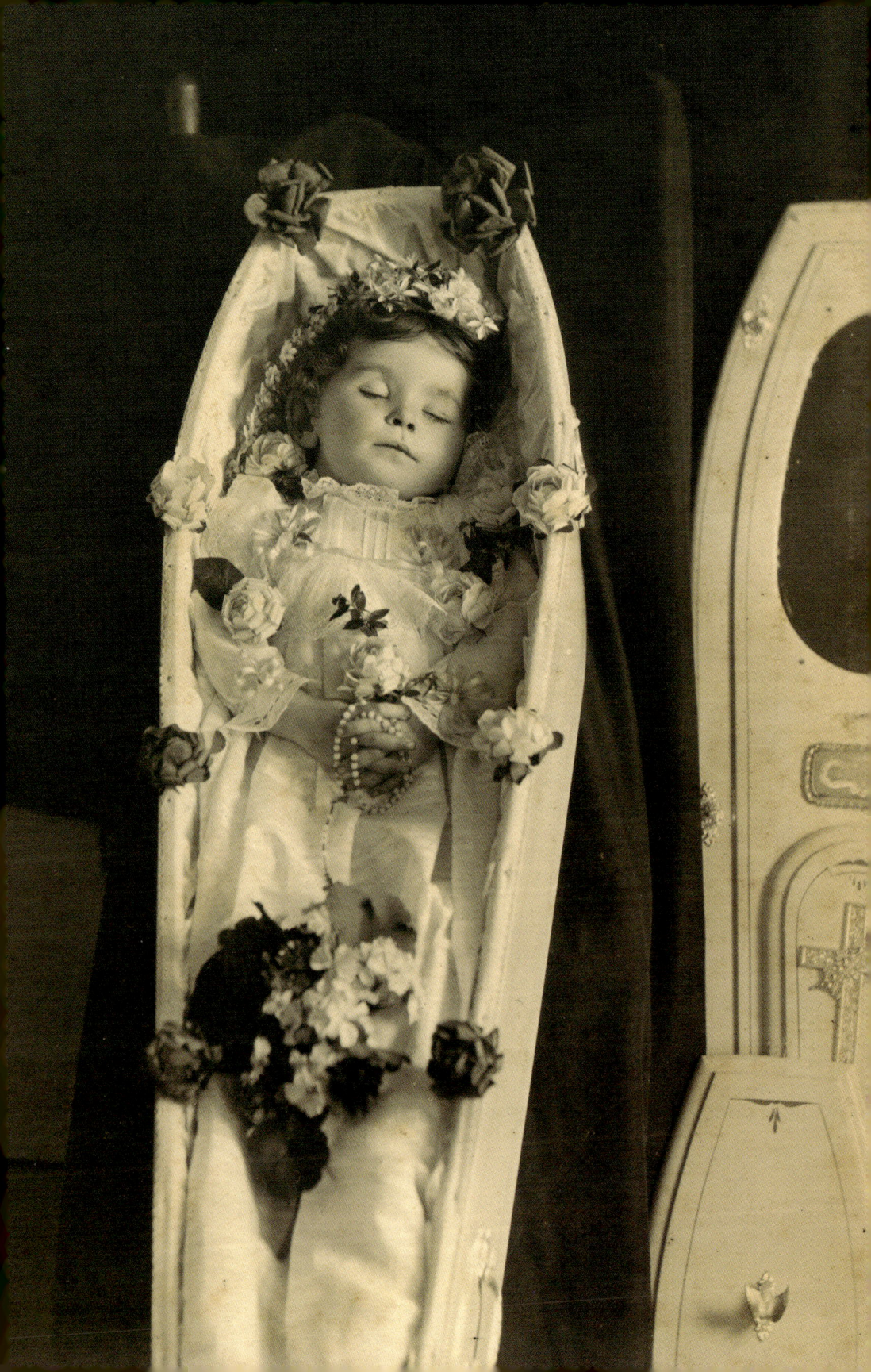

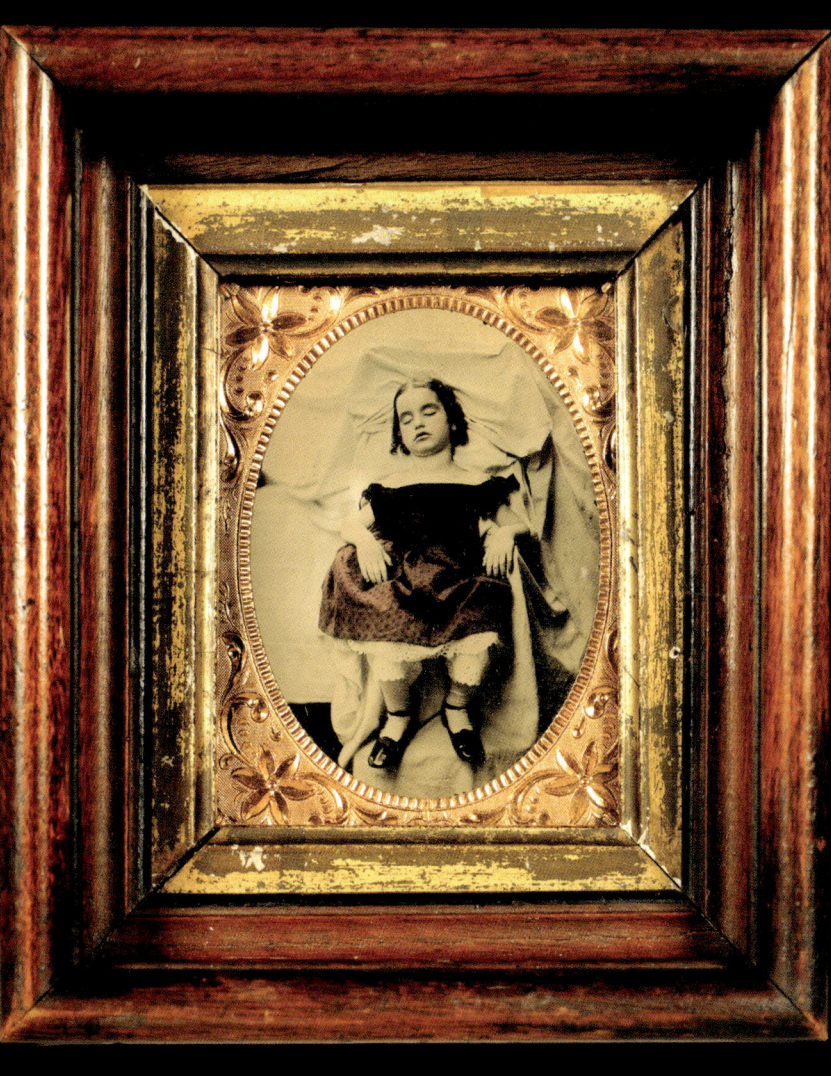

In Wisconsin circa 1895 • cabinet card • 6.5" x 4.25"

l, her coffin decorated with roses, holds a rosary. Off to one side is the coffin lid with its viewing window an

Girl in Red circa 1860 • quarter-plate ambrotype, hand colored • 7" x 5"

Little girl posed in a cloth-draped chair, which has been tipped slightly back against a wall.

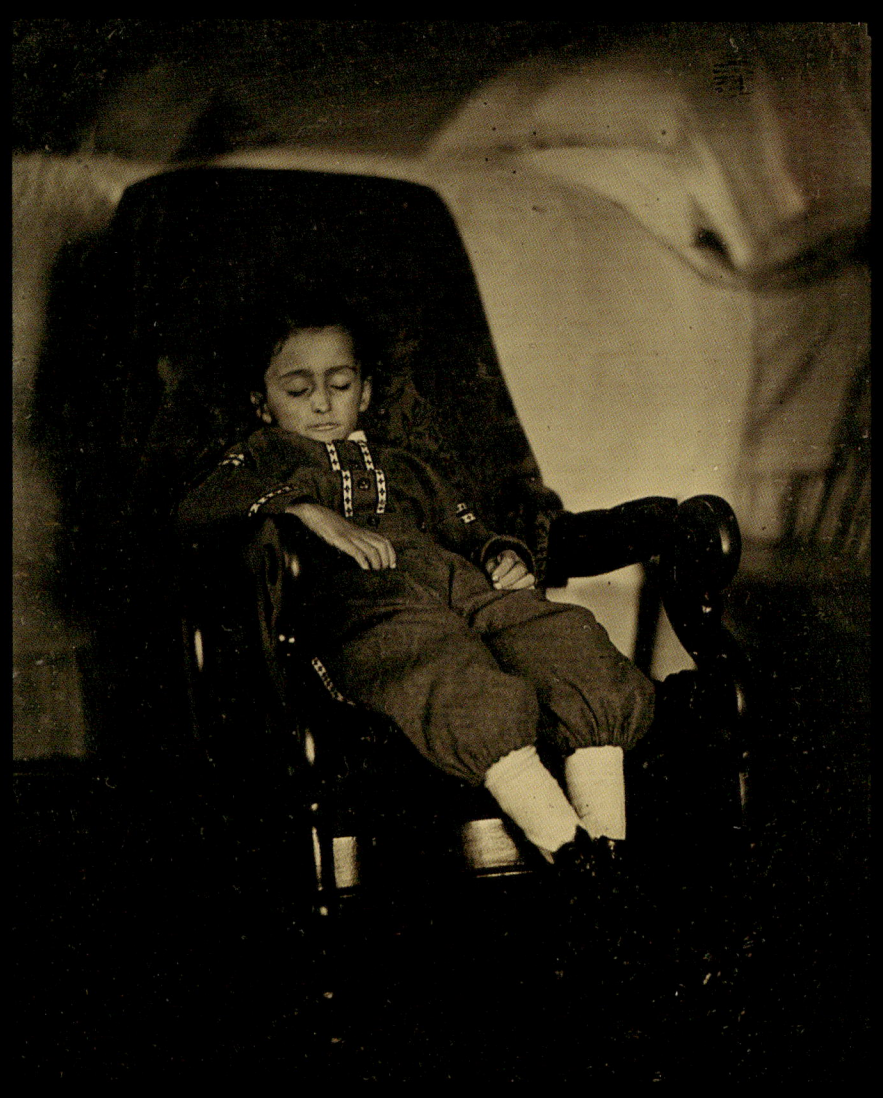

Favorite Chair
circa 1864 • quarter-plate tintype • 4.75" x 3.75"

In this image of a casually posed young boy, the photographer's intent was to portray him in as lifelike a manner as
possible. It is easy to imagine that this deceased boy has dozed off in his favorite chair.

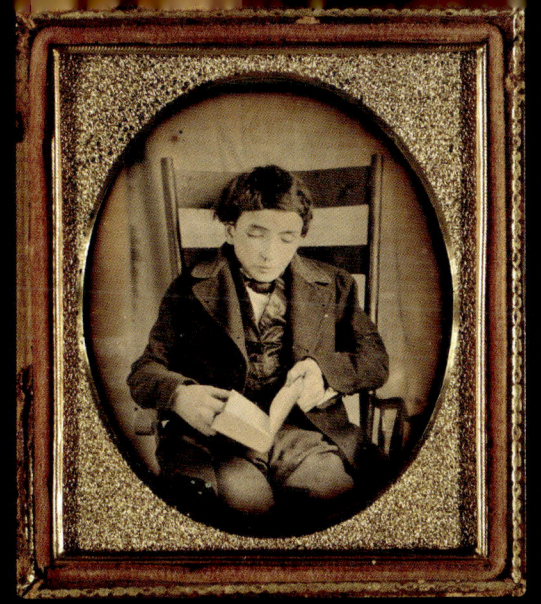
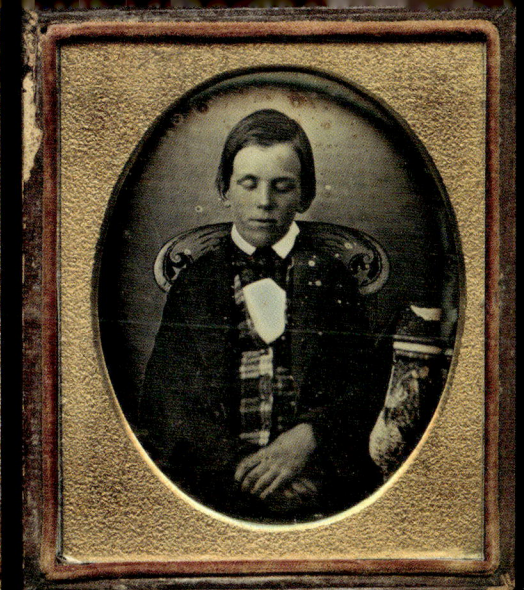

Boy with Open Book   circa 1847 • sixth-plate daguerreotype • 3.75" x 3.25"

A nicely dressed boy, posed upright and holding an open book. Note the bloody discharge running from his nose.
Due to the slower exposure times of the era, the presence of leakage in photographs would have oftentimes been unavoidable.

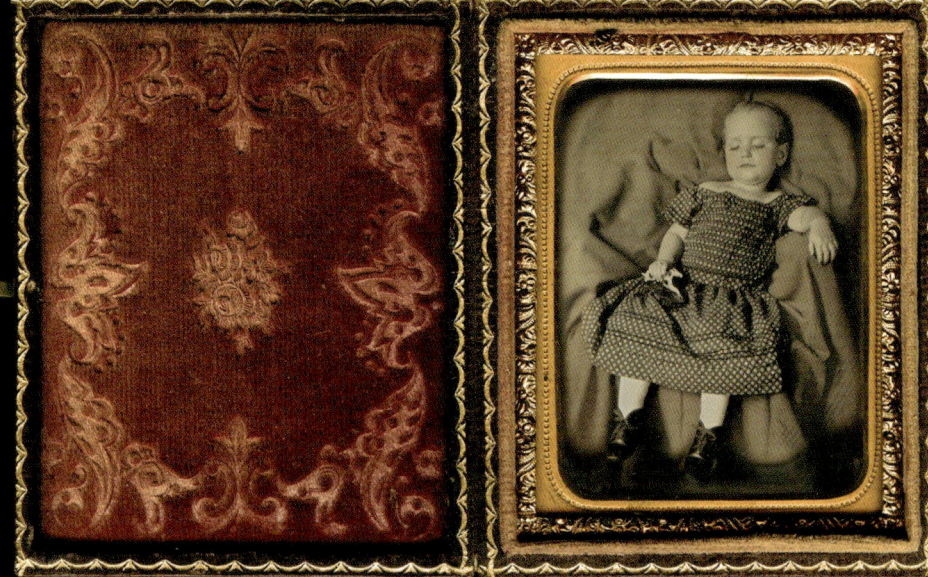

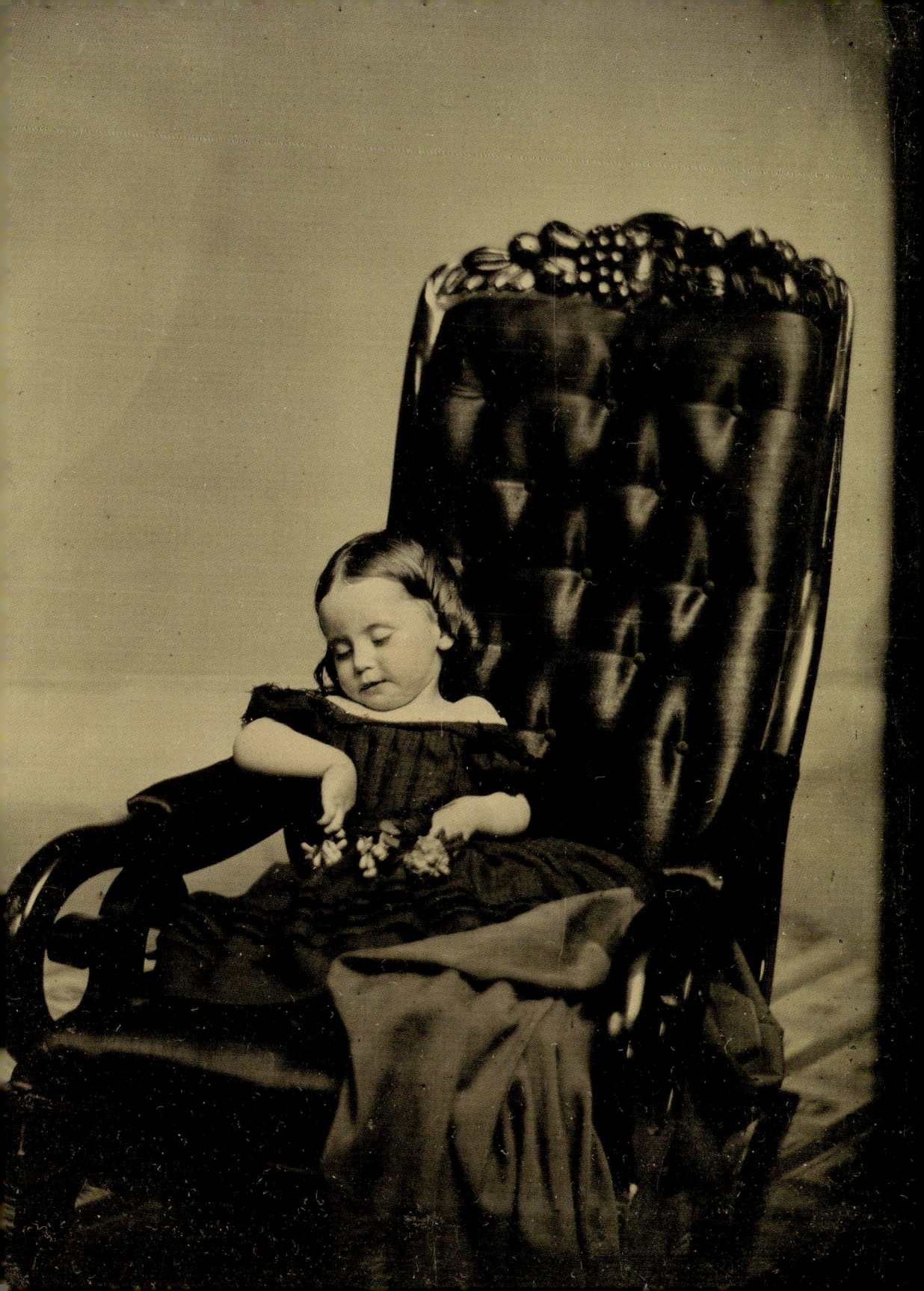

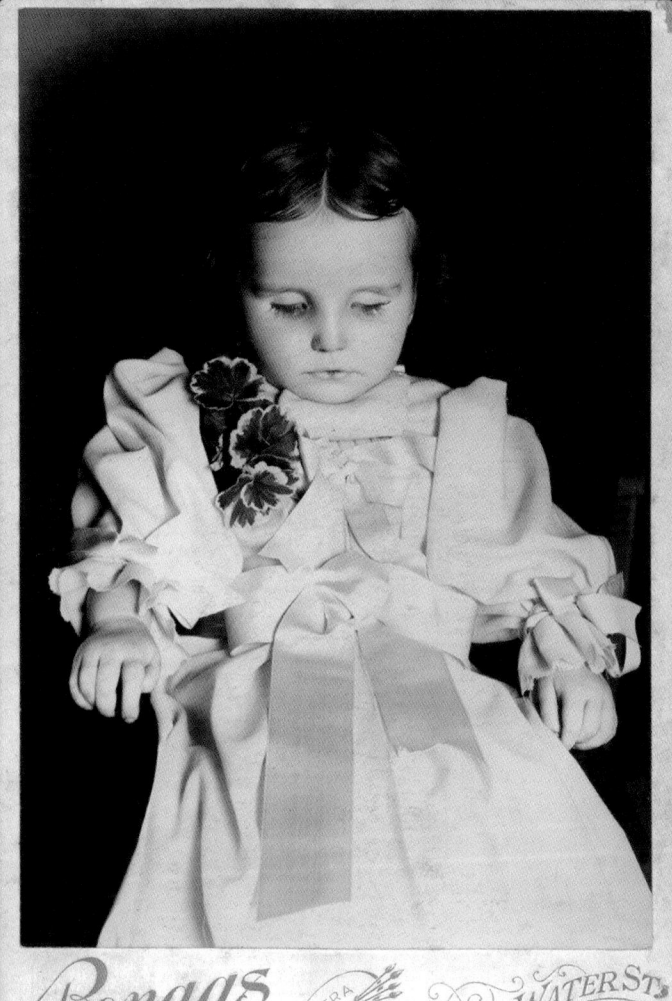

Renaas EXTRA FINISH 128 WATER ST, DECORAH, IA.

Maria Halloran circa 1893 • cabinet card • 6.5" x 4.25"

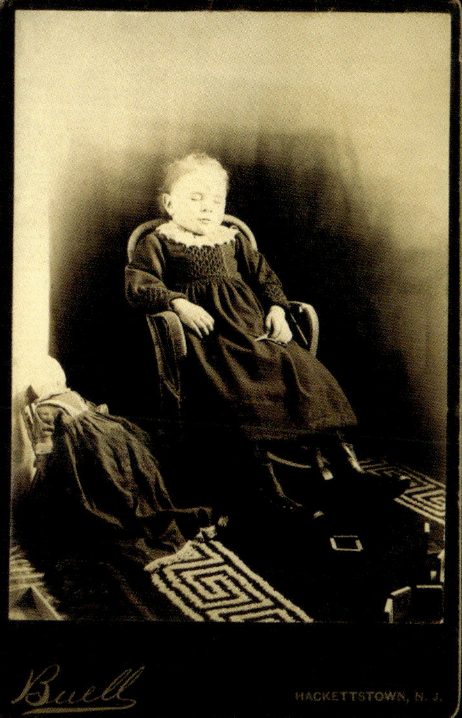

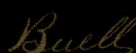

Buell   HACKETTSTOWN, N. J.

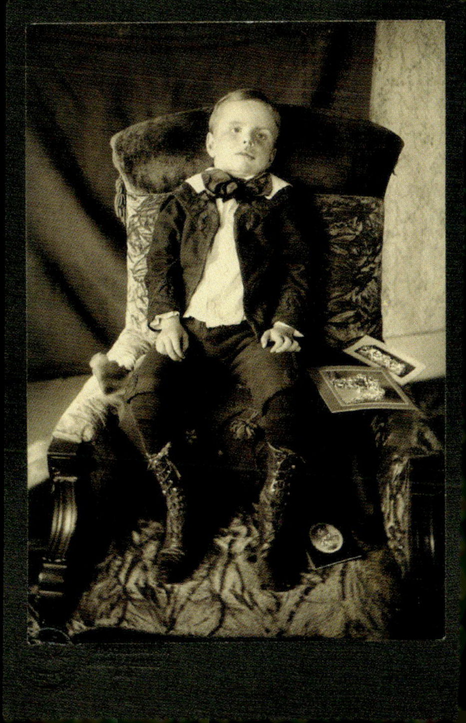

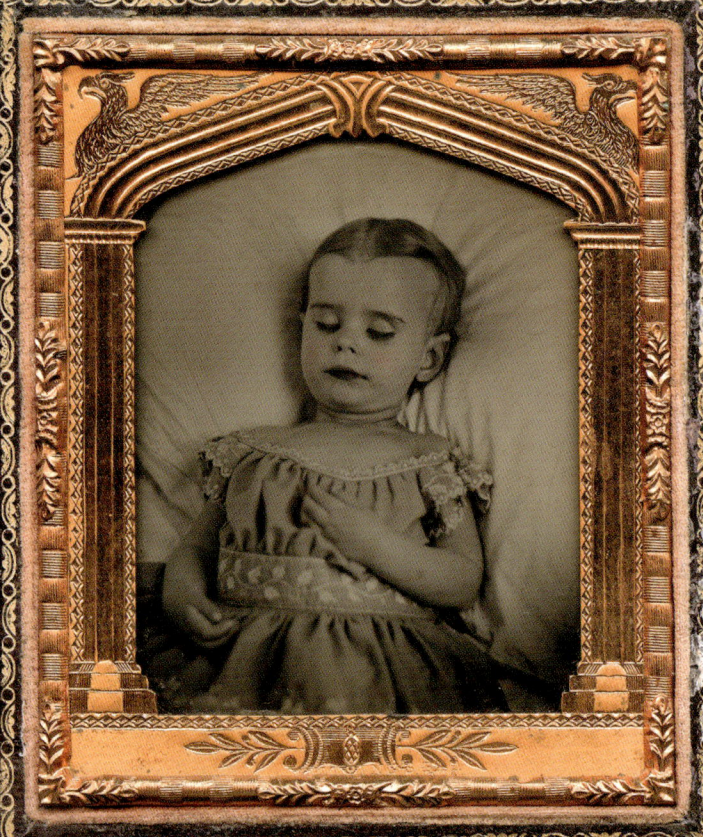

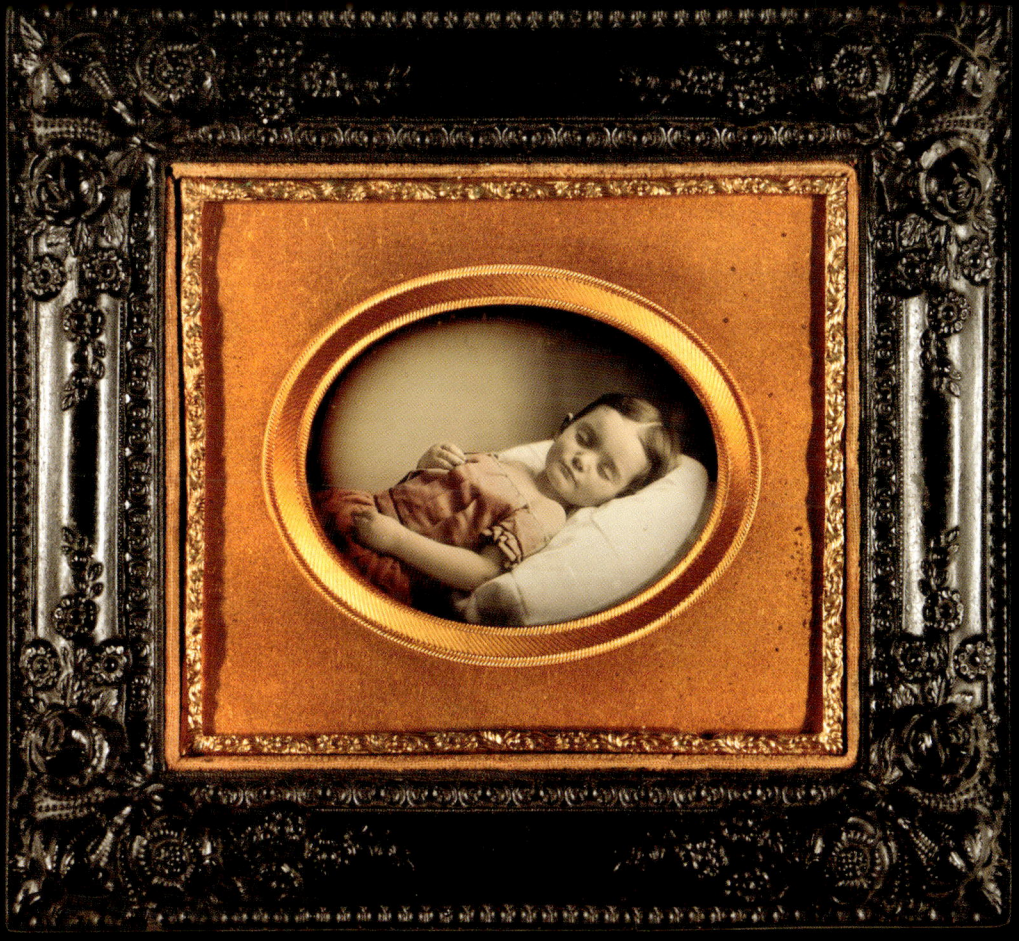

Little Girl in Pink   circa 1854 • sixth-plate daguerreotype in wall frame, hand colored • 5" x 4.5"

A little girl rests on a pillow, her dress hand-tinted a subtle pink.
A wonderfully composed scene by a masterful photographer.

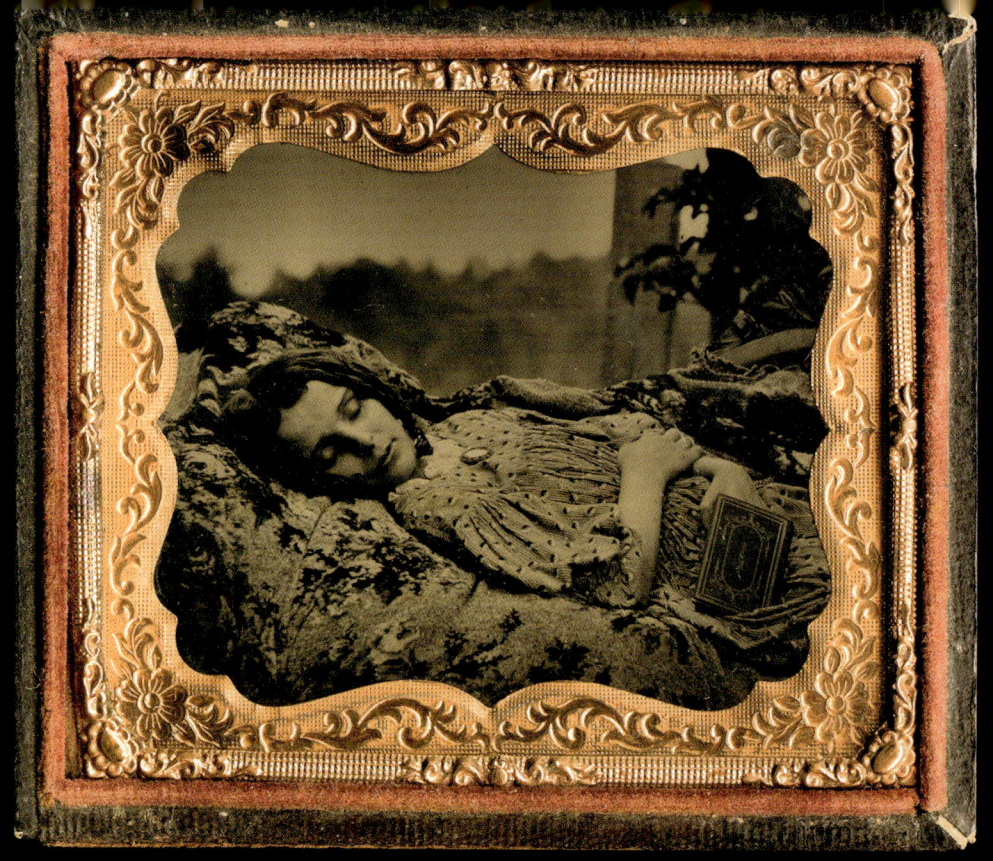

Mary Hodgkins   circa 1864 • sixth-plate tintype • 3.25" x 3.75"

Beautifully composed outdoor photo of the teenage Mary Hodgkins, whose name appears on the cover of the book she is holding, likely her diary, a book of psalms, or prayer book.

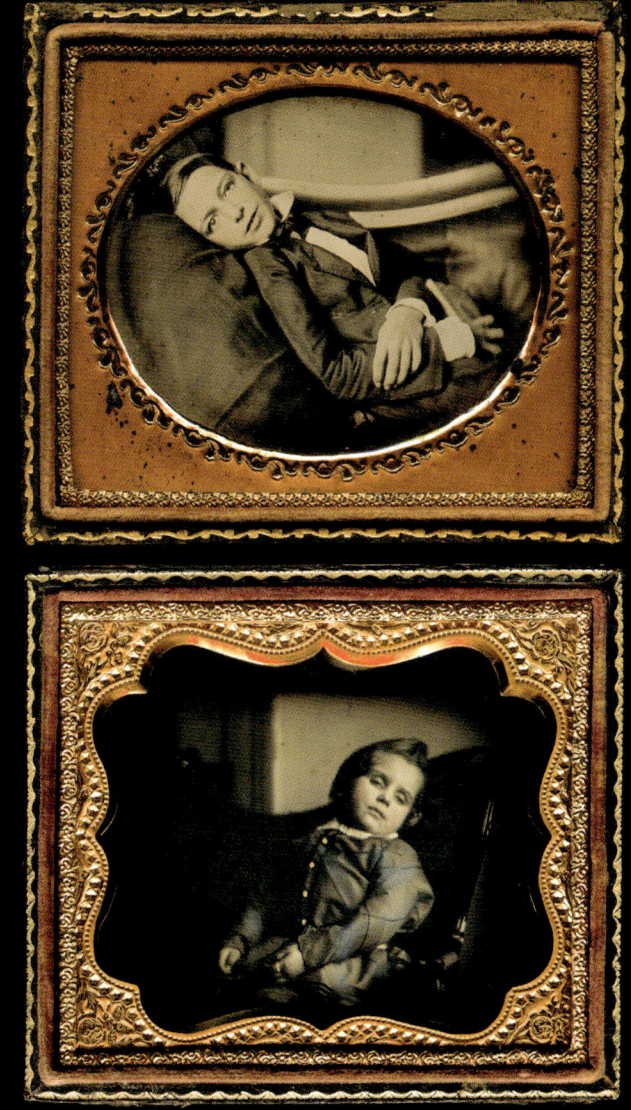

Beautiful Boy circa 1855 • sixth-plate daguerreotype • 3.25" x 3.75"

A handsome boy dressed in his best suit and laid out on a fainting couch.

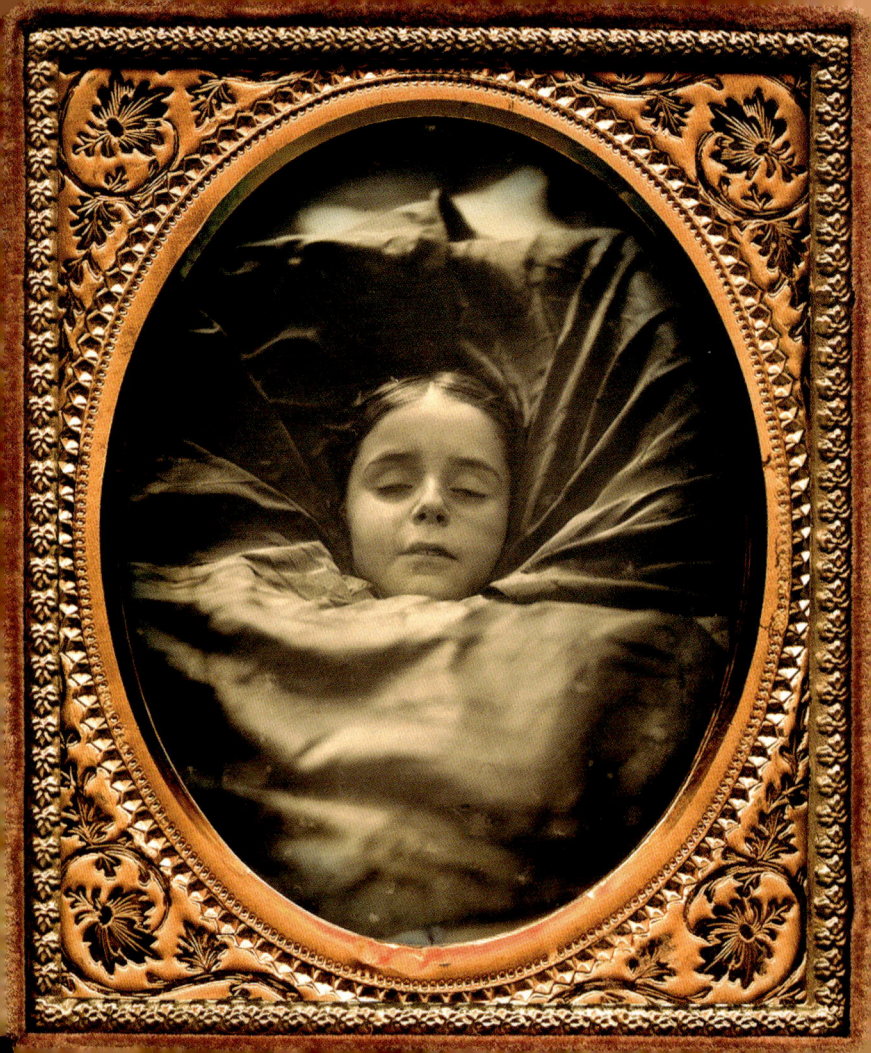

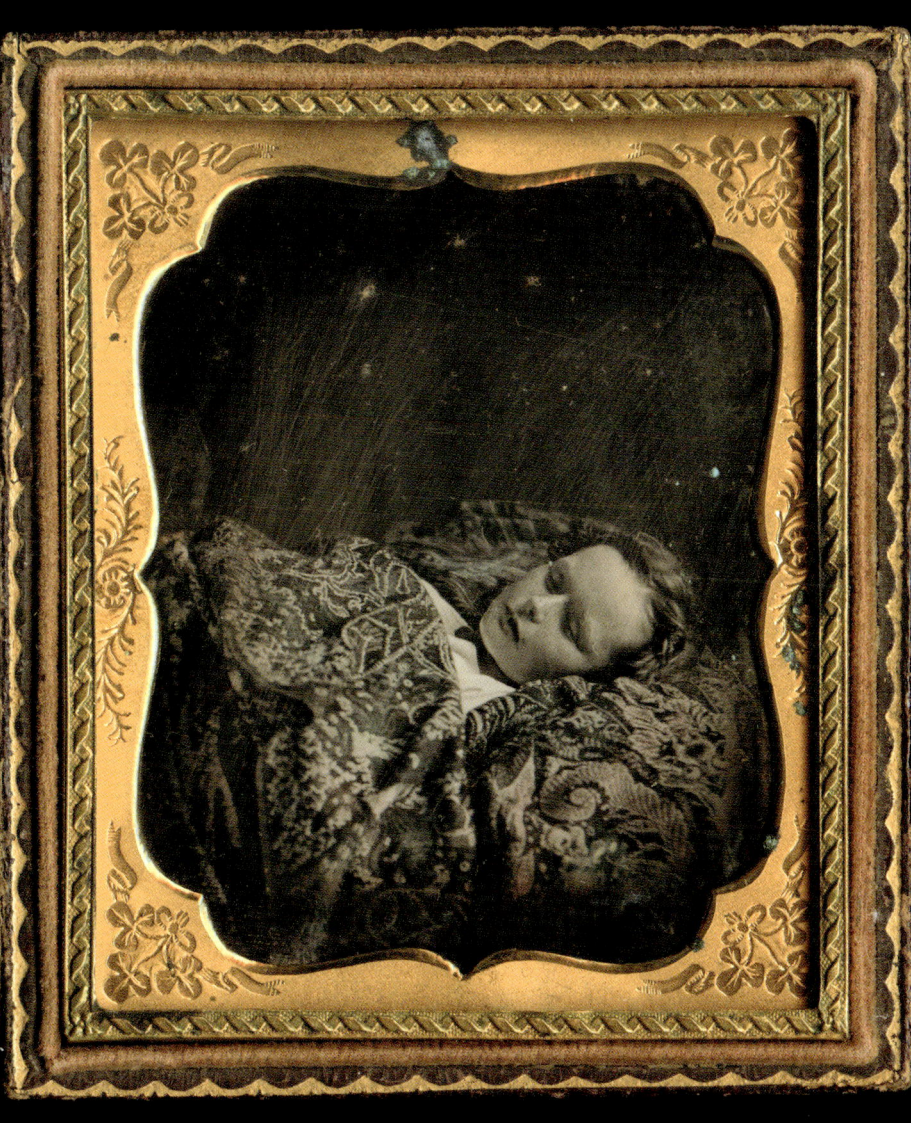

Under the Stars   circa 1855 • sixth-plate daguerreotype, hand colored • 3.75" x 3.25"

Boy bundled in a blue and pink blanket.

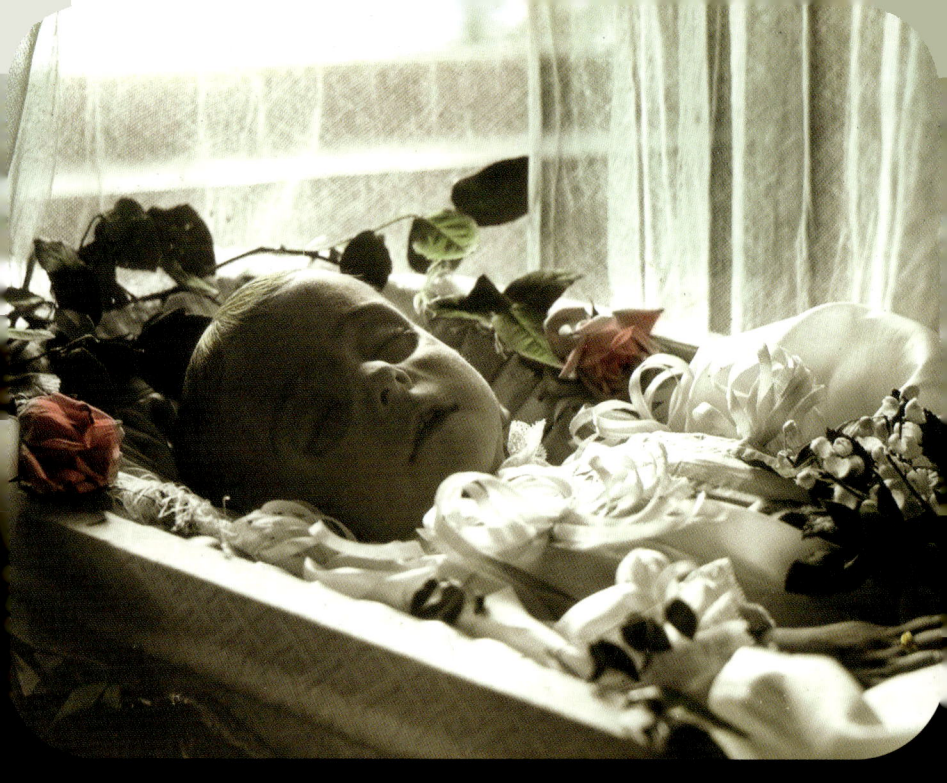

Little Boy Under Window · circa 1905 • magic lantern slide, hand-colored • 3.25" x 4"

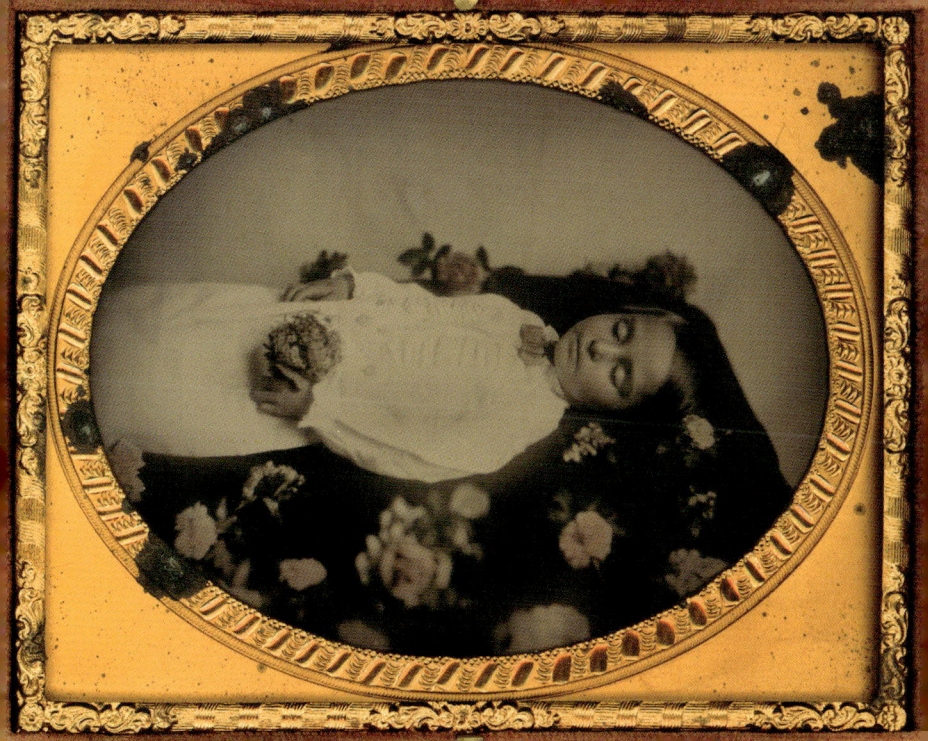

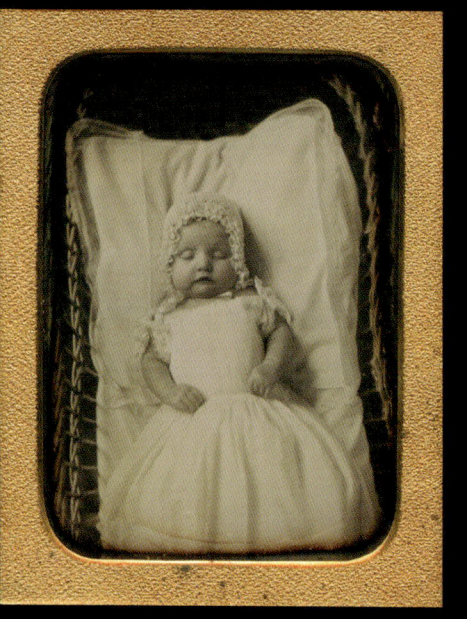
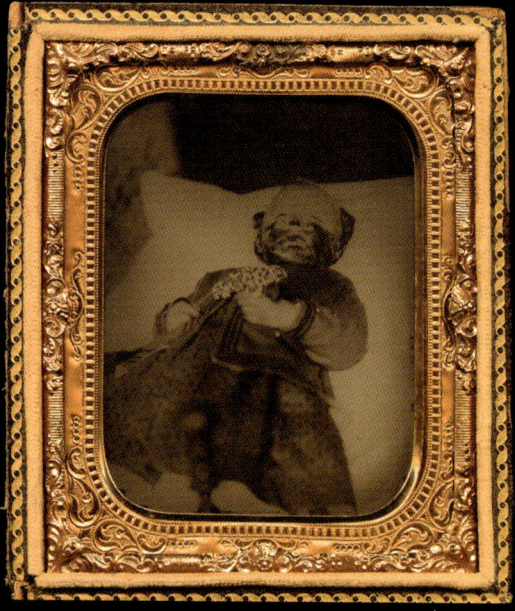

Helen Hamilton Field 1850 • quarter-plate daguerreotype • 4.75" x 3.75"

Philadelphia, Pennsylvania: A masterfully lit portrait of an identified baby in a bassinette. The back of the case has the following handwritten note: "Helen Hamilton Field, 1st child of Samuel & Mary G.P. Field. Taken after death." A second note inside the case reveals her cause of death as scarlet fever.

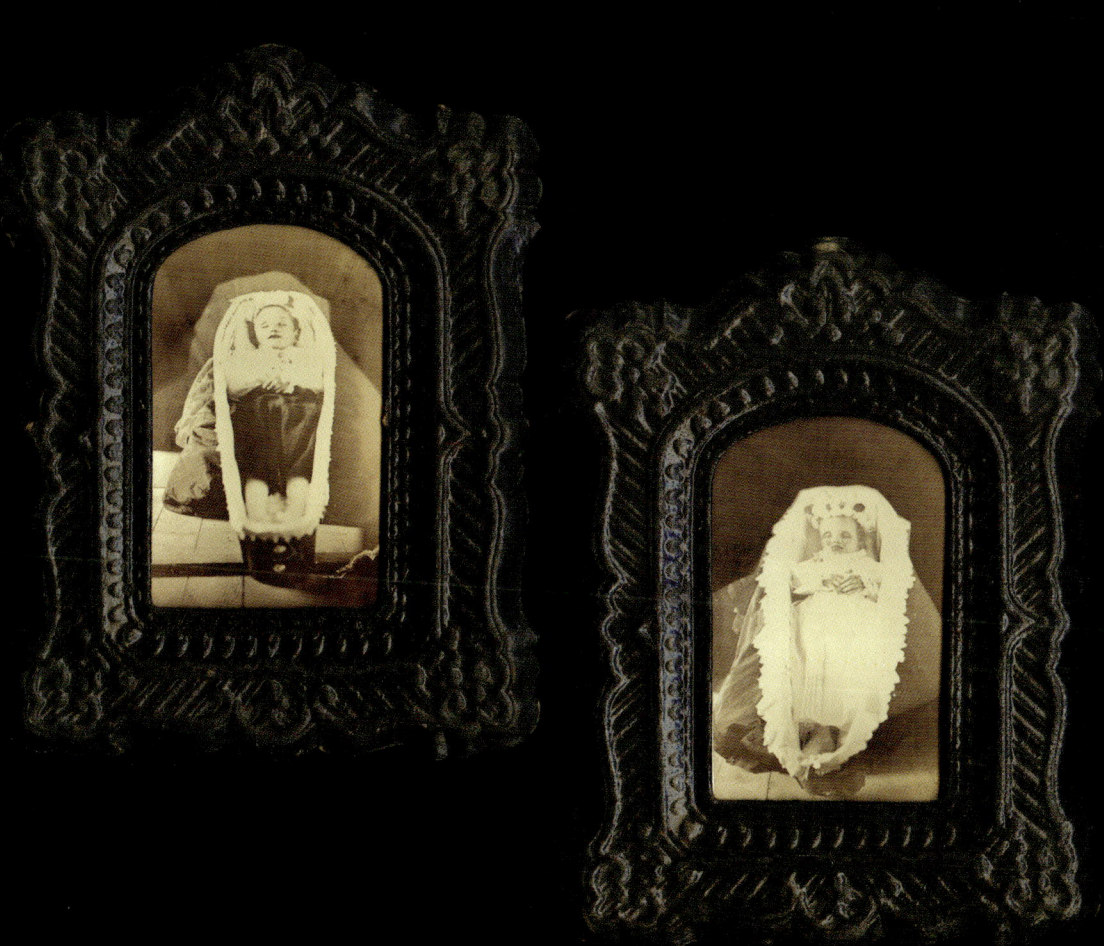

Traveling Photographer circa 1876 • carte de visites • 4" x 2.5" each

*The setting suggests that these photographs were taken by an itinerant photographer who traveled out to the family home.
Both children were likely dead several days by the time these photographs were taken. The thin netting covering their coffins
was used to keep flies and other insects away from the bodies. In matching pressed paper frames.*

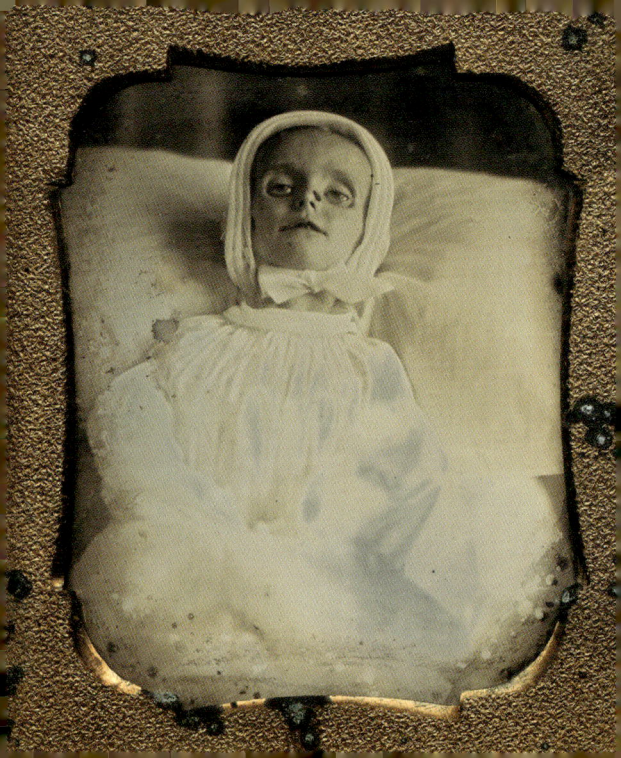

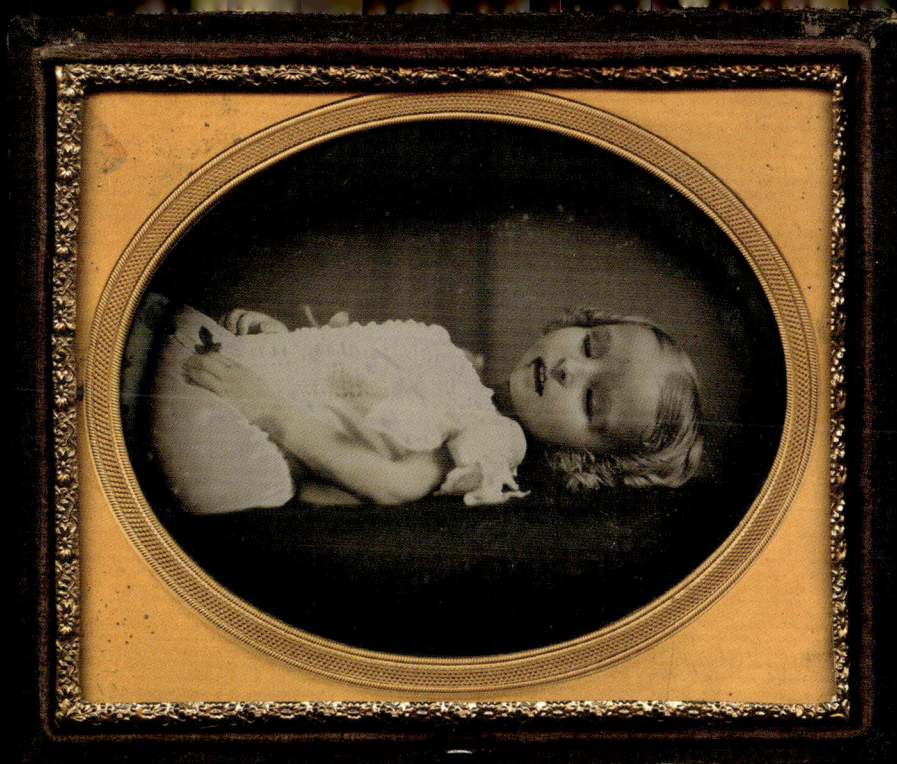

Bloody Discharge and Bruises circa 1858 • quarter-plate daguerreotype • 3.75" x 4.75"

Little girl holding a single, downturned rose. Note the bloody discharge running from her mouth, and apparent bruising on her arms and face. Though child abuse was common and largely ignored in the nineteenth century, it is much more likely, taking into consideration the care and expense that went into this quarter-plate daguerreotype portrait, that she died from an accident or sudden illness. Photographer: George Smith Cook, Root Gallery, Philadelphia, Pennsylvania.

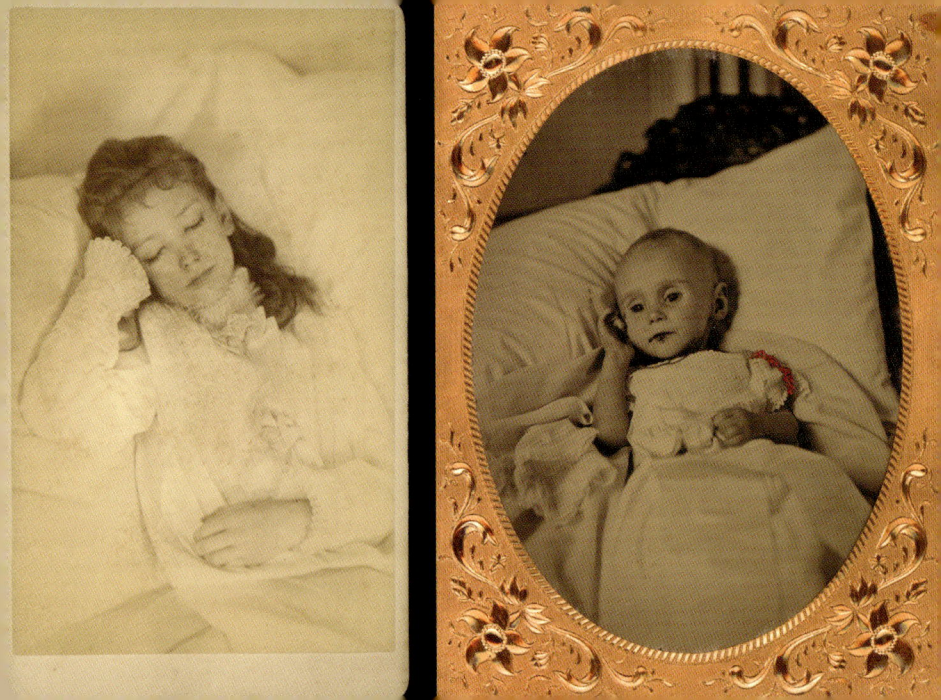

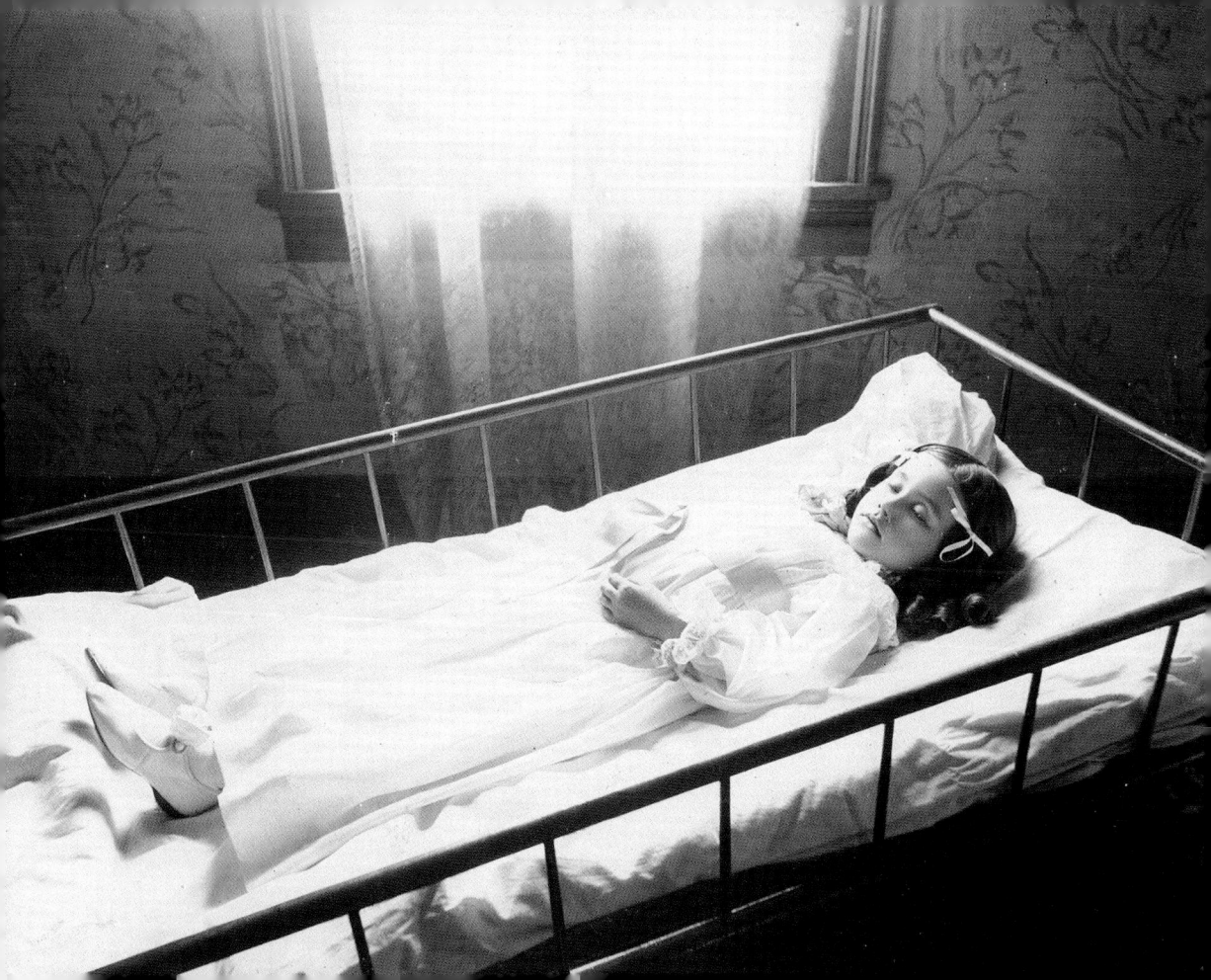

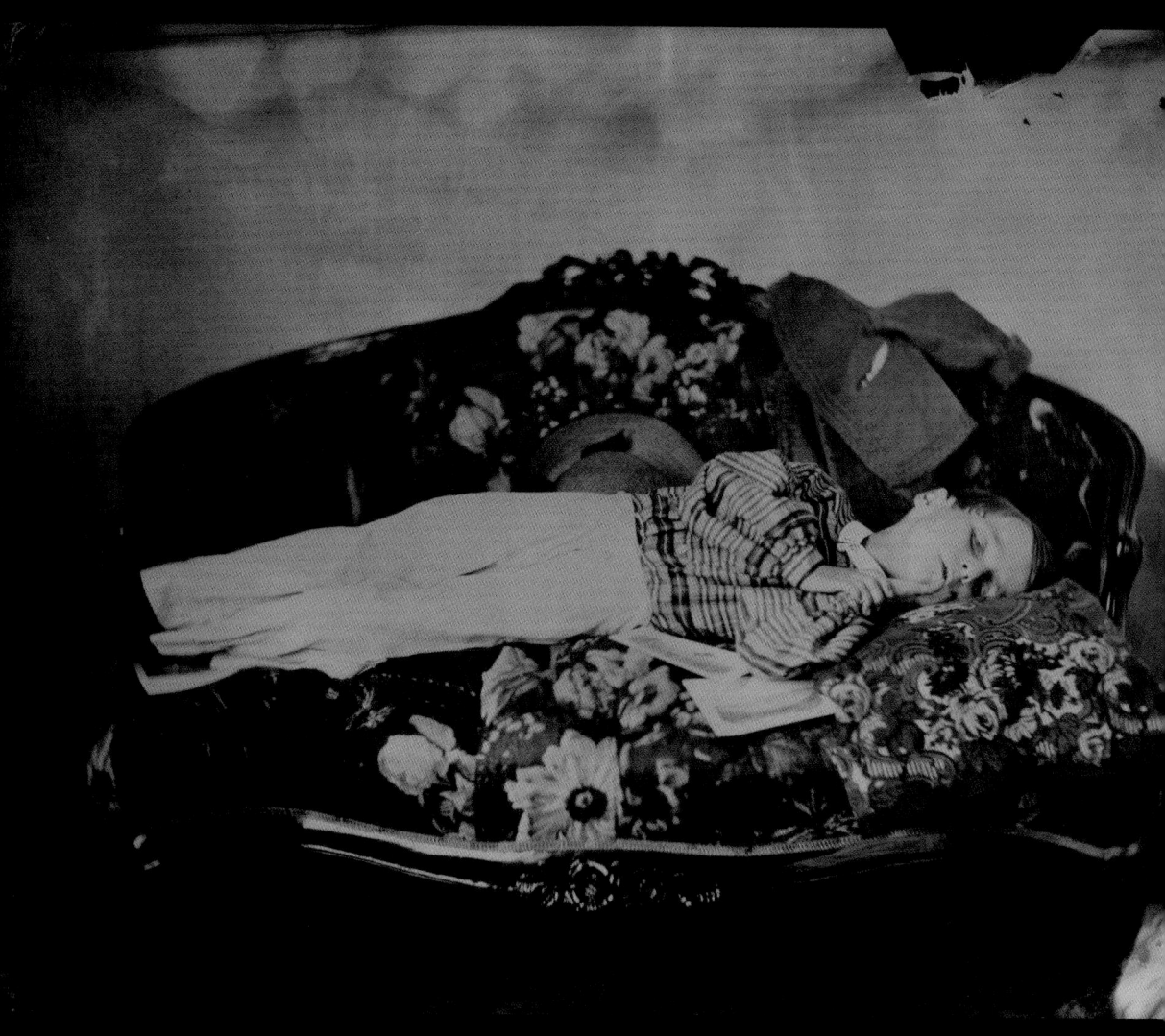

Boy on Sofa   circa 1860 • half-plate ambrotype • 5" x 6"

Large ambrotype of a boy on a couch, chin resting in his open hand. His jacket and straw hat are casually placed behind him. Also on the couch are two family photographs, or favorite prints.

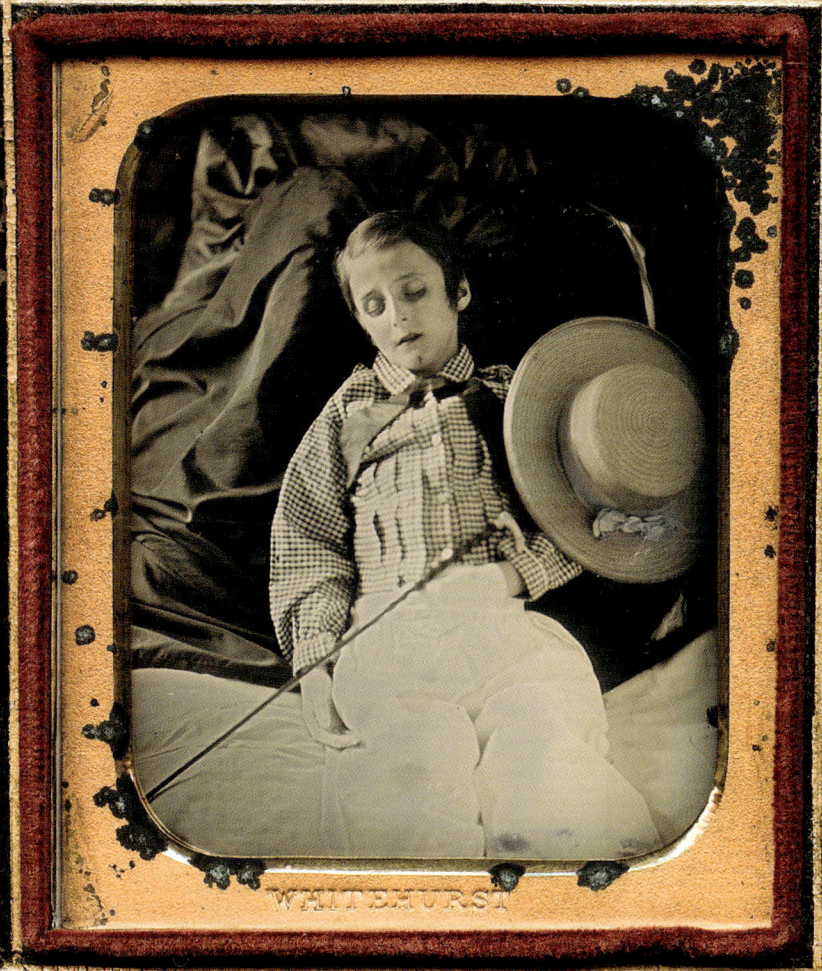

WHITEHURST

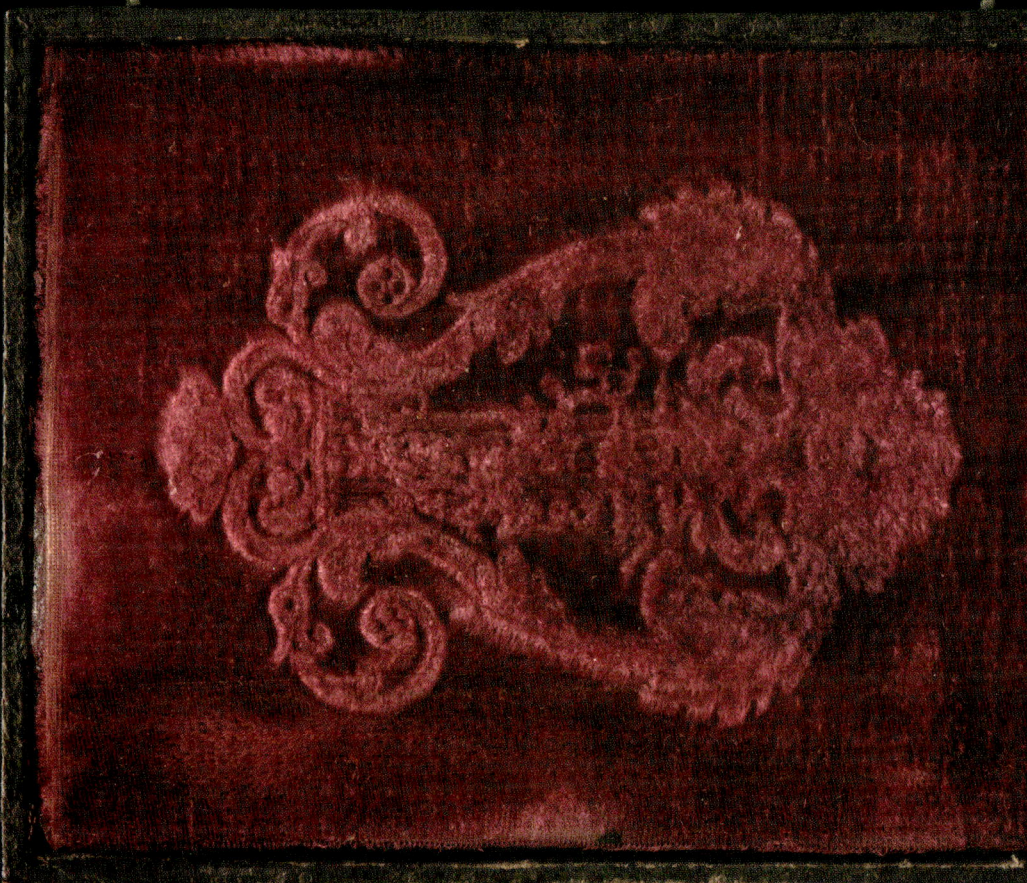

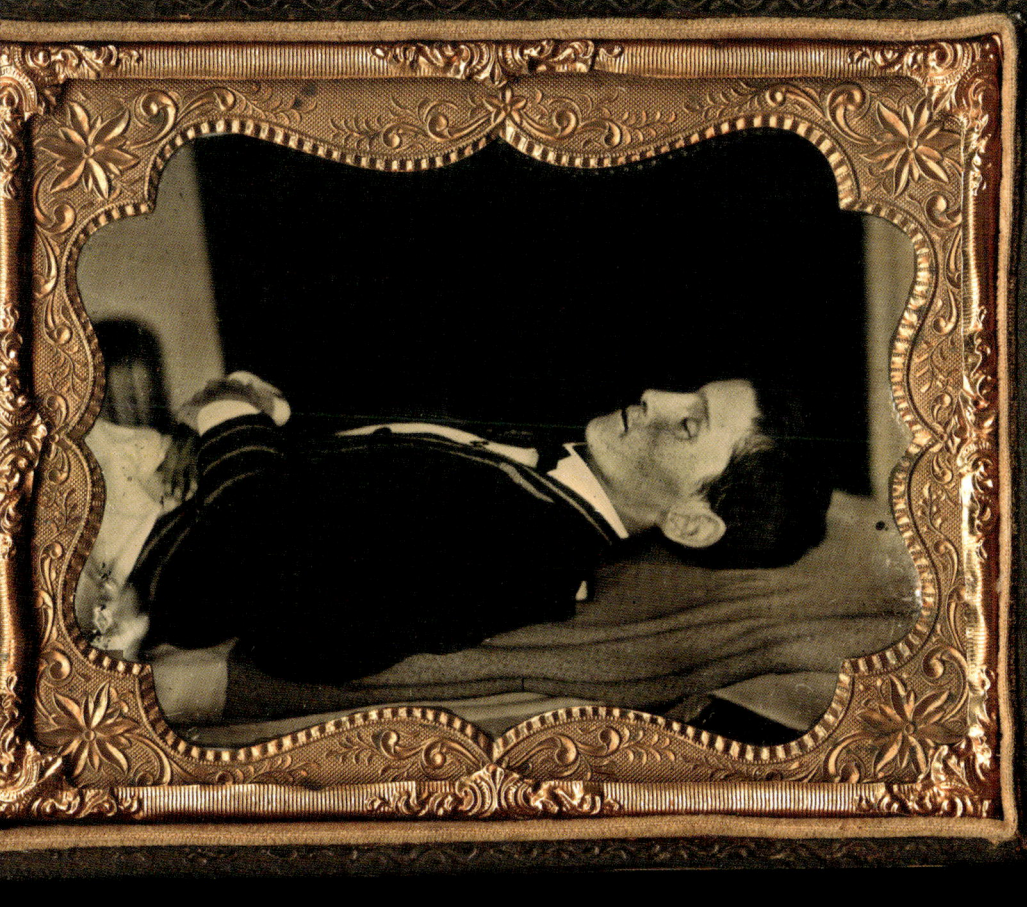

Boy Dead Several Days circa 1862 • quarter-plate tintype • 3.75" x 4.75"

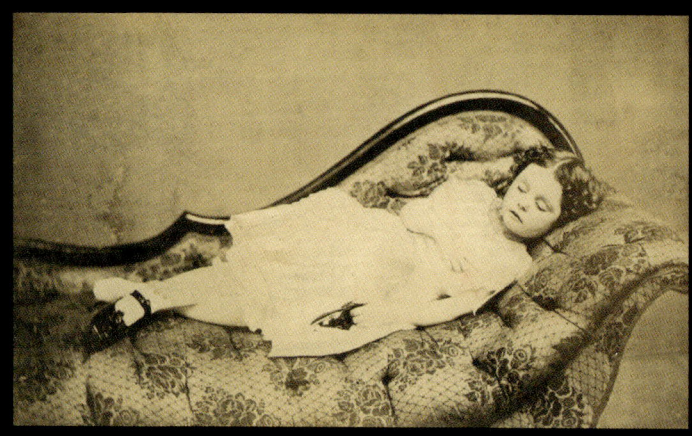

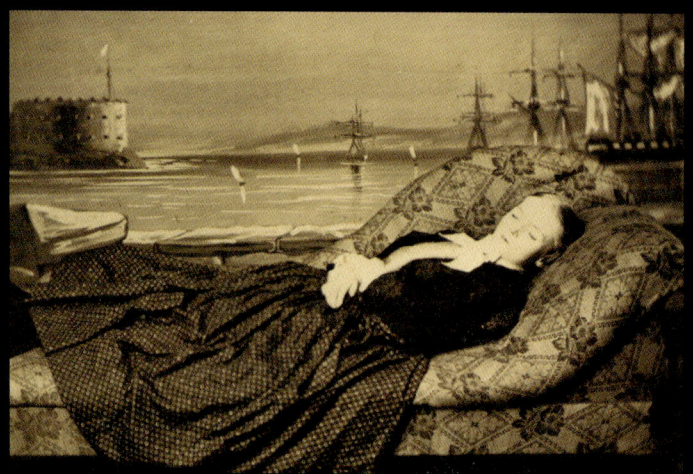

The Empty Shoe   circa 1866 • carte de visite • 2.5" x 4"

Edith Parshall, seven years old, holding a single shoe. In the Victorian Era, a pair of empty shoes, symbolizing a life cut short in childhood, was a popular prop in post-mortem photography of children. Not limited to photography, the empty shoes motif would frequently be found on children's grave markers, usually with one shoe overturned.

San Francisco Bay   circa 1868 • carte de visite • 2.5" x 4"

Sonora, California: A teenage girl is laid out in front of a wonderfully painted backdrop, possibly depicting the nearby San Francisco Bay. Backdrops such as the one seen here were quite uncommon in post-mortem photography, as typically, simple, undecorated backgrounds were favored. Photographer: Daniel Sewell.

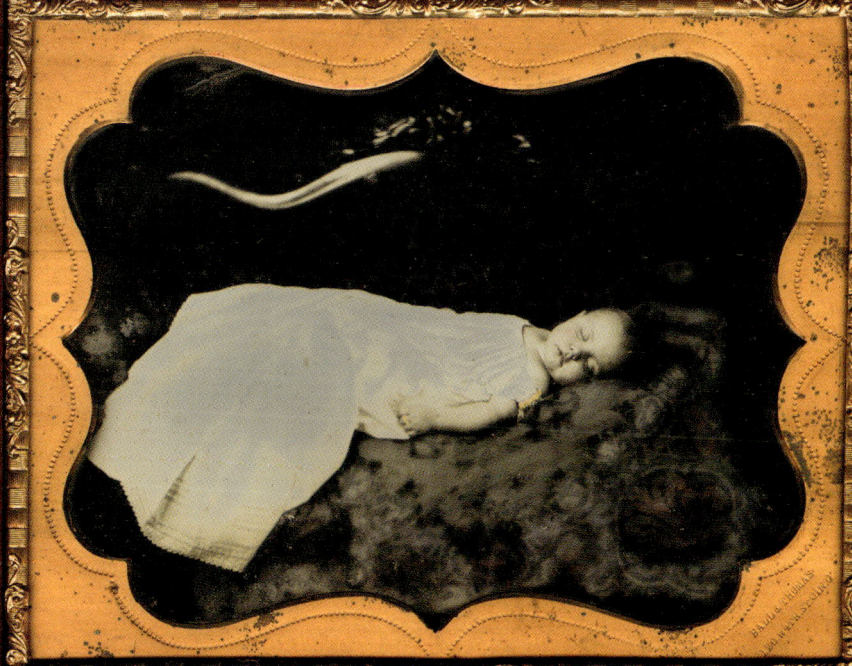

A Mother to her dying Child.

Sleep on, thou little Angel one,
  Sleep on, thou little dove;
For a mother's heart beats mournfully
  Over her dying love.

A longer and a sweet repose
  Awaits thee, sinless one;—
I'm lulling thee to a soft sleep,
  As I have often done.

A longer sleep will soon be thine,
  Among the Autumn flowers;
A sweeter song than fairies sing,
  Away in seraph bowers.

Oh! I love thee well, thou beautiful,
  And must my darling die?
Yet the purest and the fairest,
  In earth will soonest lie.

Sleep on, thou little Angel one,
  Sleep on, thou little dove;
For a mother's heart beats mournfully
  Over her dying love.   MARY.

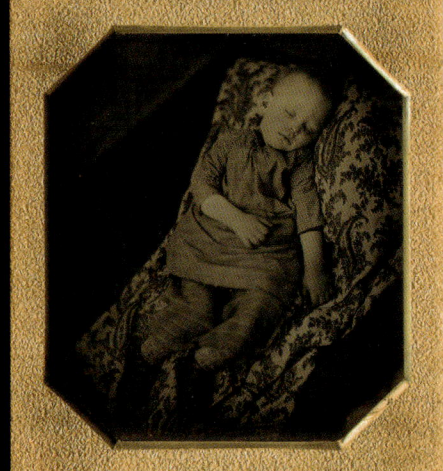

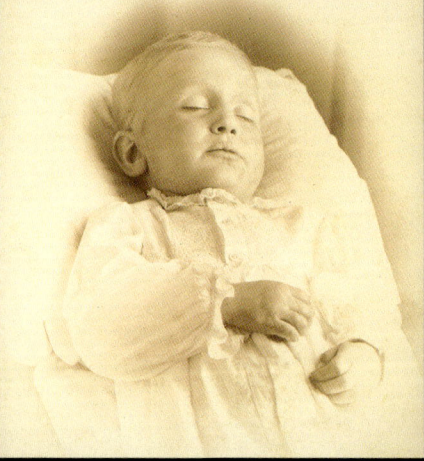

Card of Thanks.

Mr. and Mrs. W. H. Mort return their heartfelt thanks to the neighbors and friends for their kindness shown them in their sad hour of affliction in the death of their little boy, Bennie. Mr. Mort is an employe of the Rowe Stock farm. The kindness tendered to them by Col. E. L. Rowe and wife, of beautiful flowers and otherwise assisting in hour of need, was kindly appreciated. Mr. Albright, superintendent, says his little boy companion Bennie will be greatly missed by him, as he was with me in my daily walk around the farm. Benny Mort was born April 14, 1890; died March 15, 1894, aged 3 years, 11 months and 1 day.

A precious one from us has gone,
  A voice we love so well is still,
A place is vacant in our home,
  Which never can be filled.
God in his wisdom has recalled,
  The boon his love has given,
And though the little one is in
  Silent slumber here below,
The soul is safe in heaven above.

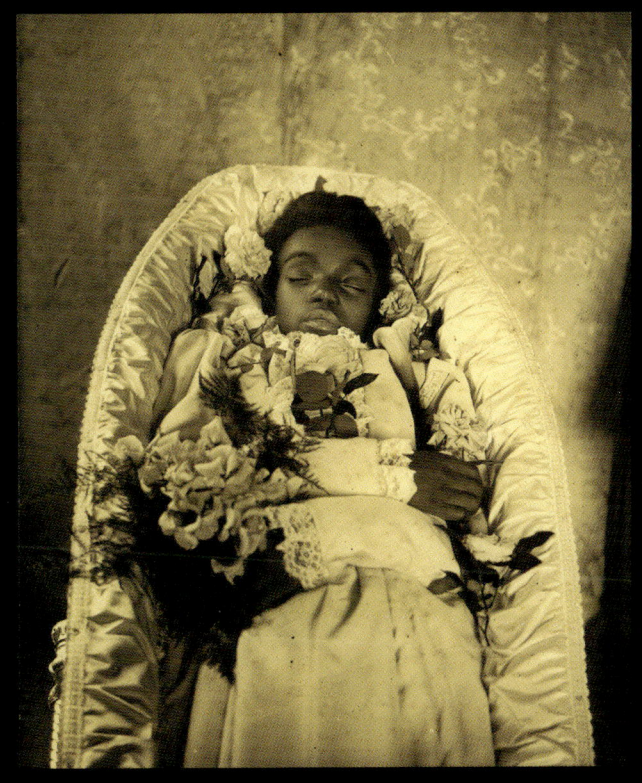

Margaret E. Bryant

Margaret E. Bryant, seventeen year old daughter of William Bryant, died at the Coatesville Hospital on Monday from an attack of pneumonia. The funeral will take place from the home of Nesbit Washington, 726 Coates street, on Thursday afternoon at one o'clock with further services at St. Paul's A. M. E. church at 2 o'clock. Interment will be made in Passtown Cemetery.

African American Teen 1924 • gelatin silver print • 7" x 5"

Margaret E. Bryant, who died of pneumonia in Coatesville, Pennsylvania, at the age of seventeen.

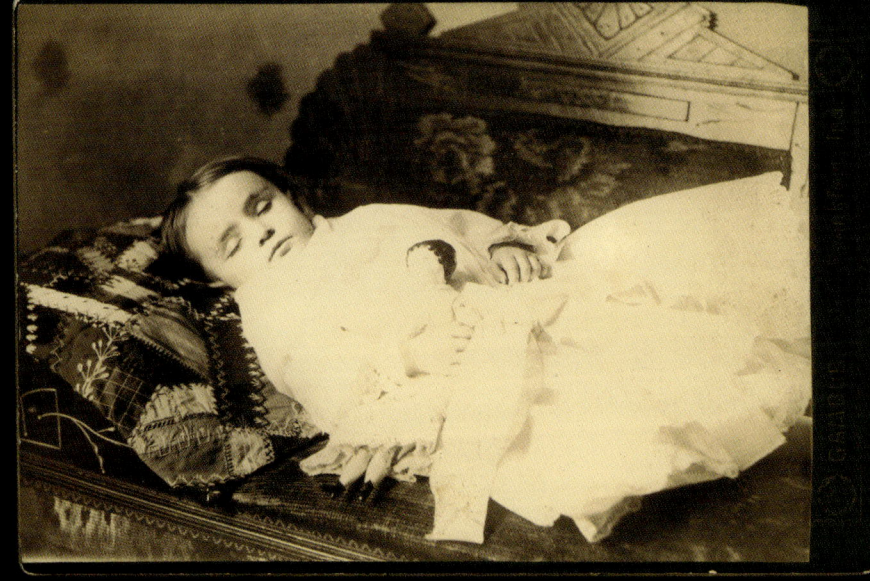

FUNERAL NOTICE.

The funeral of Eliza L. Aughe, daughter of Jesse W. and Belle Aughe, will take place at the residence, corner Columbia and Morrison Streets, at 9 o'clock to-morrow. Services by Rev. W. H. Simpson. Burial at Jefferson Cemetery. You are cordially invited to attend.

Frankfort, Ind., April 13, 1885.

Little Eliza   1885 • cabinet card • 6.5" x 4.25"
April 13, 1885: Eliza Laird Aughe resting on a patchwork pillow, with her favorite doll.

The One Gone Before   circa 1865 • opalotype • 5.5" x 4.25"
Circa 1865 post-mortem child, in rare opalotype (or milk glass) format.
A painted posthumous portrait of a female family member—perhaps an older sister—has been included in the scene

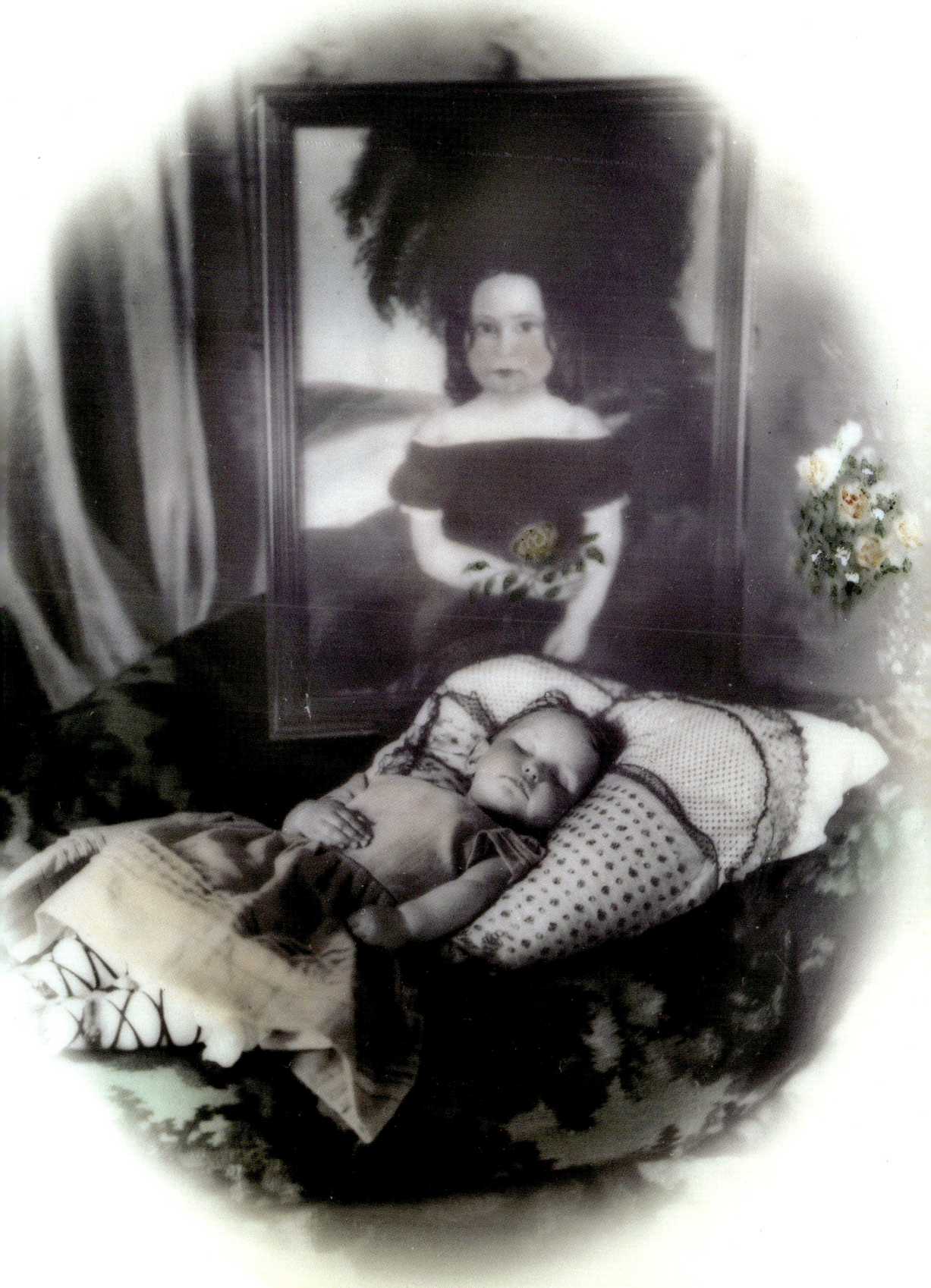

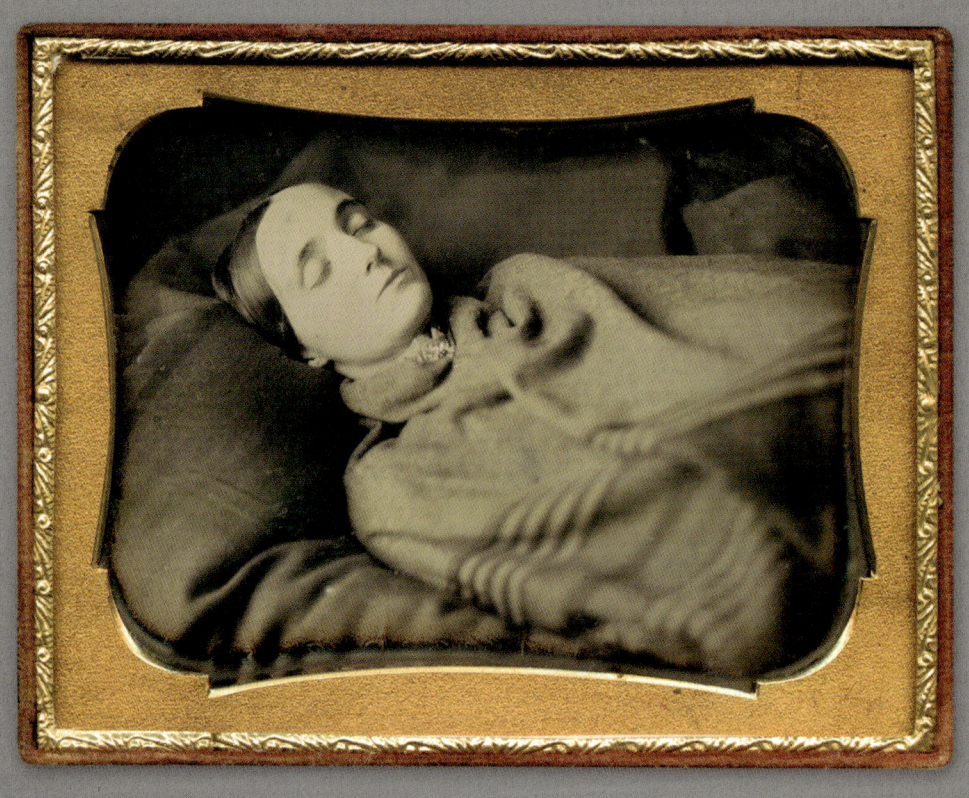

The Maiden   circa 1850 • quarter-plate daguerreotype, hand colored • 4.75" x 3.75"

A beautiful young woman wrapped in a wool blanket, cinched with a silver clasp.

ADULTS

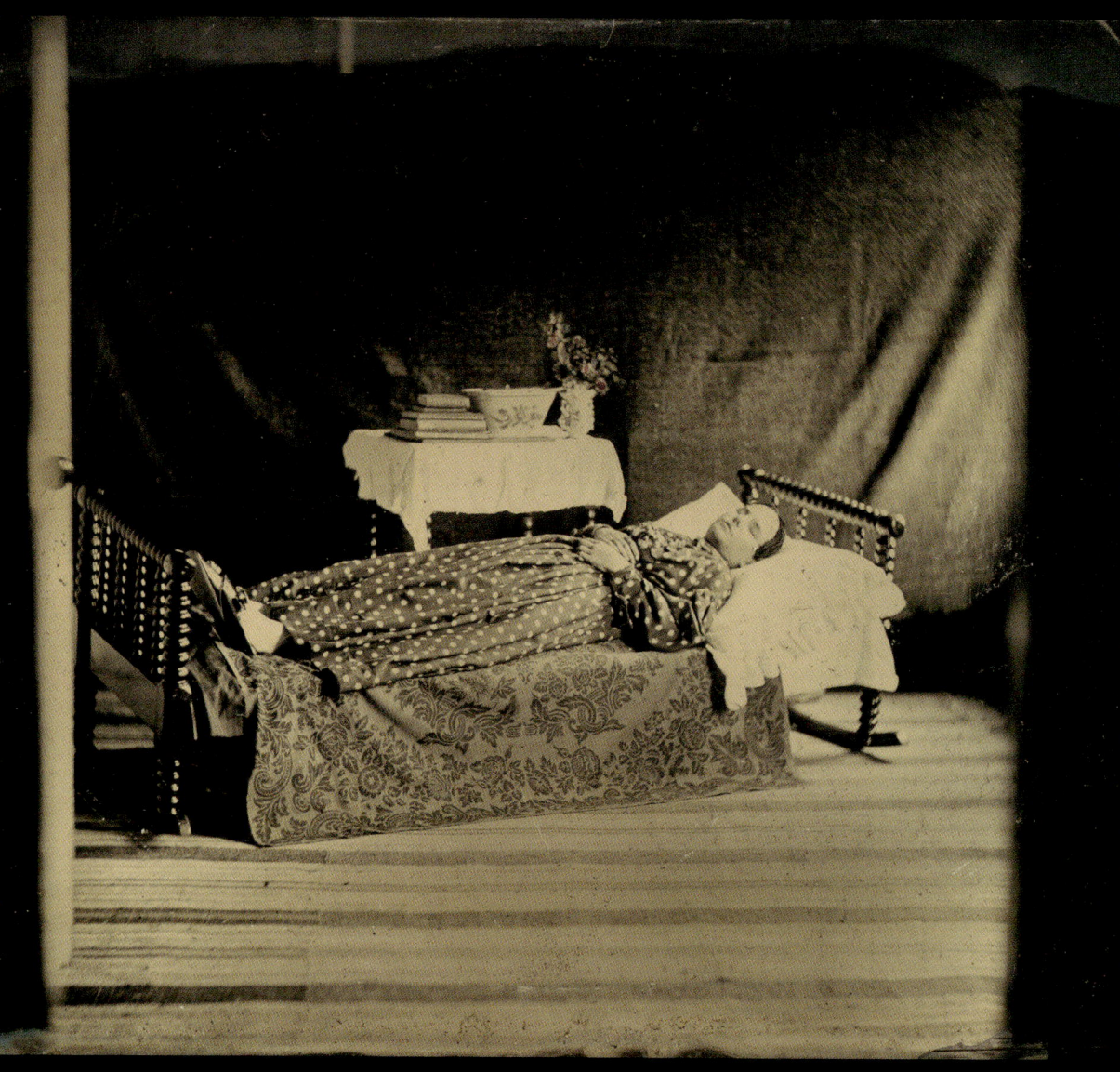

Spindle Bed circa 1865 • half-plate tintype, hand colored • 5" x 6.5"

New York, July 1865: Deceased woman in a rocking spindle bed.
This is an unusually wide shot, appearing to have been taken from outside of the room.
A stoneware pot, books, and a small vase of flowers have been placed on the small table next to her body.

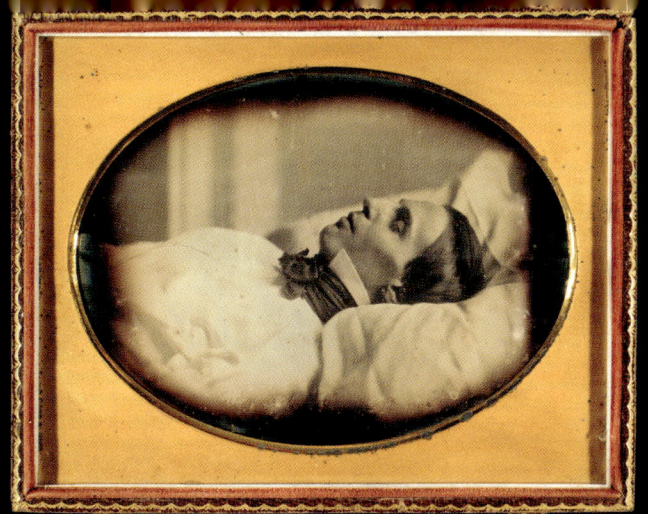

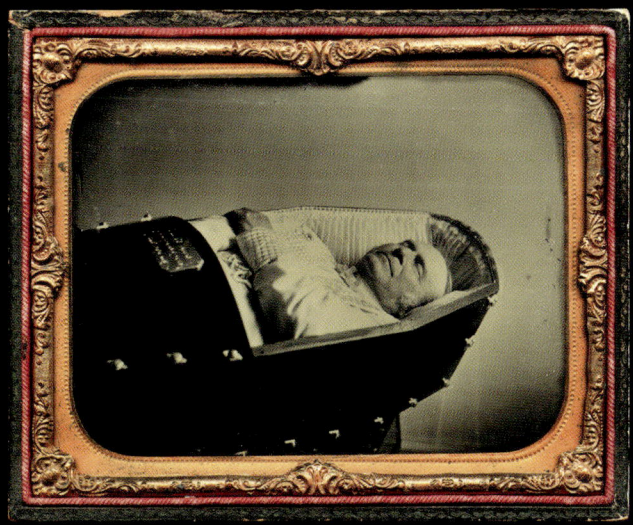

Man in Profile circa 1850 • half-plate daguerreotype • 4.75" x 6"

New York City: Large profile portrait of an affluent man, struck down in the prime of life.

- - - - - - - - - - - - - - - - - - - -

Coffin Plate circa 1864 • half-plate tintype • 5" x 6.5"

A large tintype portrait of a man in his coffin.
A silver coffin plate, which would typically bear his name, date of birth and date of death, is affixed to the front.

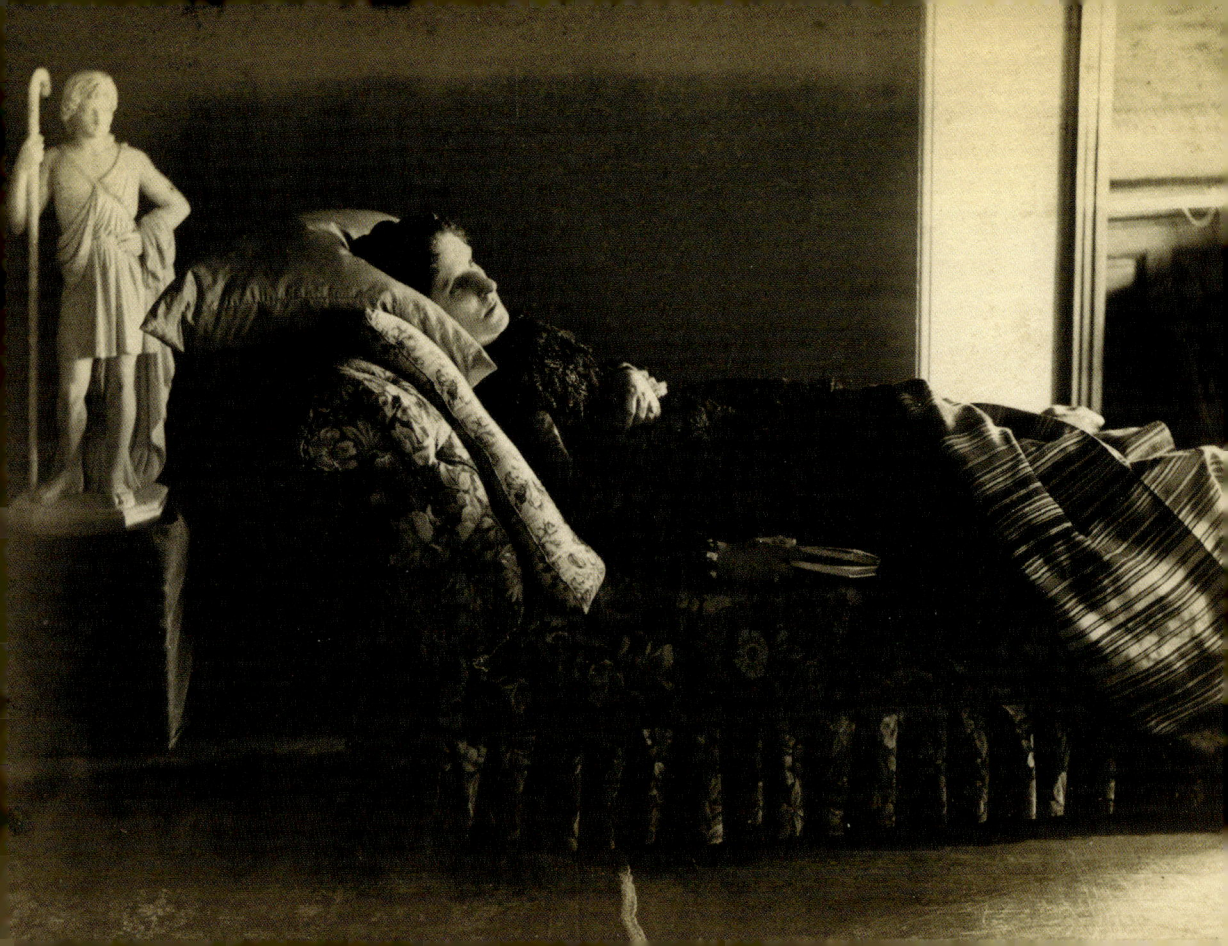

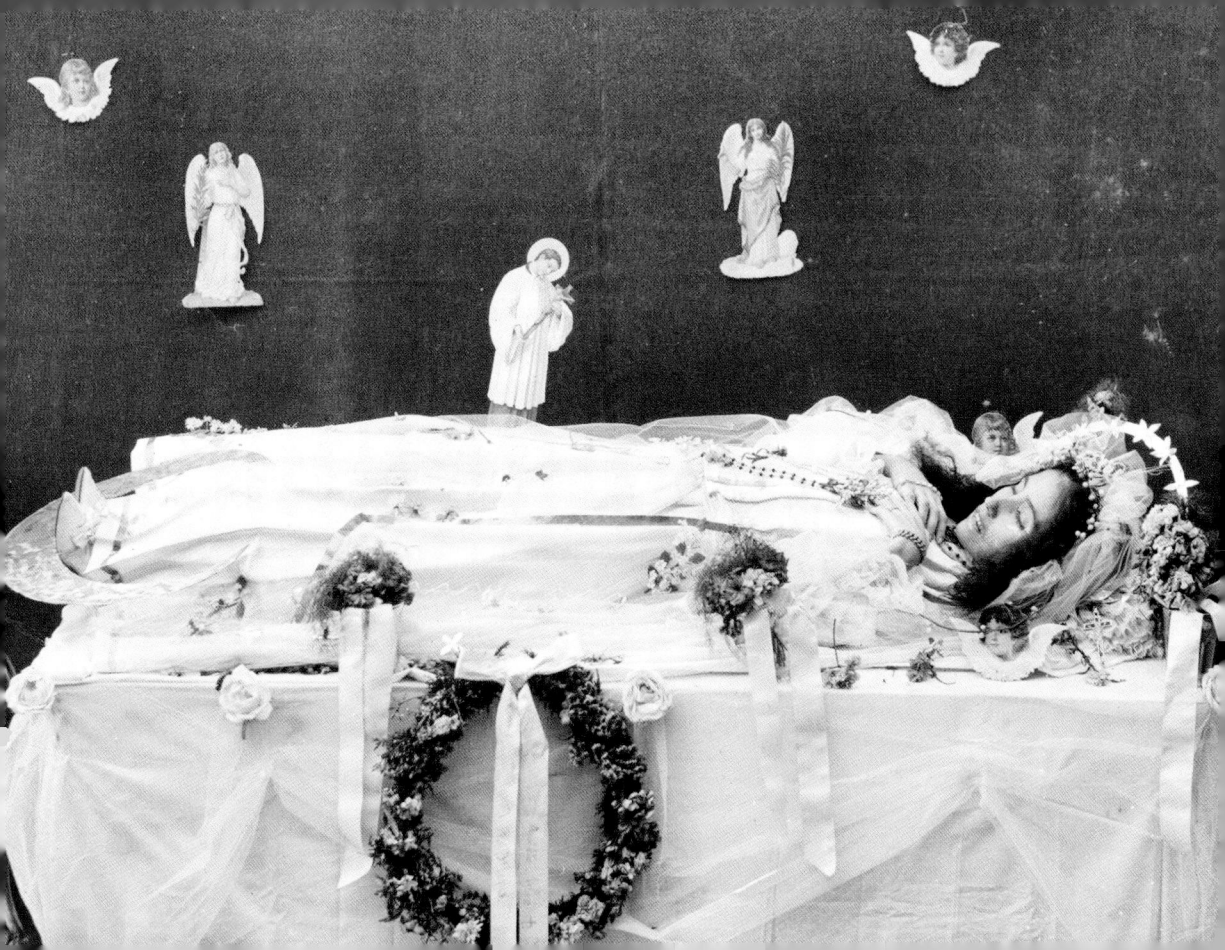

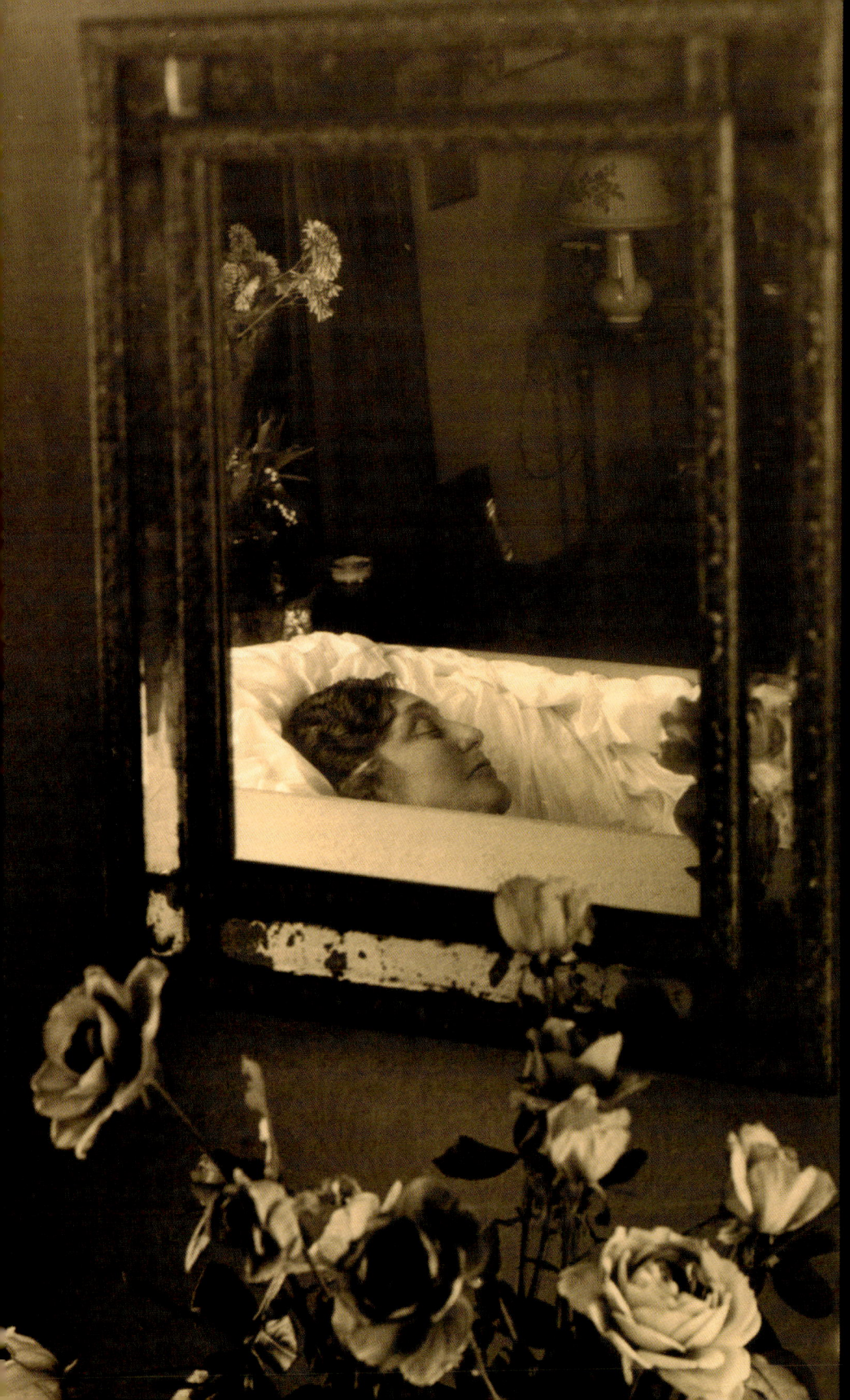

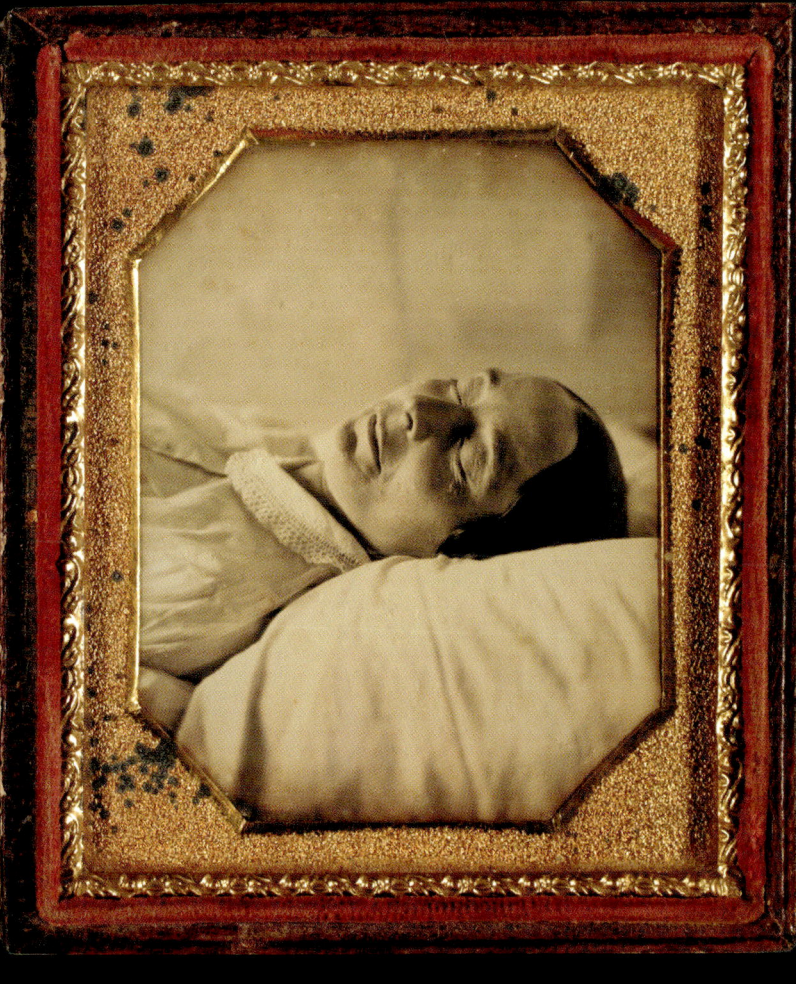

Reflection in the Mirror   circa 1920 • real photo postcard • 5.5" x 3.5"

An artistic amateur photo of Mrs. Conant in her parlor, her likeness reflected in a mirror.

Serenity in Death   circa 1846 • sixth-plate daguerreotype • 3.75" x 3.25"

A close, exceptionally detailed view of a serene looking woman in bed.

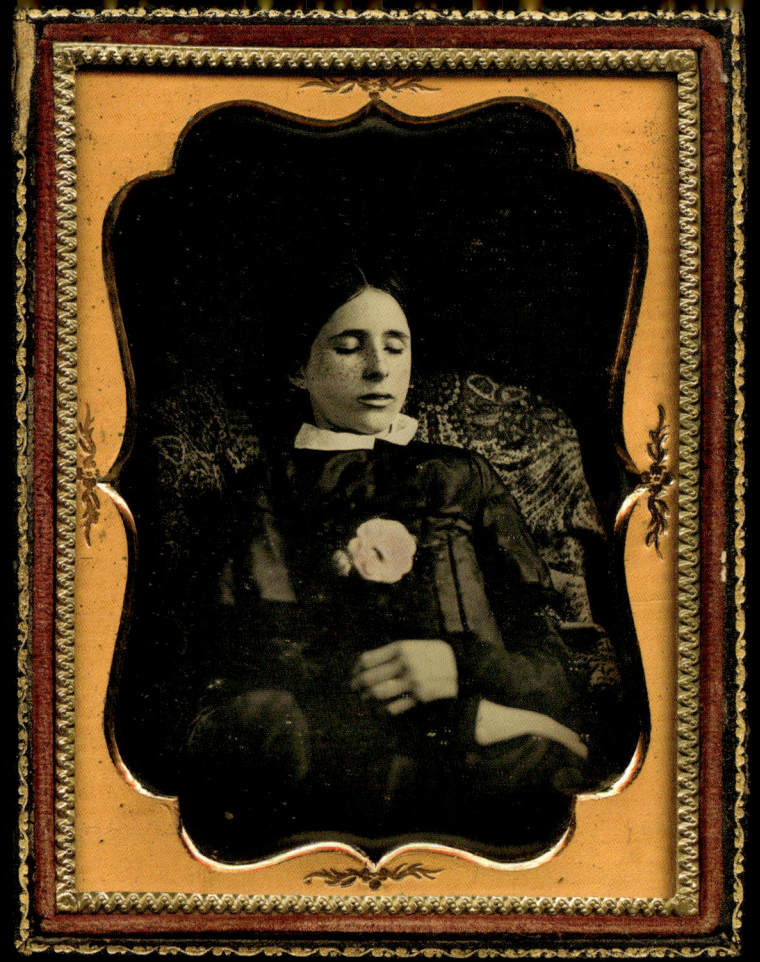

Sarah Ann   1852 • quarter-plate daguerreotype • 4.75″ x 3.75″

Sarah Ann Simonds, who died of consumption on December 18, 1852, at the age of 20, in Gloucester, Massachusetts.
Records show that on the same date, the 6–month–old daughter of Sarah and her husband Charles died of fever.

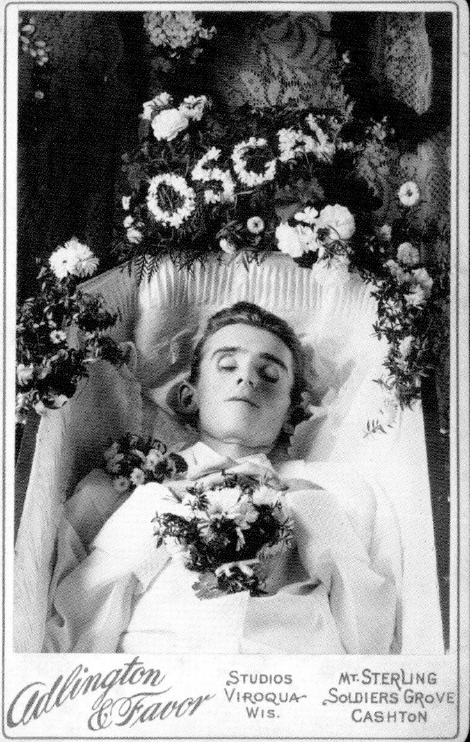

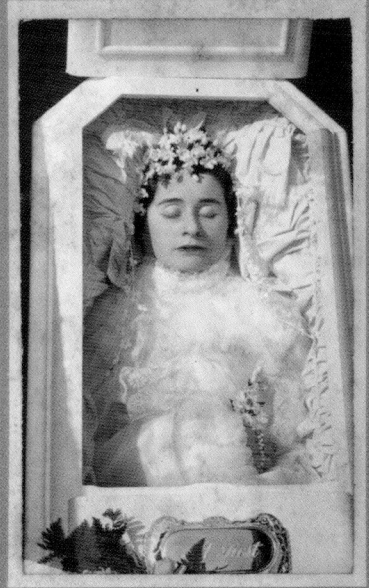

Adlington & Favor STUDIOS VIROQUA WIS.   MT. STERLING SOLDIERS GROVE CASHTON

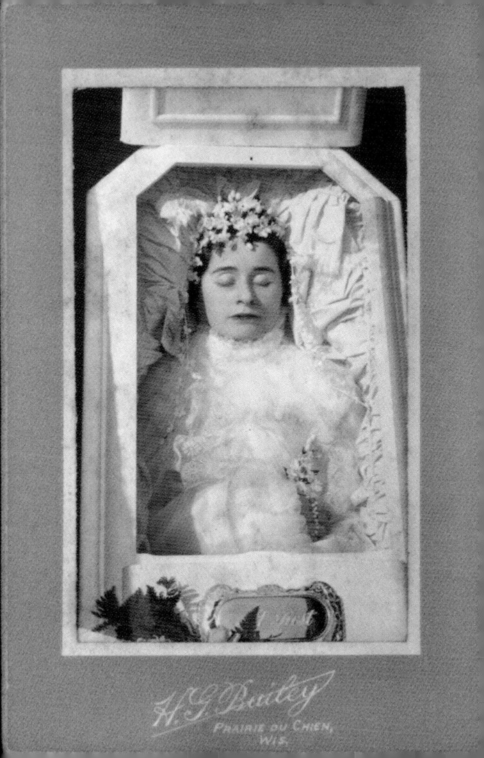

H. G. Beatey PRAIRIE DU CHIEN, WIS.

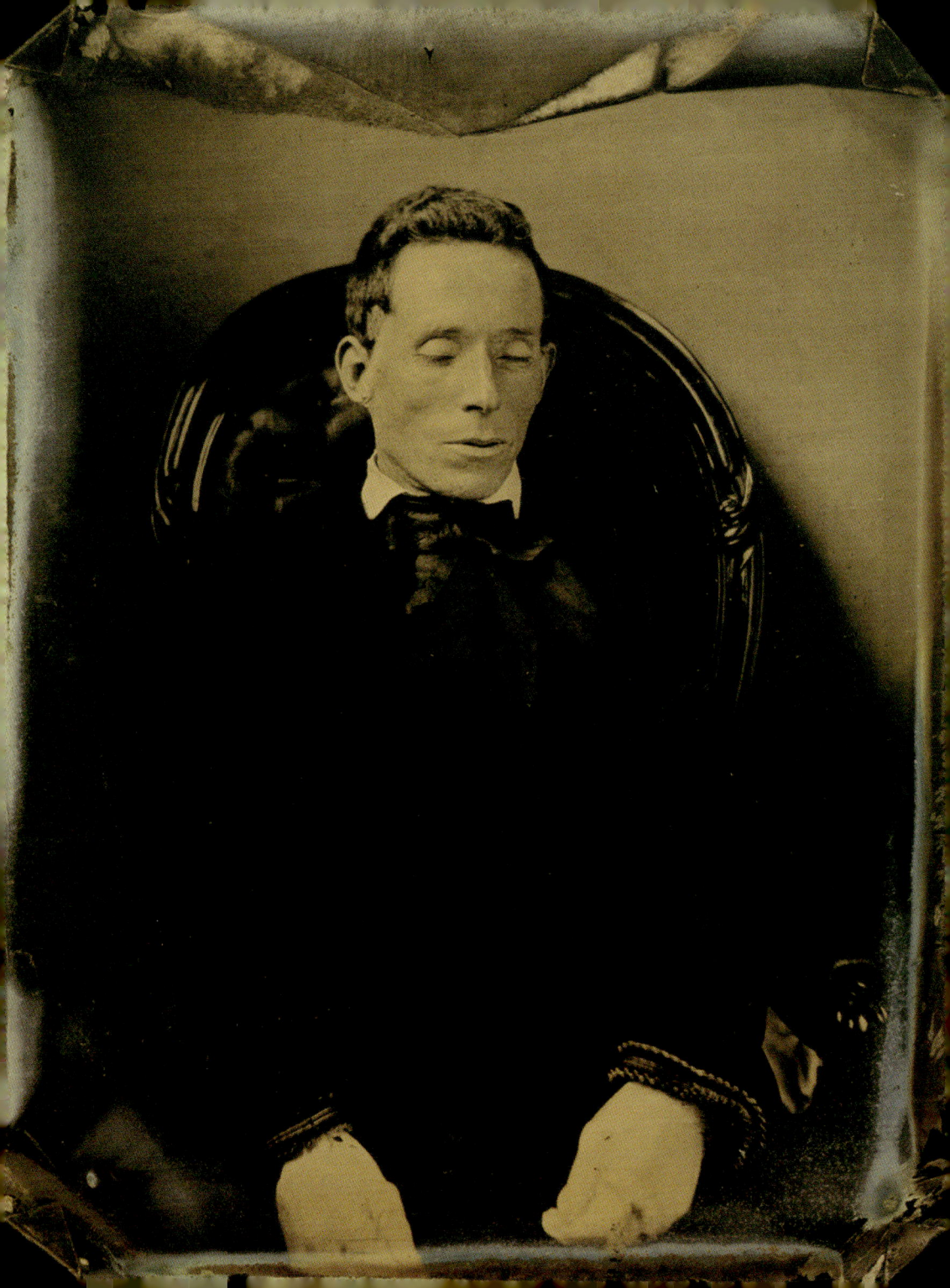

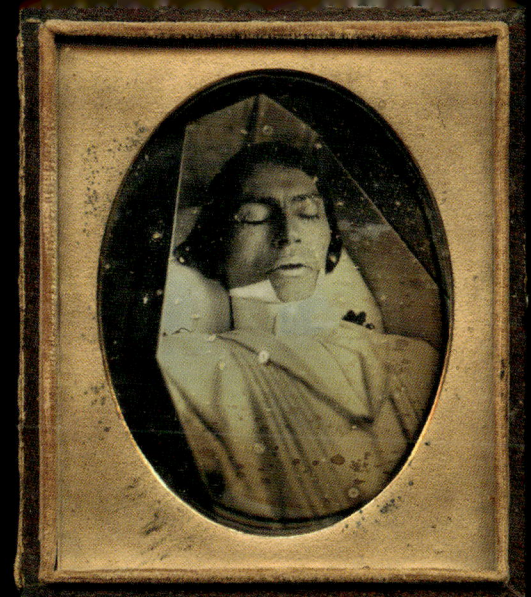 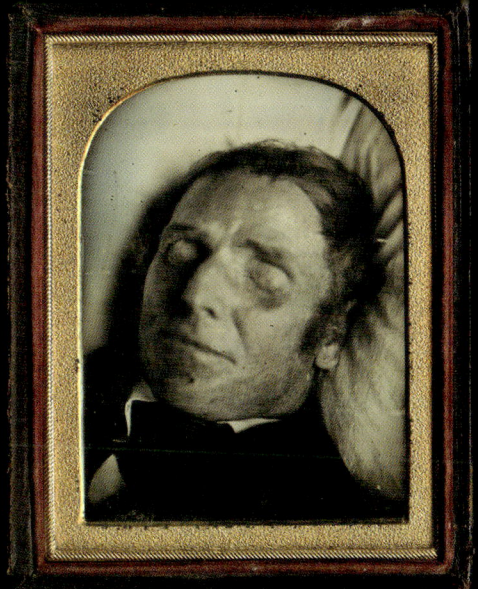

Man in Burial Robe circa 1867 • quarter-plate tintype • 4.25" x 3.25"

A man dressed in a silk burial robe and tie. On his temple is a missing, or shaved, area of hair with a small wound near its center, an injury likely associated with his cause of death.

. . . .

The Philadelphian circa 1847 • sixth-plate daguerreotype • 3.75" x 3.25"

The body of a Philadelphia man is displayed in a classic "toe–pincher"–style coffin. Photographer: Sabin W. Colton.

. . . .

Closer circa 1848 • quarter-plate daguerreotype • 4.75" x 3.75"

An unusual, extreme close-up shot of a man, his face filling most of the viewable area of the daguerreotype plate.

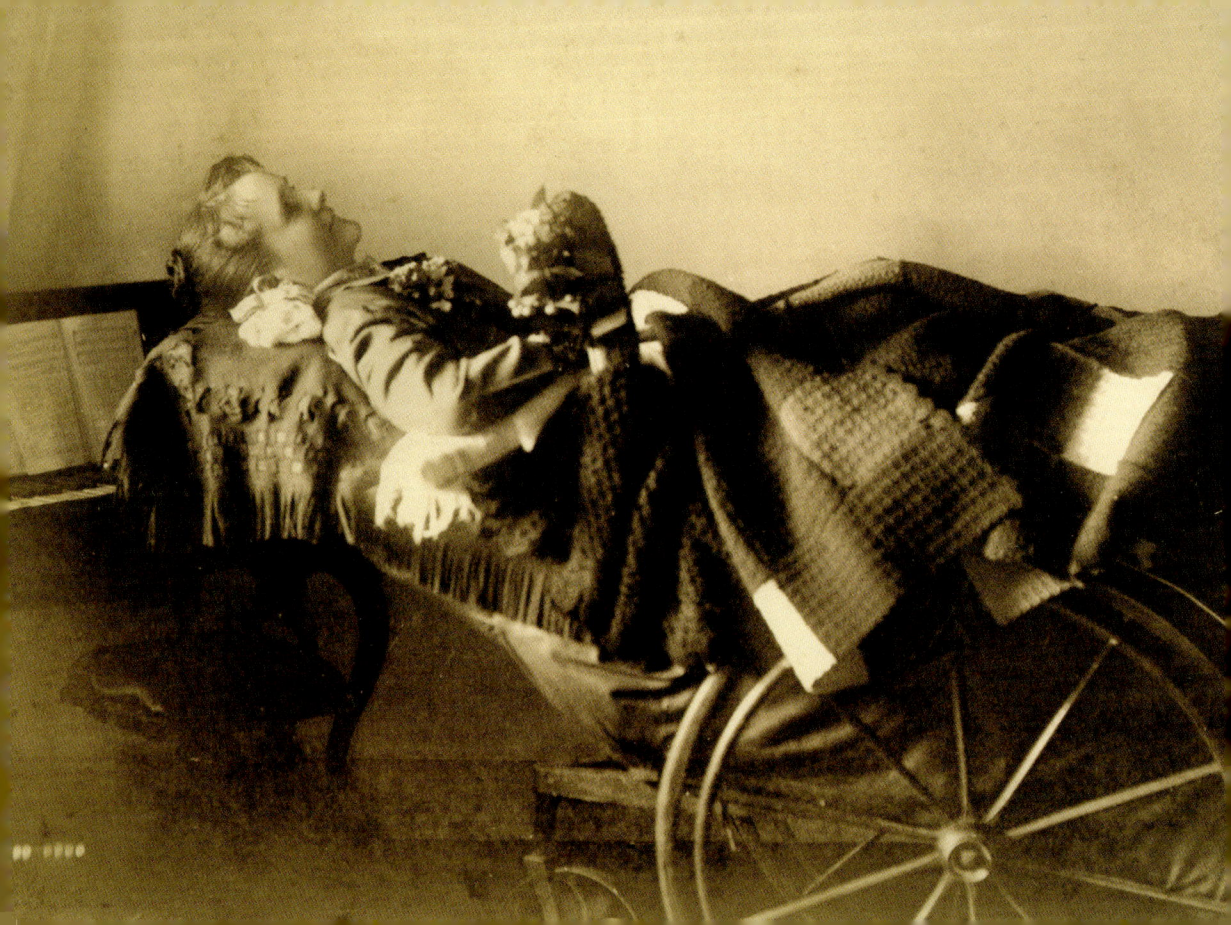

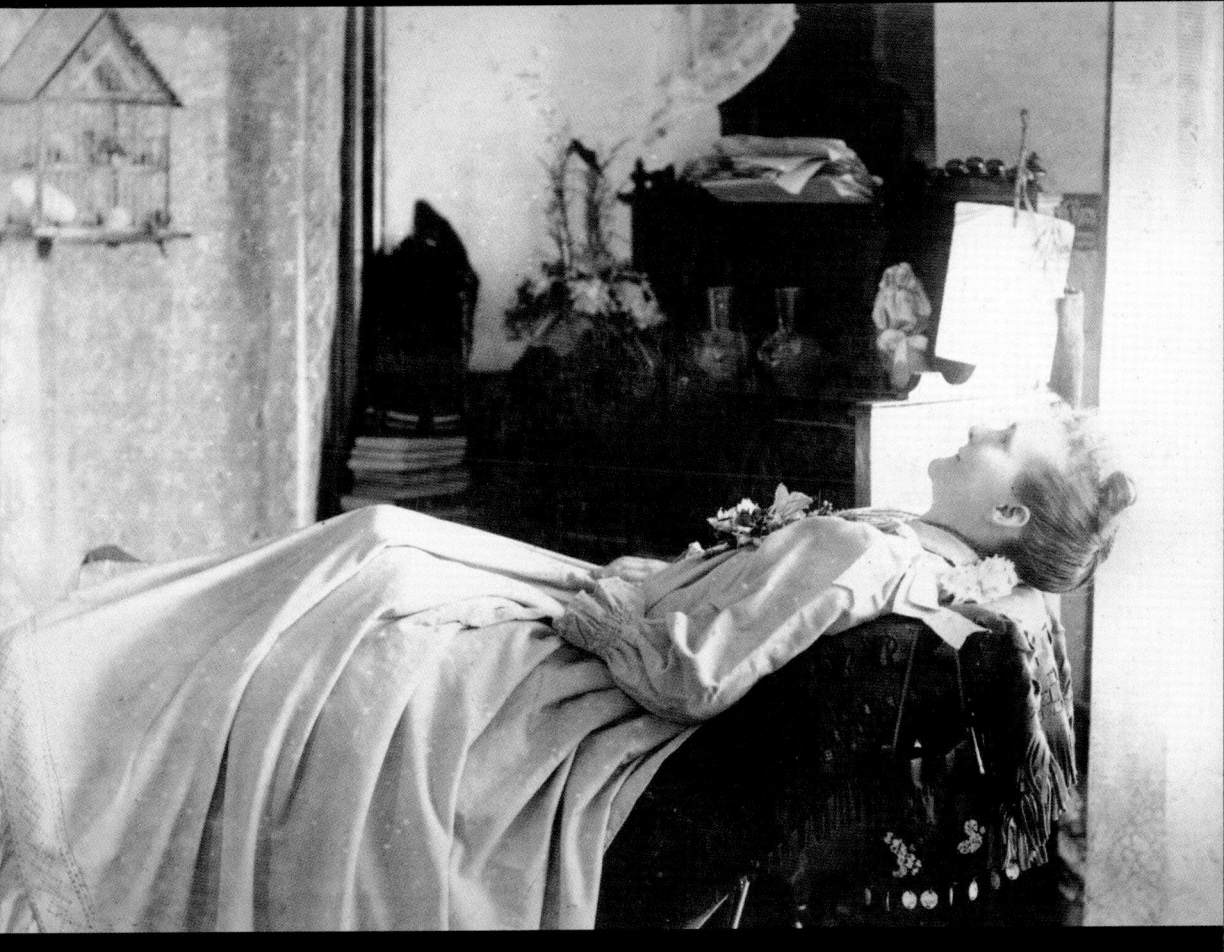

Women in Viewing Chairs   circa 1890 • cabinet cards • 4.25″ x 6.5″ each

The unusual composition of these two photos, showing a profile view of the deceased in a viewing chair,
seemed to be a favorite of the photographer John M. Brainerd, of Rome, New York.

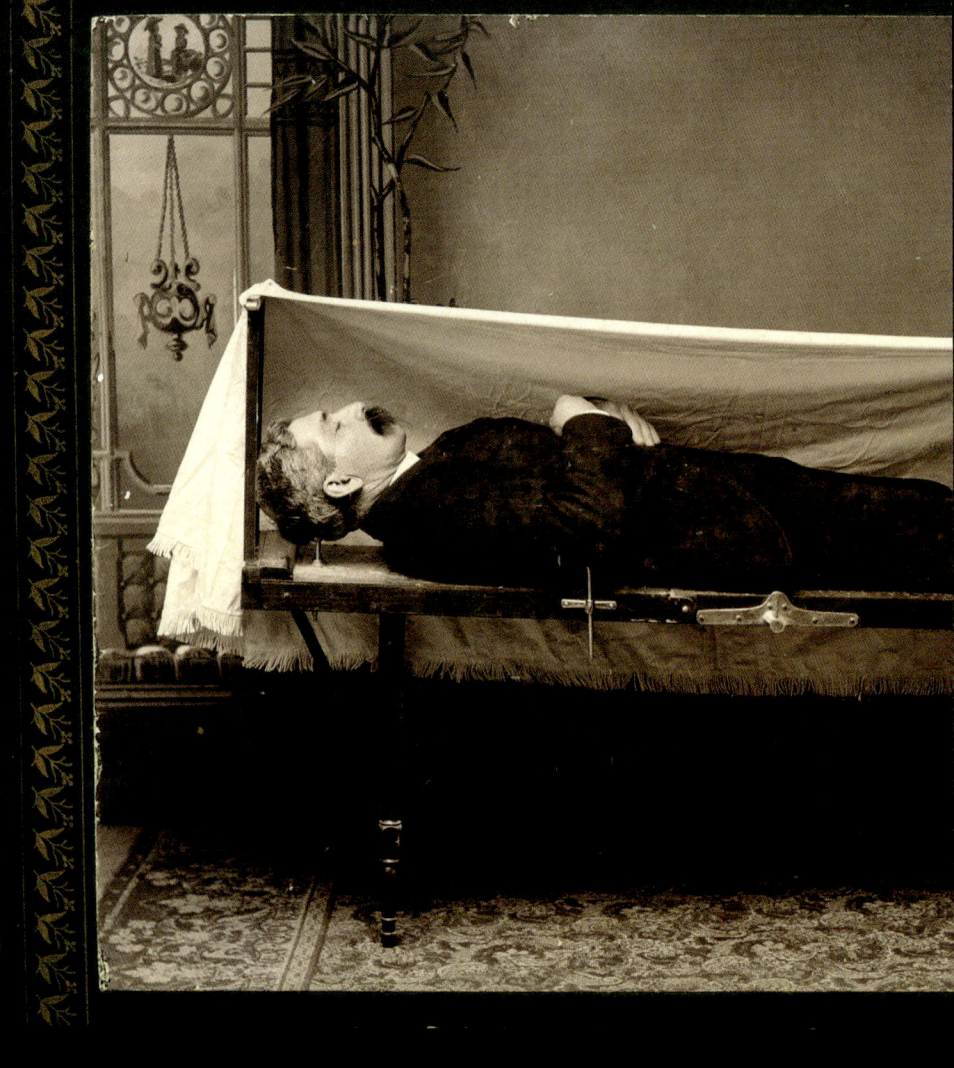

Dead Man on Cooling Board   circa 1888 • cabinet card • 4.25" x 6.5"

Tunkhannock, Pennsylvania: A very rare cabinet card showing a man on a cooling board.
Bodies were placed on cooling boards to slow down the decomposition process.
The boards had holes in them, allowing air from a block of ice placed below to keep the body cool.

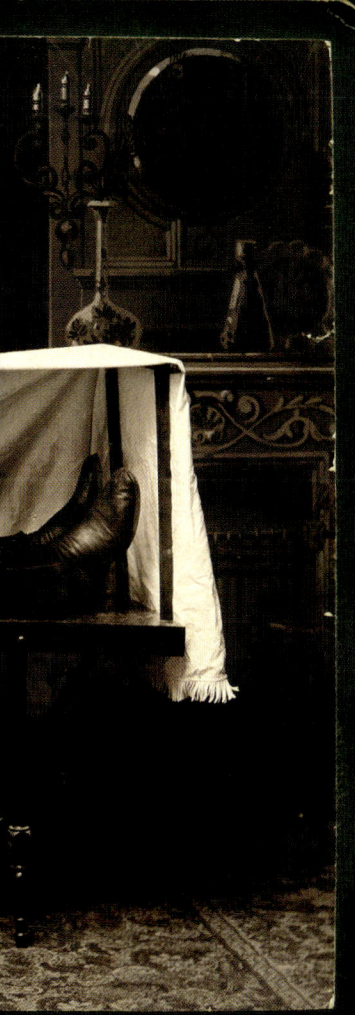

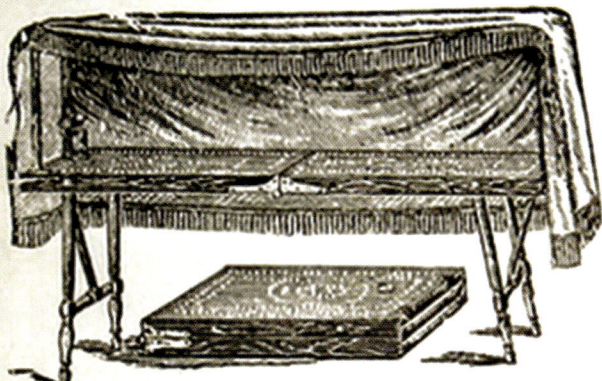
Advertisement for the B. F. Gleason cooling board

DEATH IN THE NINETEENTH CENTURY:

Tradition, Technology, & the Conflicts of the Modern

ADAM ARENSON I

Death is a part of life. It has always been so.

At once banal and profound, the absolutes of death—its finality; its unknowability; the uncertainty of its time—have been the strongest preserve of religion, offering believers answers about how to live a good life and seek a Good Death, and how to know what follows, both for the mourners on Earth and for the departed.

Death—timeless, universal, omnipresent.

And yet the modern viewer will object. Science and technology have transformed the process of dying, and they have altered our understanding of the causes of death, and our role in when and how people die. Scenes of dying are mostly hidden from us now, in hospitals. The preparation of the body and the work of burial have been taken over by professional morticians and designated burial grounds.

The fine-grained documentation of our lives has cheated, a bit, the finality of death. It is not just on television police procedurals that by the records of the life lost we remain: we keep video and audio recordings, pictures and letters, whether in print or hovering there, on the screen. We may soon see automated social-media responses from the dead, participating as they might have done, in order to allow individuals to "live on" virtually.[2]

Much as our world would seem, at first glance, unbelievable to the American of 1900, their world would have flabbergasted the American of 1800. Human needs have rarely changed over the millennia, but the ways to address them continue to transform, and the experience of death, dying, and mourning is no exception. In 1800, ice in warm months or in the tropics was an impossibility; within a few decades, it was a regular occurrence. In 1800, illumination meant the sun, or burning anything from wood to kerosene; by 1900, the widespread use of electrical lights marked the end

> *Because I could not stop for Death—*
> *He kindly stopped for me—*
> *The Carriage held but just Ourselves—*
> *And Immortality.*
> ⋯
> *Since then—'tis Centuries—and yet*
> *Feels shorter than the Day*
> *I first surmised the Horses' Heads*
> *Were toward Eternity—*
>
> —**EMILY DICKINSON**, WRITTEN ABOUT 1863; PUBLISHED IN 1890[1]

of the era of the gas lamp. In 1800, surgery had to be completed on a terrified, awake patient; over the course of the century, ether and then more and more sophisticated anesthetics were used to numb the patient to pain. Most importantly for those caring for the dead, over the century came germ theory and sterilization, offering ways to care for the dying and dead without a significant risk of joining them anon.

In 1800, the area that would become Fullerton, California, was part of the first transcontinental empire in North America— *Nueva España,* which stretched from Florida to Tejas to Nuevo México and Alta California and was governed from Mexico City. California's diverse native residents lived subject to both the priests and the military at the missions. In 1848, in the

Treaty of Guadalupe Hidalgo, California was acquired by the United States, though the most dramatic transformations in this area would await the coming of the Southern Pacific railroad, in 1883, and the network of streetcars and then the phalanx of automobiles that would lead to the orchards being dug up for suburbs.

How did Americans die in the nineteenth century, and how were they mourned? Until well into the twentieth century, Americans died at home. And, as remains true to this day, the age-old religious traditions of the mourners dictated how the body was treated, what ceremonies were held, how burial was effected, and what kinds of commemorations were to follow.

But the nineteenth century saw a transformation of the landscape of death. In 1831, the

1 Emily Dickinson, #712 ("Because I could not stop for Death-") written about 1863; published in 1890 http://www.wwnorton.com/college/english/nap/because_i_could_not_dickin.htm **2** Heather Kelly, "How to post to Facebook, Twitter after you die," *CNN* February 22, 2013 http://www.cnn.com/2013/02/22/tech/social-media/death-and-social-media

year after Emily Dickinson was born, the Massachusetts Horticultural Society established Mount Auburn Cemetery, the first garden cemetery. Rather than continuing to cram generations of burials into small church graveyards overtaken by urban development, Mount Auburn marked an effort to establish a large and permanent park-like setting for burials. Planted with native and exotic trees and flowers, Mount Auburn was intended as a place for the living as well as the dead, a healthy, pastoral, and uplifting landscape. On the outskirts of the growing city, Mount Auburn and other garden cemeteries set the tone for the next generation's large public recreation areas, such as Central Park, Prospect Park, and Boston's Emerald Necklace.

As this exhibition explores, the science of communication and documentation also changed tremendously in the nineteenth century. In the 1830s, Samuel Morse patented the first telegraph, and Louis Daguerre and his associates created the first permanent photographs, with light etching itself onto metal. In the years that followed, the photograph and the telegram, the world's first instant message, would alter how people thought about space and time. World events could be known instantly and printed in the morning paper; crop prices in Iowa could influence grocery prices in New York or London, and vice versa. Thus, into a seemingly traditional world came new technologies, with all of their creative and disruptive potentials.

For the rich or famous, the need to grasp at the dead for something tangible to remain was always stronger. It was common to carry locks of hair of loved ones, whether alive or dead. Creating a plaster mask, to be then cast, carved, or used as the model for a portrait, was the best way to document a person's features. Such masks were created in life or death for Benjamin Franklin, George Washington, and Abraham Lincoln, along with Isaac Newton, Napoleon Bonaparte, and John Keats, among others, and the significant number of extant memorial paintings suggests that such portraiture was a common practice for those who could afford it. Once photography was improved upon and made commercially viable— and then, by the turn of the twentieth century, cheap enough for any middle-class family to own a camera—the possibilities for post-mortem and mourning photography grew immensely.

In the mid-nineteenth century, foreign immigration, increased urbanization, and these scientific and technological advances led to a sense that life was speeding up, whether one was positioned at the spinning wheel of a new textile factory or crossing a busy intersection ahead of a streetcar. Growth in population and mobility meant it was possible to be a face lost in the crowd, with the possibilities and dangers of anonymity and privacy that had been impossible in the close-knit communities a generation before. And it meant a body could turn up, identity unknown, leaving the mystery to be pondered.

While forensic scientists, investigative reporters, and police detectives would develop techniques to document a crime scene (including the use of photography) by the end of the nineteenth century, fiction writers were the first to grasp the possibilities of science to reach beyond the fact of death, creating the genres of science fiction and the detective story. In 1818, Mary Shelley dreamt up *Frankenstein* as a horror story, with a monster created out of body parts of the dead. Beginning in 1841, C. August Dupin was author Edgar Allen Poe's detective character, a sleuth who used his powers of "ratiocination" to discover unseen details, reconstruct the thought process of the criminal, and bring the truth to light—much like his famous literary successor, Sherlock Holmes, who first appeared in 1887.

Most of these inventions, discoveries, and transformations were already known by 1861, but one cannot consider the state of death in nineteenth-century America without grappling with the horrific toll of the Civil War: at least 620,000 soldiers were killed, and unknown numbers of civilians. They died in horrific bursts of carnage—more than 7,800 dead at Gettysburg in three days; more than 3,600 dead at Antietam in one day—and, more commonly, from the ravages of disease, whether from battlefield wounds, contaminated water sources, or exposure to the elements. Photographers from Matthew Brady's studio rearranged bodies on the battlefield to heighten the pathos of their images. The families of officers sent urgent telegrams to local embalmers and railroad operators, and purchased stench-proof steel caskets to get their loved ones home for a final viewing before burial; common soldiers were buried, at first, in mass graves on the battlefields. If they were identified, it was often because they clasped a photograph of a loved one.

"We here highly resolve that these dead shall not have died in vain—that this nation, under God, shall have a new birth of freedom—and that government of the people, by the people, for the people, shall not perish from the earth," Abraham Lincoln said, concluding his address at Gettysburg. The fallen men were exhumed, identified, and reburied individually, in a new landscape of death: the national cemetery. The repeating rows of headstones—machined and engraved in a uniform manner—again spoke of the power of technological transformation to continue the traditional practices of death and mourning.

Death is a part of life. But, because life changes, death changes as well: its cause, and its course. While, ultimately, death is unstoppable, our manner of remembering the departed advances as society does, through the newest possibilities of science, at the cost of what is available in the marketplace. Whether locks of hair or death masks, garden cemeteries or forensic investigations, memorial photographs or intricate costumes of mourning, the techniques may change, but the desire—to reach out, once more, and touch a loved one—remains eternal.

Bibliography

Ames, Kenneth L. *Death in the Dining Room and Other Tales of Victorian Culture.* Philadelphia: Temple University Press, 1992.
Deverell, William Francis. *Whitewashed Adobe: The Rise of Los Angeles and the Remaking of Its Mexican Past.*
    Berkeley: University of California Press, 2004.
Downs, Jim. *Sick from Freedom: African-American Illness and Suffering During the Civil War and Reconstruction.*
    New York: Oxford University Press, 2012.
Faust, Drew Gilpin. *This Republic of Suffering: Death and the American Civil War.* New York: Alfred A. Knopf, 2008.
Fuller, Randall. *From Battlefields Rising: How the Civil War Transformed American Literature.* New York: Oxford University Press, 2011.
Isenberg, Nancy, and Andrew Burstein. *Mortal Remains: Death in Early America.* Philadelphia: University of Pennsylvania Press, 2003.
Kropp, Phoebe S. *California Vieja: Culture and Memory in a Modern American Place.* Berkeley: University of California Press, 2006.
Laderman, Gary. *The Sacred Remains: American Attitudes Towards Death, 1799-1833.* New Haven: Yale University Press, 1997.
Roach, Joseph R. *Cities of the Dead: Circum-Atlantic Performance.* New York: Columbia University Press, 1996.
Sachs, Aaron. *Arcadian America: The Death and Life of an Environmental Tradition.* New Haven: Yale University Press, 2013.
Sandweiss, Martha A. *Print the Legend: Photography and the American West.* New Haven: Yale University Press, 2002.
Solnit, Rebecca. *River of Shadows: Eadweard Muybridge and the Technological Wild West.* New York: Viking, 2003.
Srebnick, Amy Gilman. *The Mysterious Death of Mary Rogers: Sex and Culture in Nineteenth-Century New York.*
    New York: Oxford University Press, 1995.

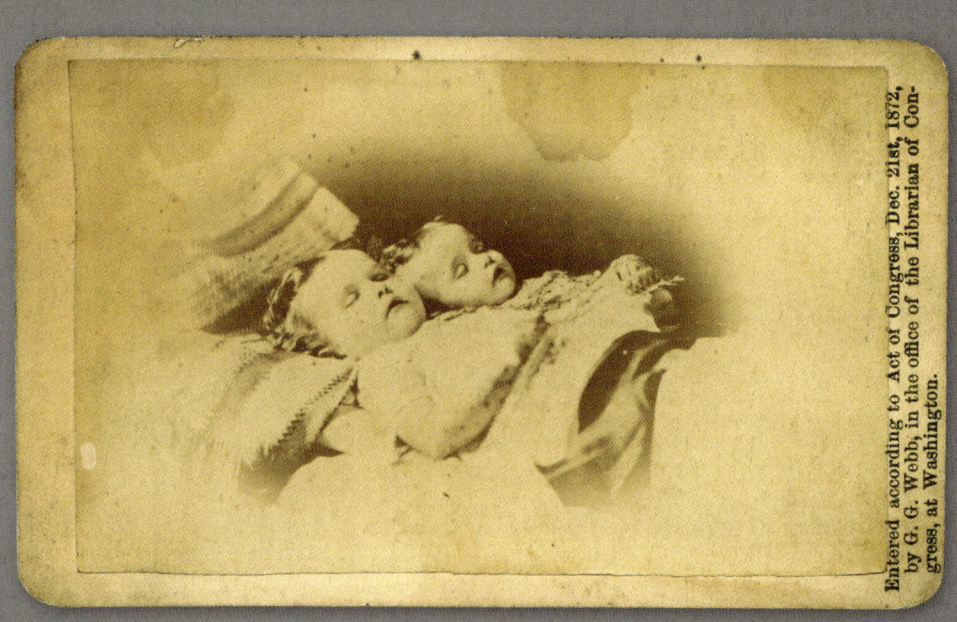

Entered according to Act of Congress, Dec. 21st, 1872, by G. G. Webb, in the office of the Librarian of Congress, at Washington.

The Murdered Children 1872 • carte de visite • 2.5" x 4"

Columbiana, Ohio: 3-year-old Minda and 1-year-old Adelaide Porter, murdered with a hatchet by their father,
Irwin (or Erben) Porter, on December 12, 1872. Porter was tried, convicted, and sentenced to life in prison.
Shortly after his incarceration, he was said to have become "raving mad" and confined to an iron cell.
He died in prison on November 15, 1875.

CRIME

—

MURDER

—

TRAGEDY

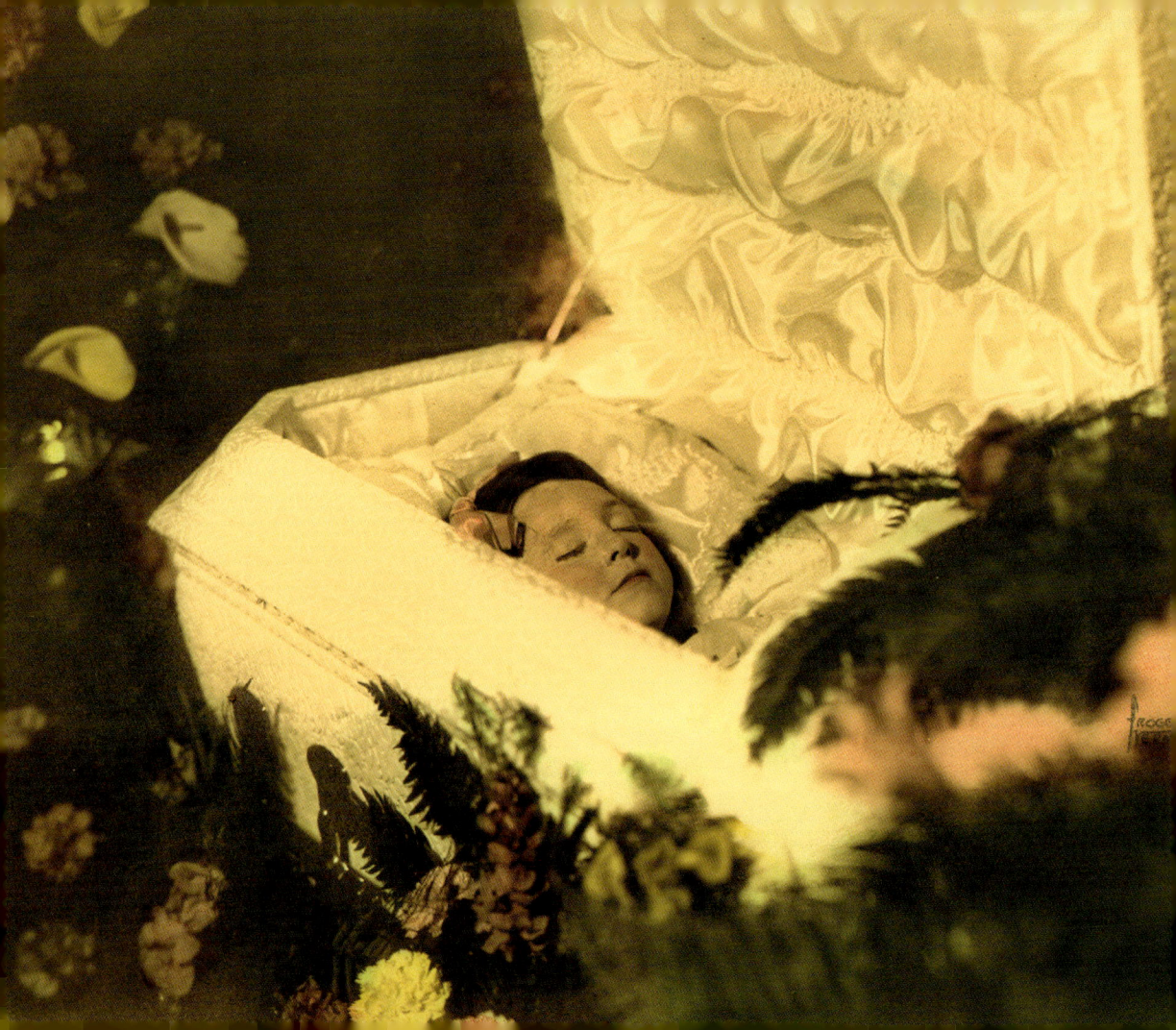

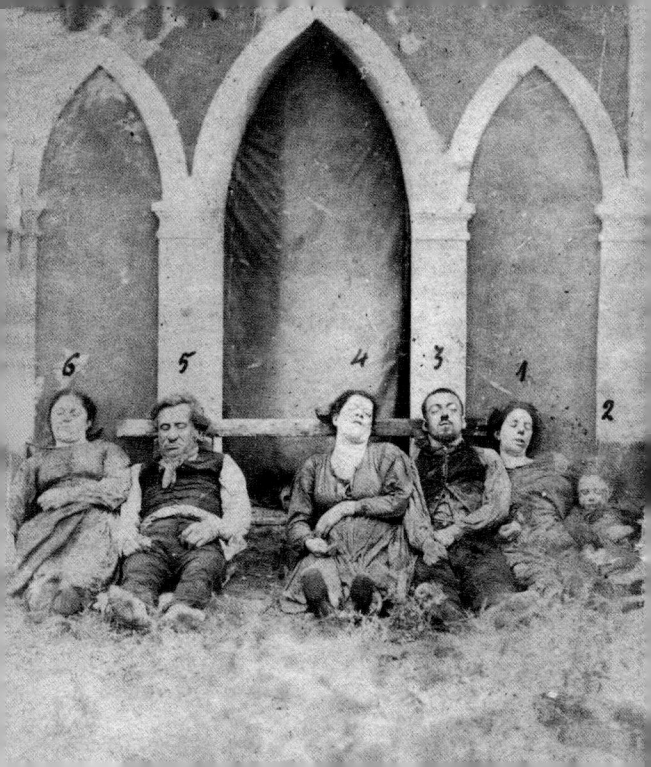

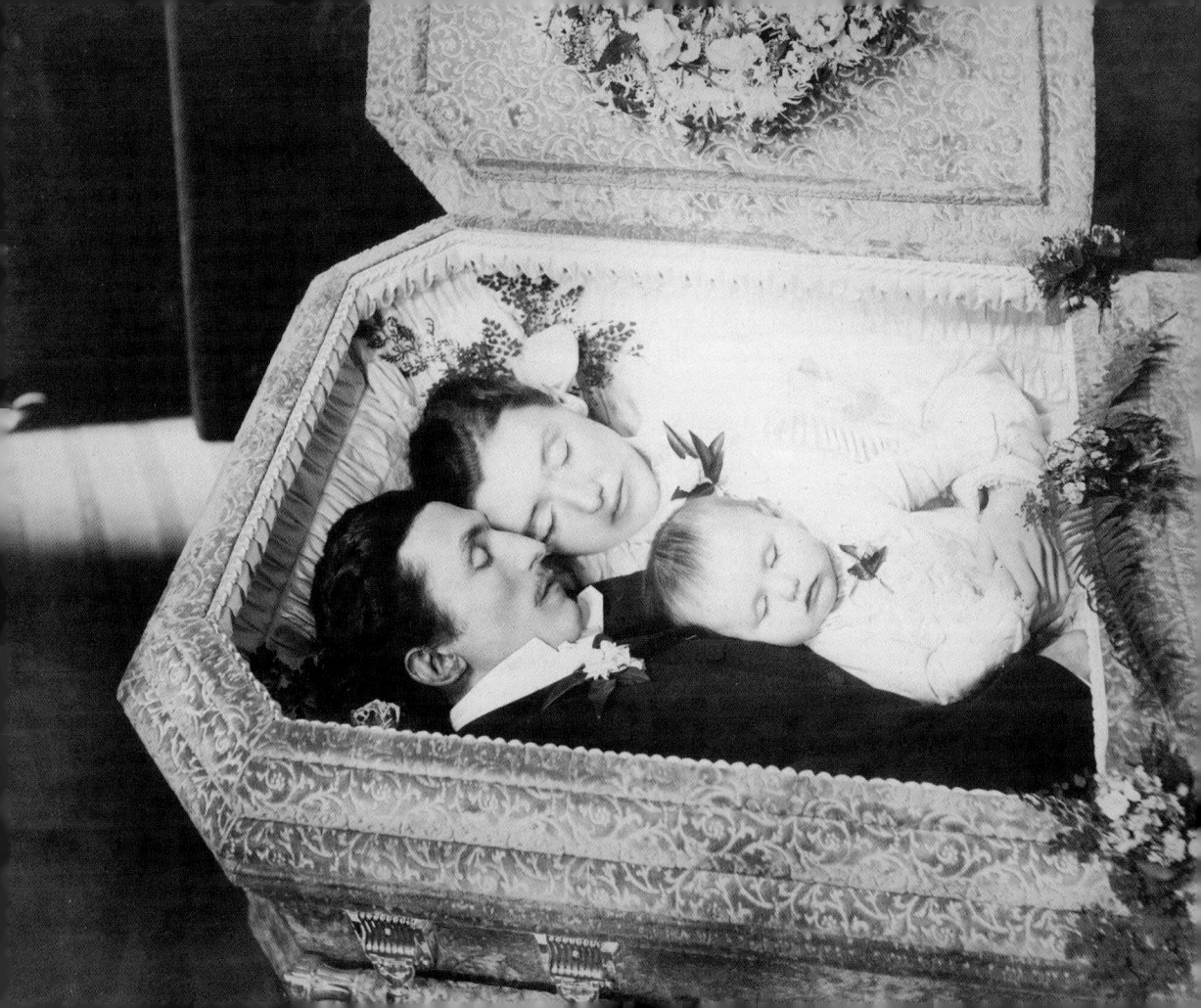

THREE IN ONE CASKET.

EMIL KELLER, WIFE AND BABY UNITED IN DEATH.

The Little One Died at the City Hospital Last Night—The Funeral Will Be Held from the Universalist Church To-morrow Afternoon.

Shortly after 6 o'clock last evening death came to the relief of little Anna Keller at the City hospital. It was found that the bullet from the mother's revolver had penetrated the infant's right lung and came out on the left side.

The body of the child was removed to Gross' undertaking room and prepared for burial with its parents.

Throughout the day throngs of people have visited the undertaking rooms to view the remains.

Father, mother and daughter will be buried in the same casket, which is a special order, about 4 inches deeper and 9 inches wider than the ordinary, and covered with gray embossed plush. The plate reads :

```
EMEL KELLER,
Aged 30 years.
MARY, his Wife,
Aged 29 years.
```

Another plate is inscribed "Our Darling."

The head of Mrs. Keller rests on the left shoulder of her husband, thus hiding from view the wound in her temple and partly covering a discoloration of the right eye. There are traces of suffering in the woman's face but her husband looks as if he was in slumber. His left arm encircles the body of his wife while his right rests on his hip. Between the mother and father is the infant, a handsome, plump child. Its right hand is clasped by the left of its mother while its left rests on the mother's left arm. The mother and the infant are laid out in plain white shrouds while the husband and father has a coat and vest of plain black and trousers of a dark pattern.

The funeral will take place tomorrow afternoon at 2:30 from the Universalist church and the interment will be in Fort Hill.

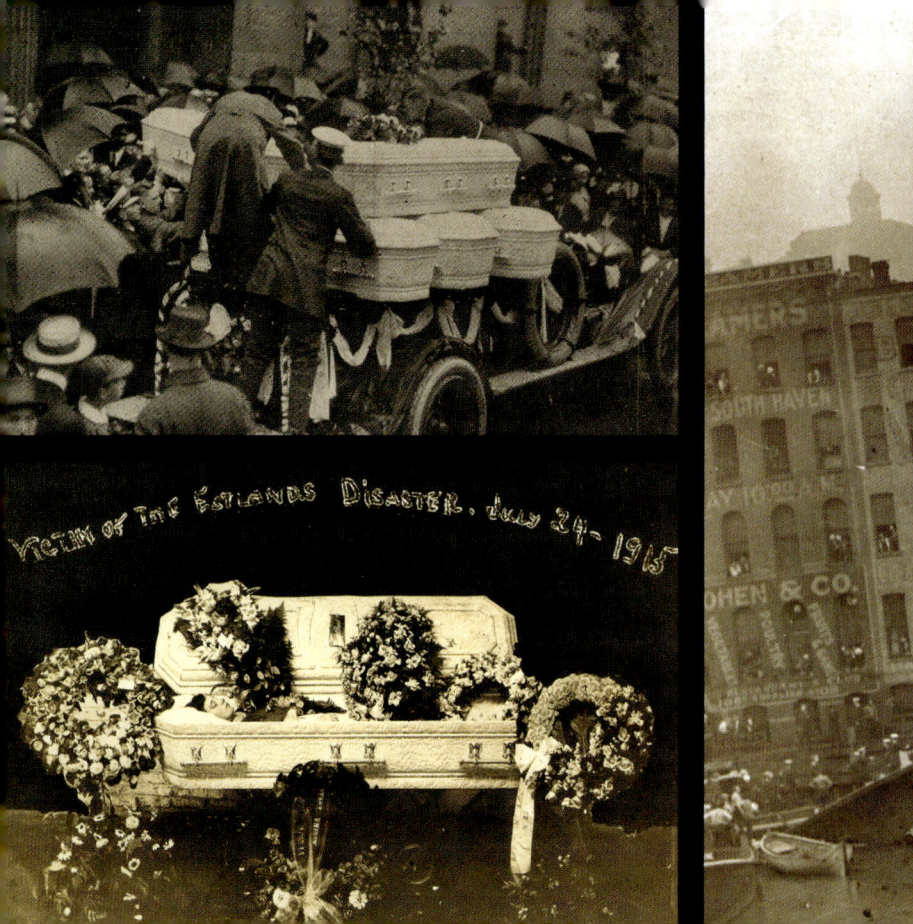

VICTIM OF THE EASTLAND DISASTER, JULY 24 - 1915

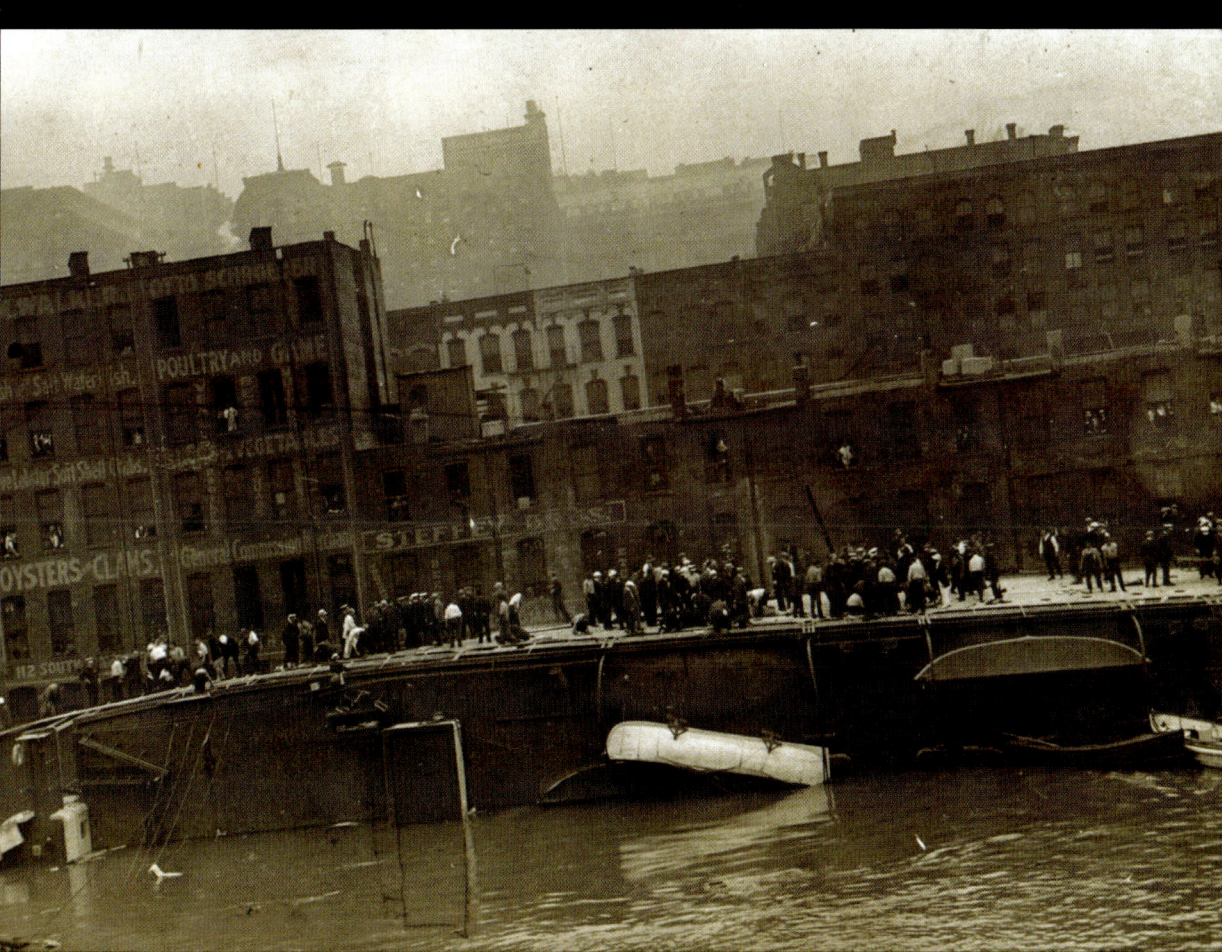

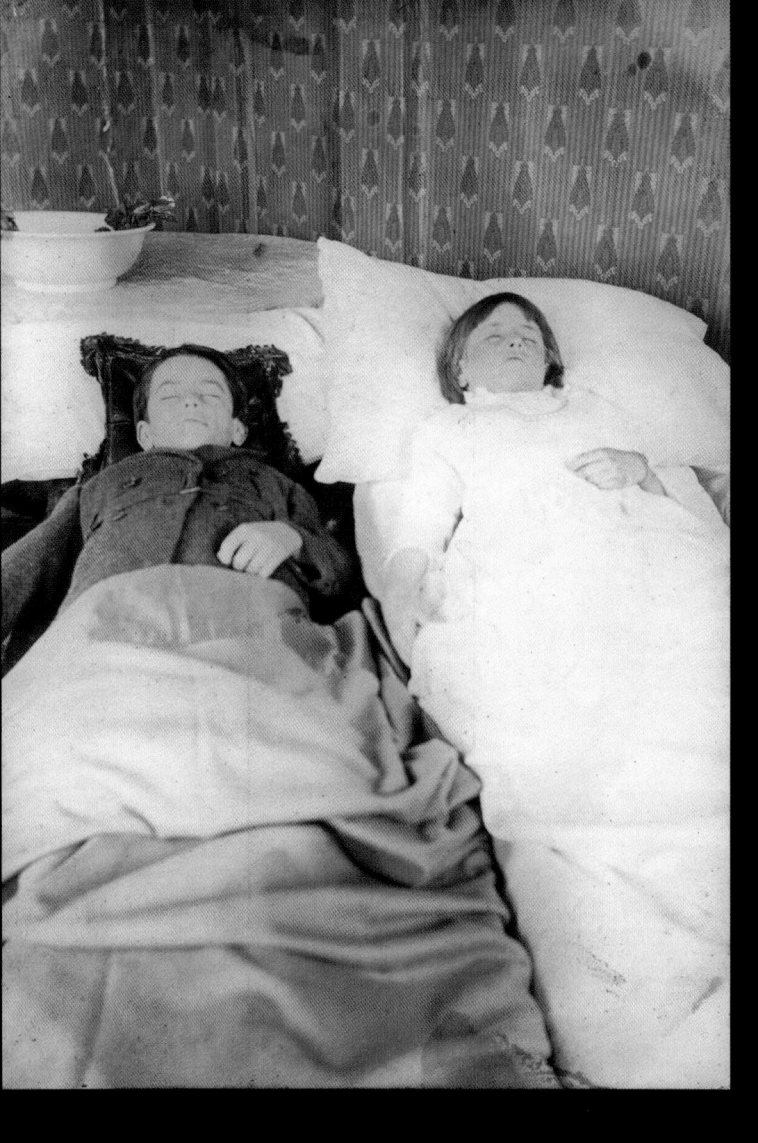

Spranger Children   1923 • gelatin silver print • 6.5" x 4.5"

"Maxie" Spranger and his sister Johanna, who drowned after falling through thin ice while sledding,
Williamsville, Michigan, January 6, 1923

An Accident That Stirs The Sympathies of All

Seldom is the county shocked by an accident which touches the heart strings of the people like the one which recently happened at what is known as Williamsville, at Williams lake, in Unadilla township. The two children of Mr. and Mrs. Leo Spranger, Maxine, a boy aged nine, and Johanna, a girl aged eight, were being drawn on the ice by a neighbor boy, Earl Carr, when the ice gave way precipitating all into the water. The Carr boy managed to climb out by the aid of some bushes that were overhanging the water and ran for help. Men soon arrived and finding the body of the boy, bore it to the house only to be confronted with the question from the frantic mother, "Where is my little Johanna?" They had not known before that it was a double drowning. They hastened back and soon found the body of the little girl.

The accident is especially sad as it was the only children of the Sprangers. Sheriff Bod and Coroner Crittenden decided that the drowning was accidental and that an inquest was unnecessary.

BROTHER AND SISTER DROWNED IN POND AT WILLIAMSVILLE

Saturday afternoon, while three children, Max Spranger, 8 and his sister Johanna, 10 and Earl Carr, 9, were playing on the ice, the Spranger children were drowned.

The little Carr boy was drawing the others on a sled when the ice gave way under the sled and all three fell into the alke. He hurried to the nearest house for help but when the little boy and girl were recovered life was extinct.

Mr. and Mrs. Spranger, the parents of the little ones are almost prostrated by the fatal accident have the sympathy of the entire community of Gregory and vicinity where Mr. Spranger works as a painter.

The double funeral was held at the home in Williamsville, Tuesday afternoon.

FIND EIGHT MURDERED ON NORTH DAKOTA FARM

Man, His Wife, Four Children, Farm Hand and Another Were Slain.

BISMARCK, N. D., April 24.—The bodies of Jacob Wolff, his wife, their four children and a farmhand were found by a neighbor today on the Wolff farm, near Turtle Lake, north of here.

Later still another body was found. A bloody hatchet was discovered in the cellar and this, it is believed, figured in the tragedy.

Numerous empty shotgun shells lay scattered about the place, indicating that the seven had been shot. Mystery surrounds the affair.

QUARREL OVER DOG WIPED OUT FAMILY

Farmer, Wife, Five Children and Chore Boy Murdered by a Neighbor.

Washburn, N.D., May 14.—Injuries administered to one farmer's cattle by another farmer's dog started a quarrel, resulting in the murder of Jacob Wolf, his wife, five children, and a chore boy, near Turtle Creek, N.D., according to a confession made here by Henry Layer, the police say.

The confession attributed to Layer is a record of cold-blooded atrocity rare in the annals of crime. Layer, whose farm adjoins the Wolf place, was arrested at his home Tuesday night and yesterday, after making the confession, was sentenced to life imprisonment by Judge Nuessle.

According to the statement, there was ill-feeling between the two farmers for some time, culminating in a quarrel over Layer's cattle being worried by Wolf's dog. On April 22, Layer went to the Wolf farm, and was ordered away by the owner. When he refused to go, Wolf, he says, secured a double-barrelled shotgun. As the two men struggled in the doorway to the kitchen for possession of the weapon, it was discharged twice.

One of the shots killed Mrs. Wolf, and the other a 13-year-old chore boy. Layer by this time had taken the gun away from Wolf. He went into the sitting room, obtained a handful of shells from a bureau drawer, and hurried outside. Wolf was running toward the barn, and Layer fired, hitting Wolf in the back. He then shot Wolf again in the back as he lay on the ground, according to the alleged confession.

Layer then ran to a barn and shot two of the girls while they pleaded for mercy. Attracted by the screams of three little girls in the house, Layer shot two of them and killed the third with a hatchet.

After the seven members of the family and the chore boy had been killed Layer went to the barn, covered the two bodies with hay and dragged Wolf's body into the shed and buried it under a pile of hay.

He then went into the kitchen, opened the cellar door and threw in the bodies of Mrs. Wolf, three children and that of the boy. He then took the gun, broke it in two, and threw the pieces into a slough north of the Wolf farm, where they were later found.

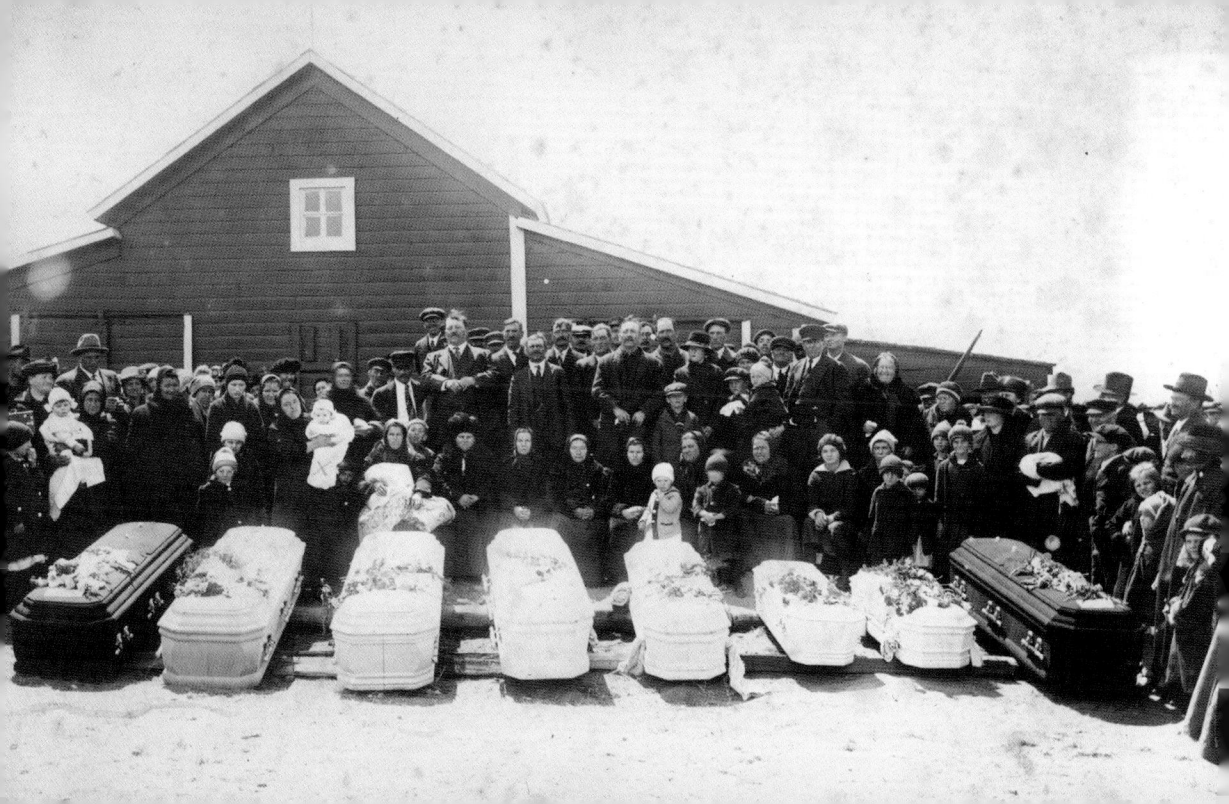

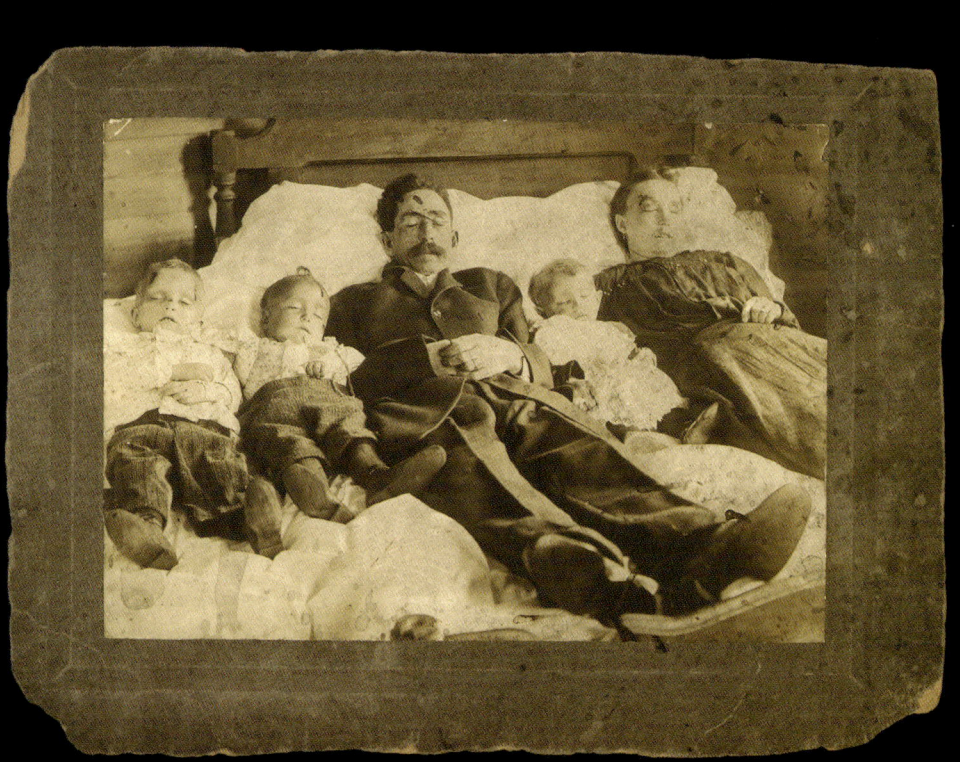

EXECUTION A HORROR

20-Year-Old Led on Scaffold Twice. First Rope Broke and Body Writhed in Agony.

Houston, Mo., Dec. 21—The execution here today of Joda Hamilton, the 20 year old farmer boy, for the murder of five members of the family of Barney Parsons, a farmer, was a horrible affair. The first rope broke.

At the first attempt Hamilton shot through the trap with a jerk and the spectators were horrified to see the rope part. The body dropped to the ground and lay there writhing in pain. Partially conscious he was picked up and carried to the scaffold. The rope was again hurriedly placed about the boy's neck and the trap again sprung. This time it was successful.

The attending physician expressed the belief that Hamilton was fatally injured by the first fall and died before he dropped the second time. The body was turned over to Hamilton's father.

MURDERS ENTIRE FAMILY AND TELLS HOW HE DID IT

Negro Fiend Shoots Father, Brains Mother, and Cuts Throats Of Children

SPRINGFIELD, Mo., Oct. 14.—News of the murder of the family of Barney Parsons on Friday—the father, mother, and three children—near Houston, a town seventy miles east of Springfield, has reached here. Joda Hamilton, who is reported to have confessed to the murders, is in the Houston jail guarded by a force of deputies to prevent a threatened lynching.

Parsons, who was a farmer, sold his crops to Hamilton. A quarrel followed the sale. As Parsons and his family were driving home they were confronted by the murderer, armed with a shotgun. He shot Parsons, who fell to the ground. Hamilton clubbed him with the butt of the gun. He then clubbed the mother and children to death, after which he put the bodies in the wagon, took them to Big Piney Creek, and threw them into the creek, where fishermen found them

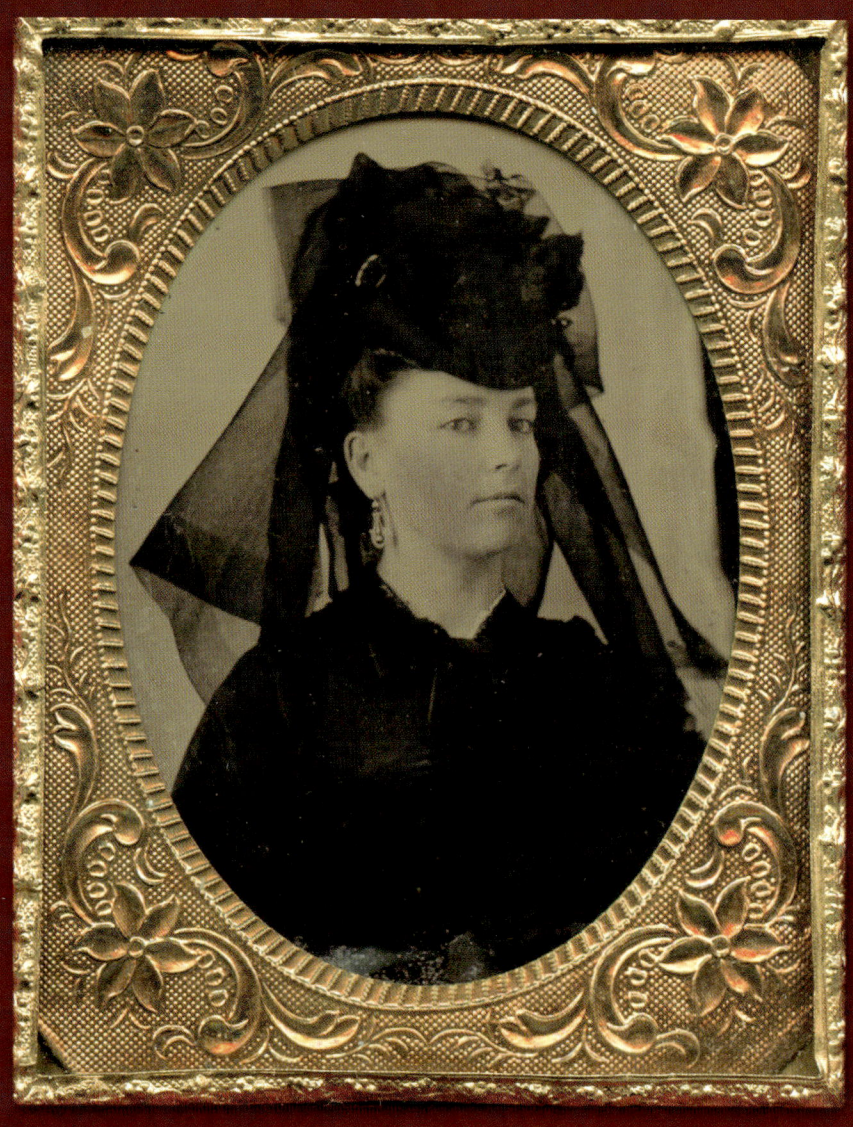

Young Widow circa 1862 • ninth-plate tintype • 3" x 2.5"
Portrait of a young widow wearing a black mourning dress, hat, and veil.

MOURNING AS MEMORY:

A Brief Primer on Victorian Mourning Customs

BESS LOVEJOY

For the Victorians, the Angel of Death was always close. He lurked in the slums, spreading typhoid and scarlet fever, and stalked the battlefields of the Civil War, riding the bullets that blew young men to bits. He wandered the sewers, dousing them in cholera, and sneaked into drawing rooms, sprinkling tuberculosis onto the handkerchiefs of young women. He made sure the cook didn't wash her hands before preparing the stew, and that she didn't think twice about drawing water from the well next to the graveyard. He was the reason parents often didn't name their children for a year, and why women who could afford it always had a mourning outfit ready.

But death wasn't necessarily terrifying for the Victorians. The end was often seen as a relief from the sorrows of this world and a chance to be reunited with family members who had gone before. Many Victorian mourning customs focused on preserving family bonds with the departed. "Mourning is a form of memory,"

wrote one widow in 1887. "When we mourn, we keep our loved ones alive in memory." The preeminent example of this kind of mourning, and all Victorian mourning, is the woman who gave her name to the era. When Prince Albert died of typhoid fever in 1861, Queen Victoria plunged into a mourning from which she never emerged. She rarely wore colors, and then only the violet shades permitted in half-mourning. She stayed in seclusion, making sure Albert's room was kept just as he'd left it, and sleeping with a post-mortem photograph of him above her head. Although Victoria was criticized for the depths of her mourning—and years of refusal to appear in public—many other widows copied the outward signs of her devotion to grief. Scholars say the development of Victorian mourning customs was also encouraged by new forms of Christianity (Evangelicalism) that emphasized the importance of the deathbed, and new movements in art (Romanticism) that encouraged outpourings of emotion. It also helped that there was a new middle class with money to spend, and new department stores to help them spend it.

The primary locus of death in Victorian life was the home. Victorians almost always died where they had lived, surrounded by family, friends, and neighbors. The departed's body was kept in the parlor until the funeral, the face daubed with plaster to create a death mask, the corpse arranged for post-mortem photographs with family members. On the day of the funeral, usually the first Sunday after the death, the facade of the house was swathed in black crepe, which also covered all the mirrors and doorknobs. The funeral service itself was often accompanied by a feast of ham, cider, ale, and special cakes, with much lively talk of the deceased, who was treated as a guest of honor. The procession to the cemetery often featured a richly ornamented coffin carried on a hearse festooned with black feathers, drawn by specially bred (or dyed) black horses wearing tall ostrich plumes. After the funeral, elaborately embossed and pierced memorial cards were frequently sent out to mourners as tokens of remembrance. Originally, these were meant as

reminders to pray for the soul of the deceased.

The prescribed mourning period was dictated by the mourner's relationship to the person who had died. Widows mourned for a total of two-and-a-half years, widowers mourned for three months, and everyone else followed a complicated series of regulations set out by the (frequently conflicting) etiquette books. The first stage of mourning attire was dominated by the use of black crepe—a scratchy, coarse, expensive fabric made from silk treated with heat. Crepe appeared in flounces, cuffs, and hems for women, in cloaks, armbands, and hatbands for men, and in various trimmings added to pets, birdcages, beehives, and sometimes even nearby trees. Shoes were black, as were gloves, hats, fans, ear trumpets, handkerchief borders, stationery edges, and the ribbons on women's underwear. The cuts of mourning dresses differed year by year (posteriors puffed in the 1870s, sleeves ballooned in the 1890s), but fabric was key: for the first period of mourning, only crepe, dull paramatta, bombazine, or other drab fabrics were permitted. After a year and a day, widows could wear dull silks trimmed with crepe, and after eighteen months, the crepe could come off. Two years in, grey and the purples of half-mourning were permitted—mauve, pansy, lilac, and heliotrope, a range made possible by the invention of synthetic dyes in 1856.

If crepe was the fabric of mourning, jet jewelry was the adornment. Made from the fossilized driftwood of the prehistoric monkey-puzzle tree, the gemstone was admired for its naturally matte surface. (As with fabrics, shine and gloss had to be avoided in the first stages of mourning due to old superstitions about reflections encouraging the dead to steal the soul of the deceased.) Jet was believed to have magical powers: the ancients said it could ward off the evil eye, neutralize poison, and drive away serpents. Blackest onyx, glass, enamel, and early forms of plastic were also worn, fashioned into brooches, earrings, pins, necklaces, and tiaras. Memorial jewelry incorporating pictures or hair of the deceased was also popular, the hair often in the form of simple twists added to enamel or jet settings, or braided or woven to make bracelets, necklaces, and watch chains. Hair jewelry, which all but died out with the Victorians, was an important way of keeping the deceased physically close at hand, as were the post-mortem photographs.

Why don't we mourn as the Victorians did? For one thing, the Angel of Death is less present in our lives. Antibiotics, vaccines, and better sanitation have lengthened our time on earth. We know to wash our hands, to drink clean water. Charles Darwin ushered in an age where death seems more like a fact of nature and less like a flower-strewn pathway to a paradise where we'll meet our families again. But it was the mass casualties of World War I—thirty-seven million dead—that sounded the death knell for Victorian mourning customs. Families of English soldiers were encouraged to avoid mourning, lest the whole nation appear swathed in depressing black. The soldier dead were buried in foreign mass graves, far from family members who could make photographs and death masks, snip hair for rings, hold wakes with hours of drinking and talking around the coffin. For us, death is more abstract, less domestic. Memory is digital, not material. Grief is individual, not communal. The Victorian customs may be gone for good—gone, but not forgotten.

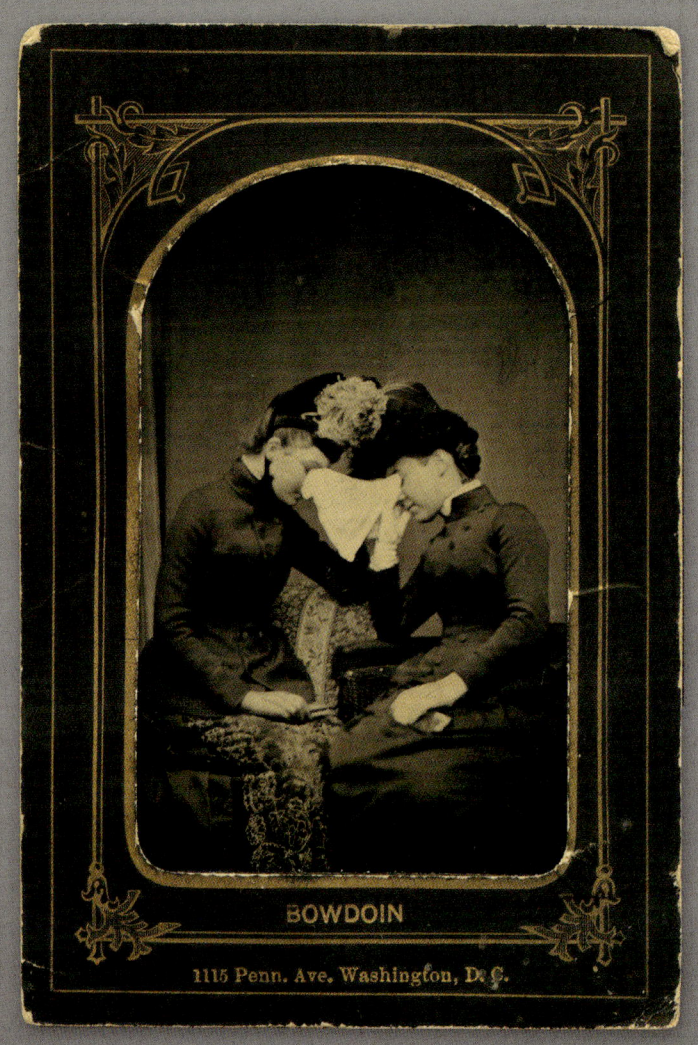

BOWDOIN

1115 Penn. Ave. Washington, D. C.

Poor Frank! 1886 • tintype • 4" x 2.75"

Crying women sharing a handkerchief.
On the back is written, "Me and Mary; Poor Frank Howard! Alas! Washington, DC, 1886."

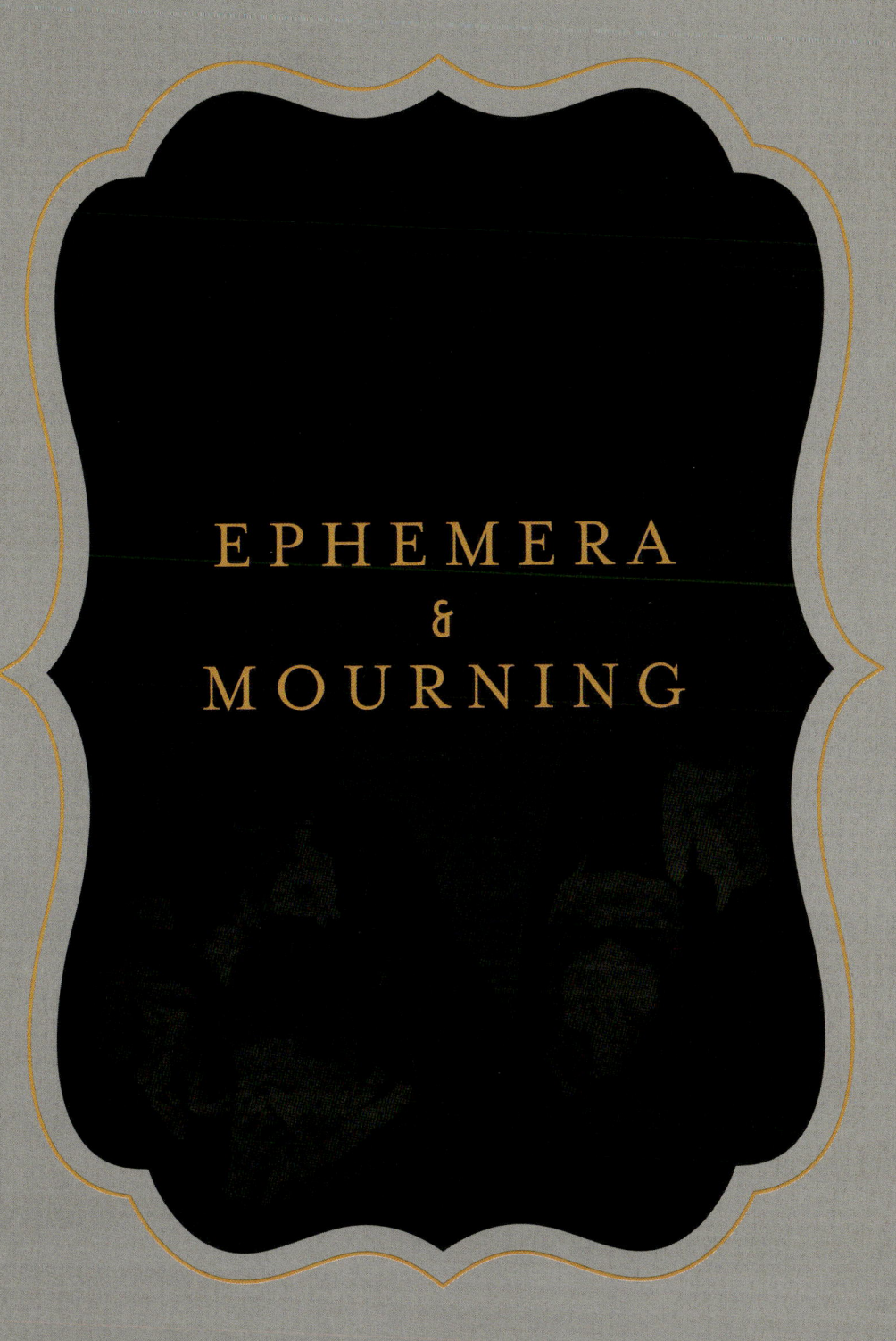

EPHEMERA
&
MOURNING

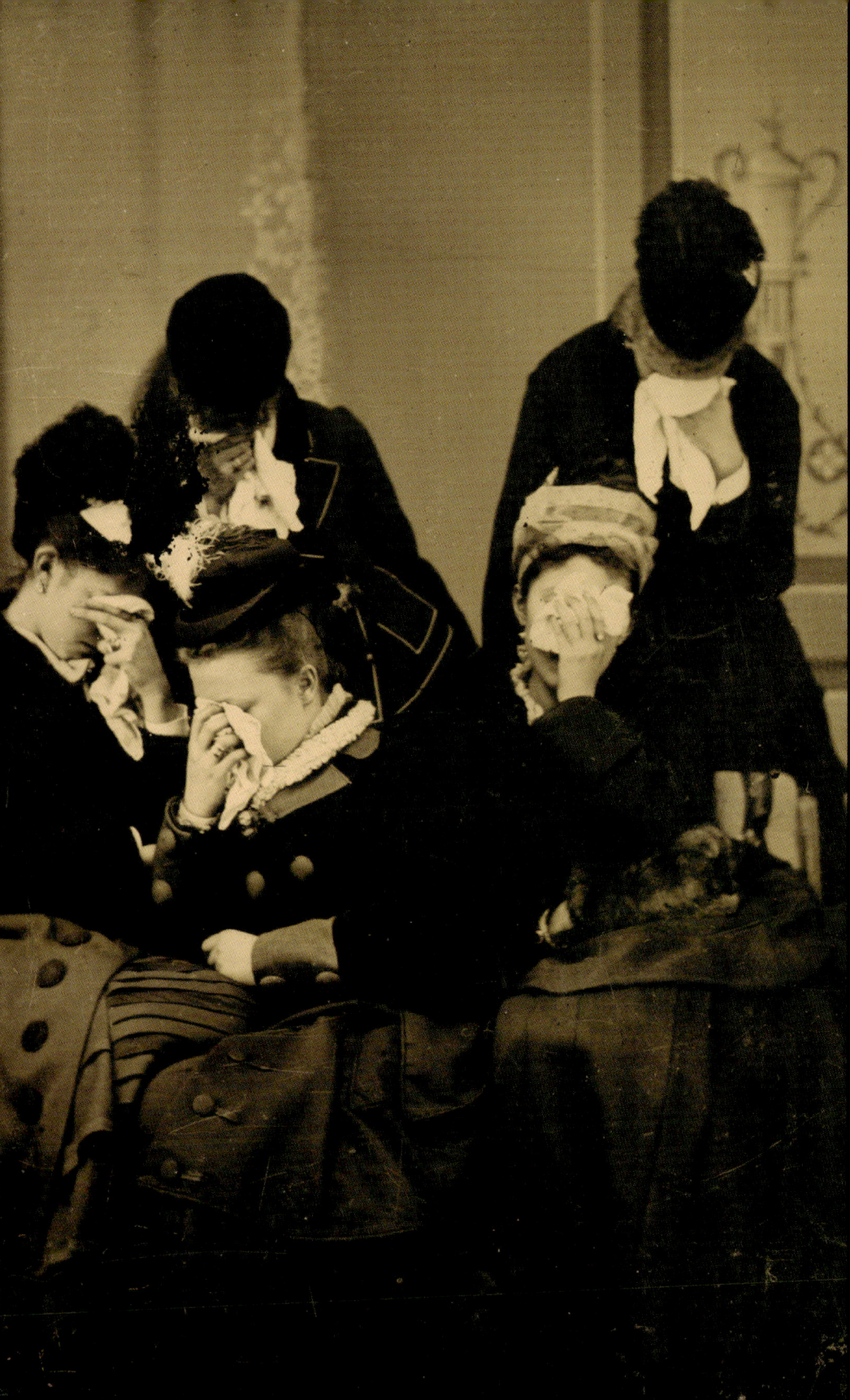

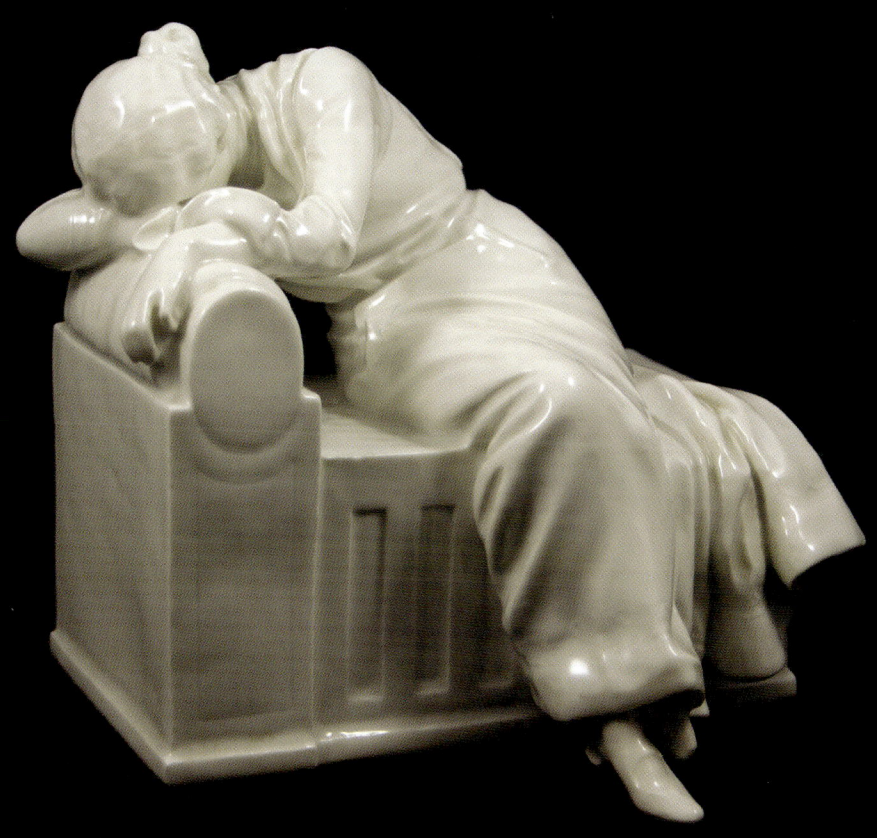

The Weepers circa 1886 • tintype • 4" x 2.5"

During the 1870s, photographs of women crying and families posing with portraits and other
mementos of deceased loved ones increased in popularity. Although scenes like the ones seen here were not
spontaneous expressions of grief, the sentiment behind them was genuine.

White Weeper 1901 • sculpture • 6.75" x 8" x 6"

Porcelain sculpture of a weeping woman. The use of weeping women in cemetery sculpture, memorials,
and photography as symbols of grief was especially popular during the Victorian Era.

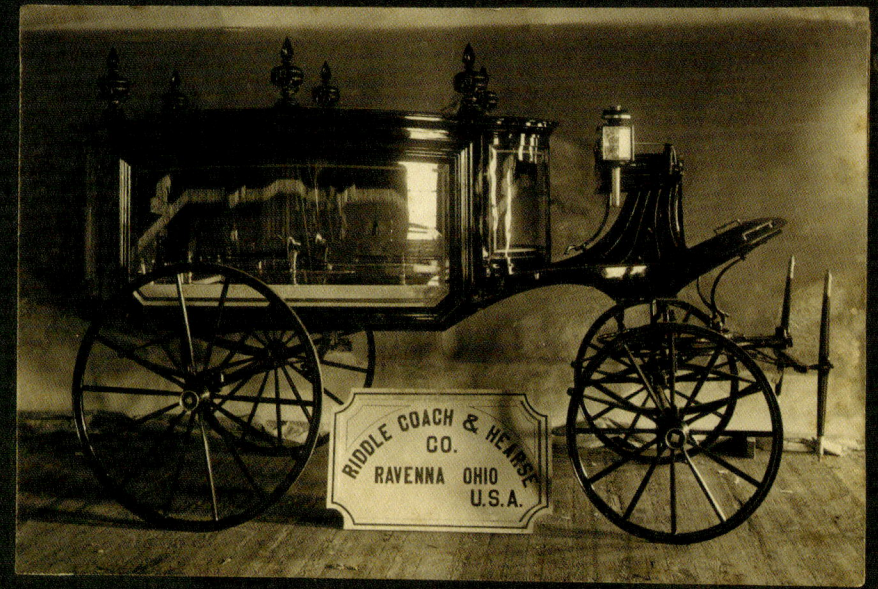

RIDDLE COACH & HEARSE CO.
RAVENNA OHIO
U.S.A.

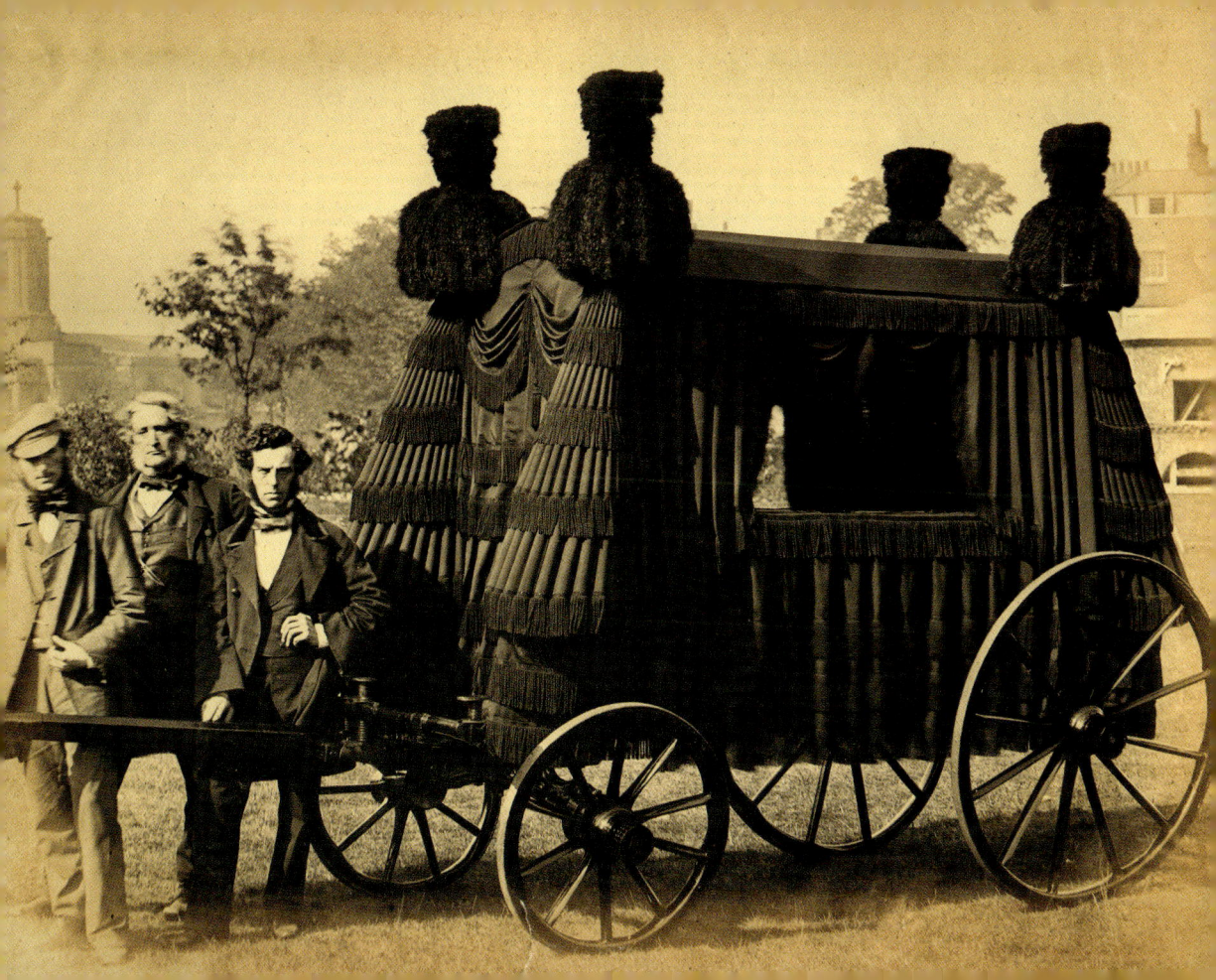

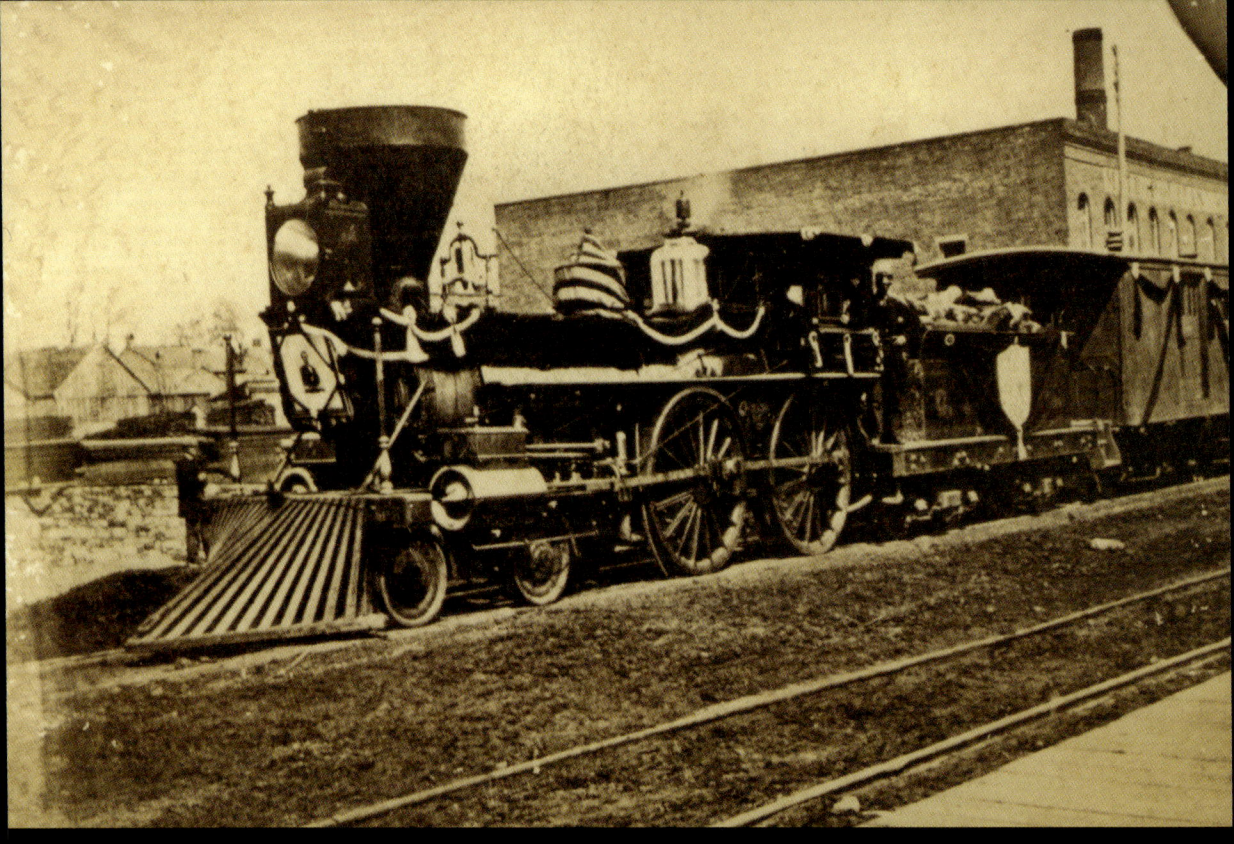

Lincoln Funeral Train   1865 • carte de visite • 2.5" x 4"

The funeral train bearing the bodies of slain President Abraham Lincoln and his son William.
On the train's two-week journey to Lincoln's final resting place in Springfield, Illinois.

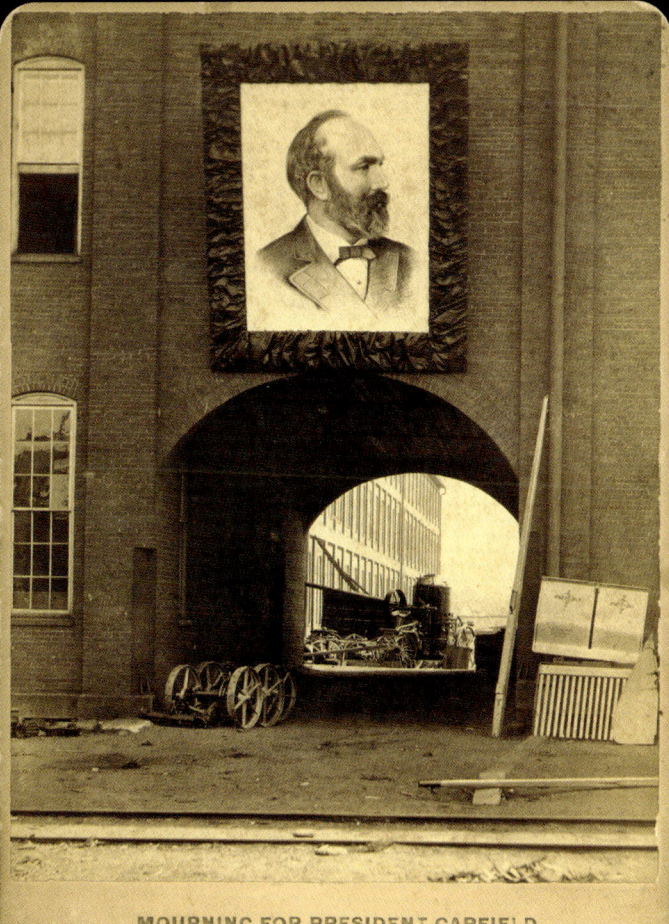

MOURNING FOR PRESIDENT GARFIELD.

"The most striking emblem of the general sorrow that we have seen anywhere is the picture of Garfield exposed on the north wall, near the central part of C. Aultman & Co's Agricultural Works. The picture is about 12x14 feet in size, reaching nearly to one of the high stories of the immense building. Seen from the ground it has all the beauty of a steel engraving. Being heavily framed in black crape, and being in plain view from cars and street, it has arrested the attention of thousands, adding to the many souvenirs of this sad day one of such pre-eminent impressiveness that time can never efface it."—Canton, Ohio, *Repository*, Sept. 24, 1881.

Mourning for Garfield   1881 • cabinet card • 6.5" x 4.25"

ember 24, 1881: a massive 12' x 14' portrait of the assassinated President James A. Gar s above the entrance to C. Aultman & Co. agricultural works building in Canton, Oh

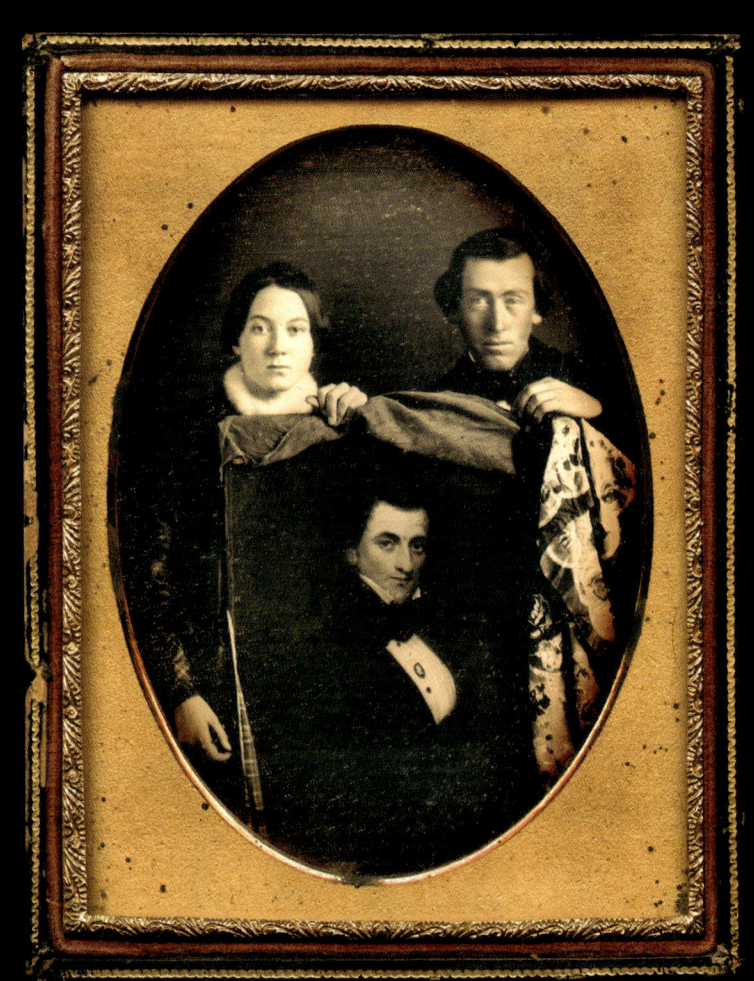

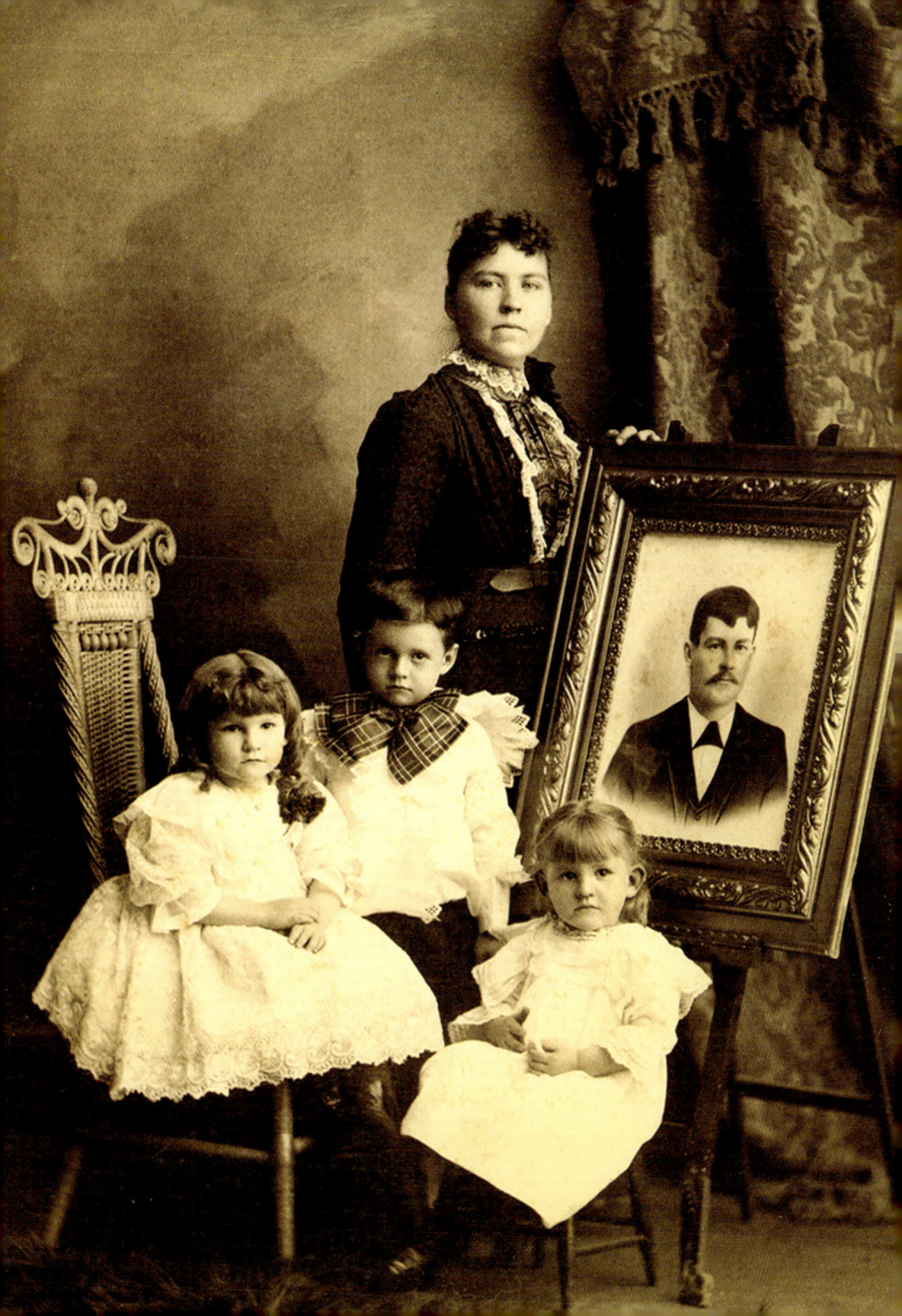

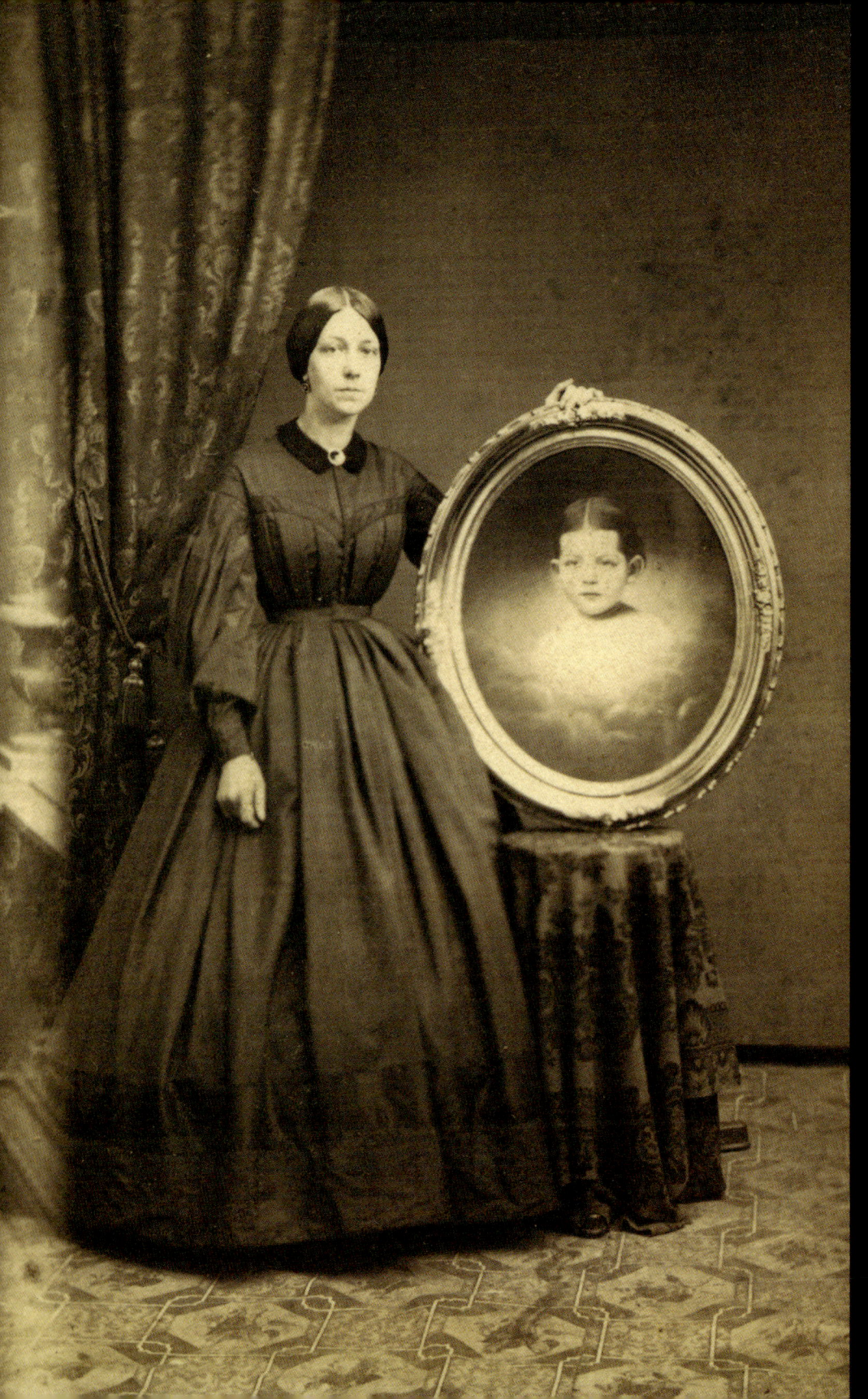

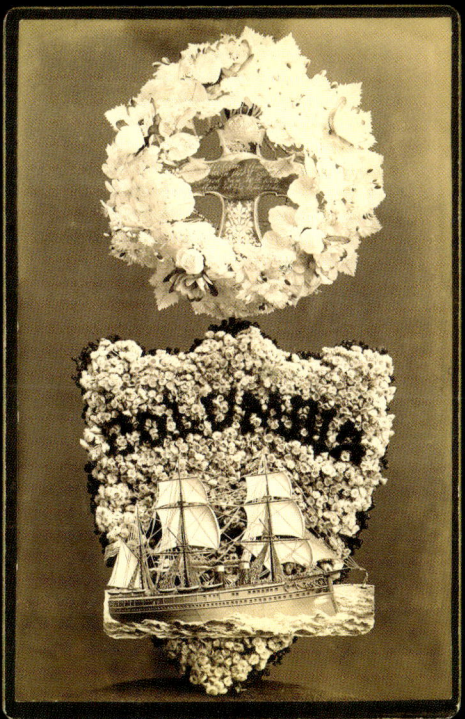

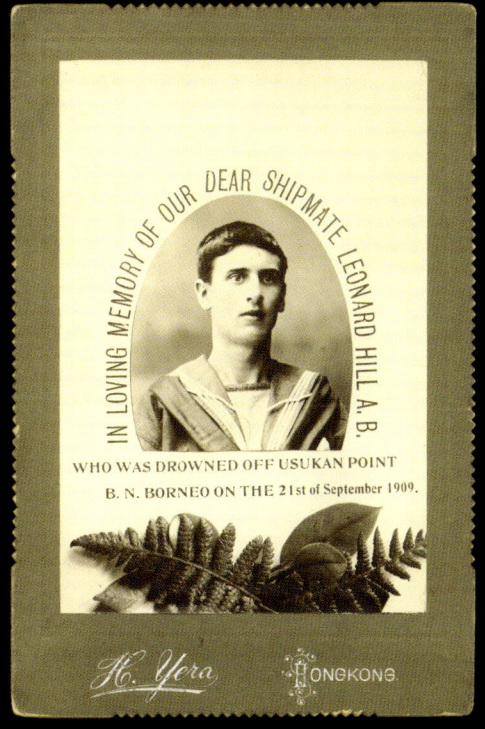

Mourning Portrait circa 1866 • carte de visite • 4" x 2.5"

Woman in mourning clothing displays a memorial painting of a little girl,
likely her daughter, who is surrounded by heavenly clouds.

Funeral Arrangement for Sailor circa 1888 • cabinet card • 6.5" x 4.25"

A floral funeral display for a lost sailor, featuring a large paper ship. The ship represents the USS Columbia,
a frigate on which the sailor would have likely served during the American Civil War

A Watery Death 1909 • cabinet card • 6.5" x 4.25"

Memorial cabinet card for Leonard Hill, A.B. (able seaman) of the British Royal Navy.

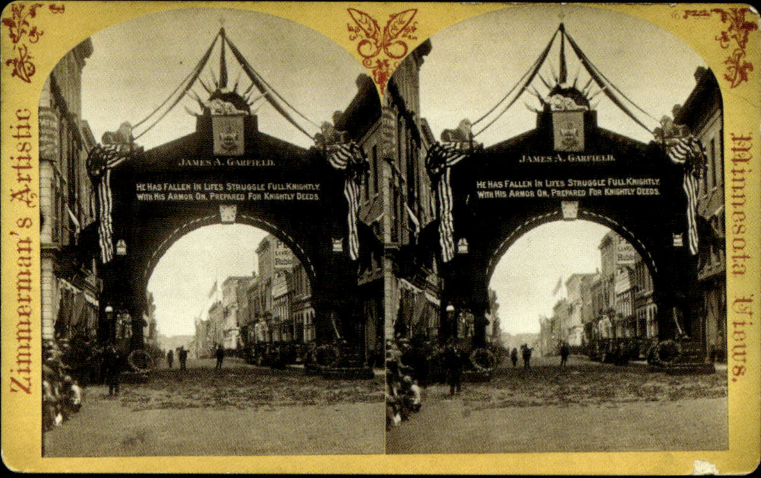

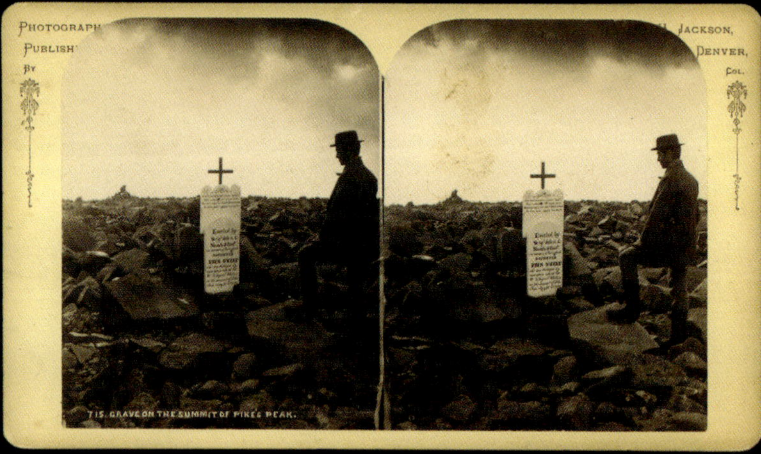

Garfield Arch 1881 • stereoview • 3.5" x 7"

Detail of a stereoview showing the huge memorial arch constructed in memory of the assassinated President James A. Garfield in downtown Minneapolis, Minnesota.

Eaten by Mountain Rats circa 1880 • stereoview • 3.5" x 7"

the summit of Pikes Peak, Colorado, a man visits the grave of Erin O'Keefe, who, according to the
her marker, was "devoured by mountain rats." The story was eventually revealed to be an elabor

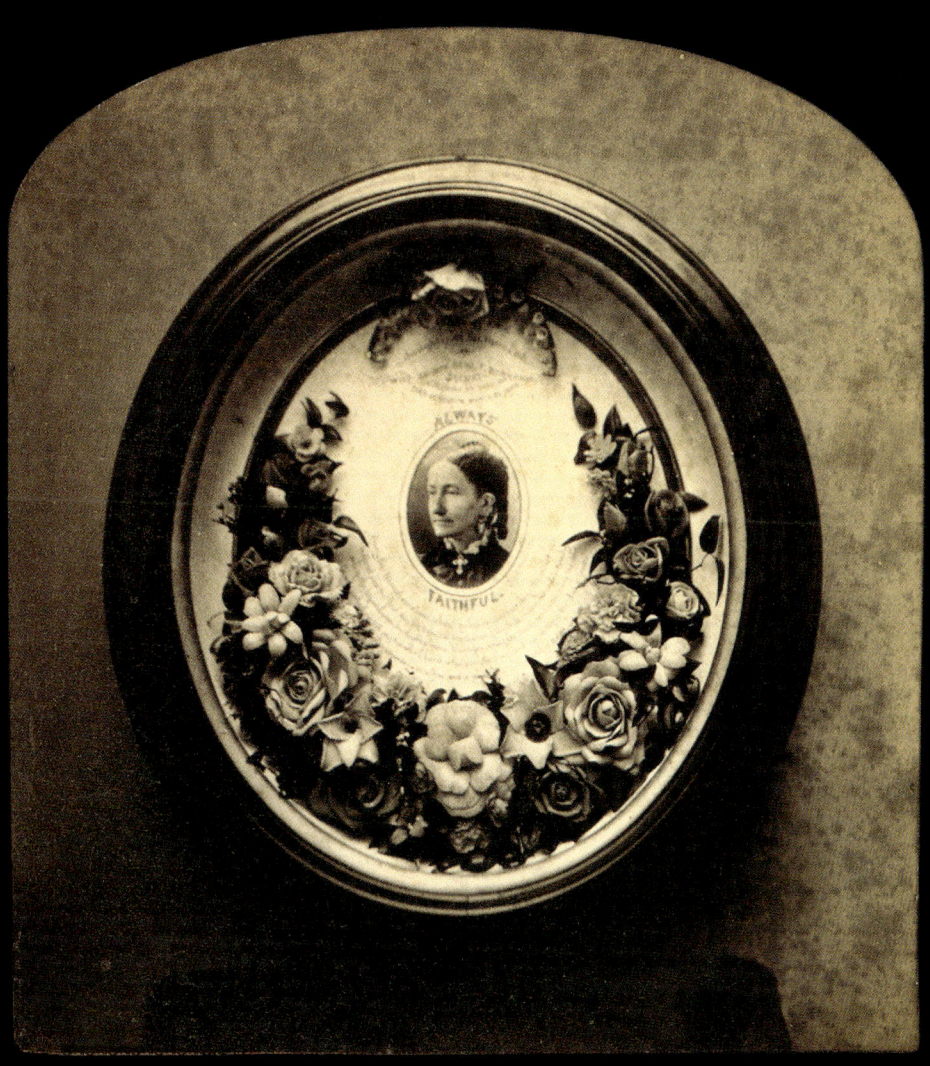

Tribute to a Teacher   1874 • one-half of stereoview • 7" x 3.5"

*Stereoview memorial for Sunday school teacher Celeste Shute Burnham.
Assembled by Miss A.F. Osgood. her pupil at South Boston Sunday School.*

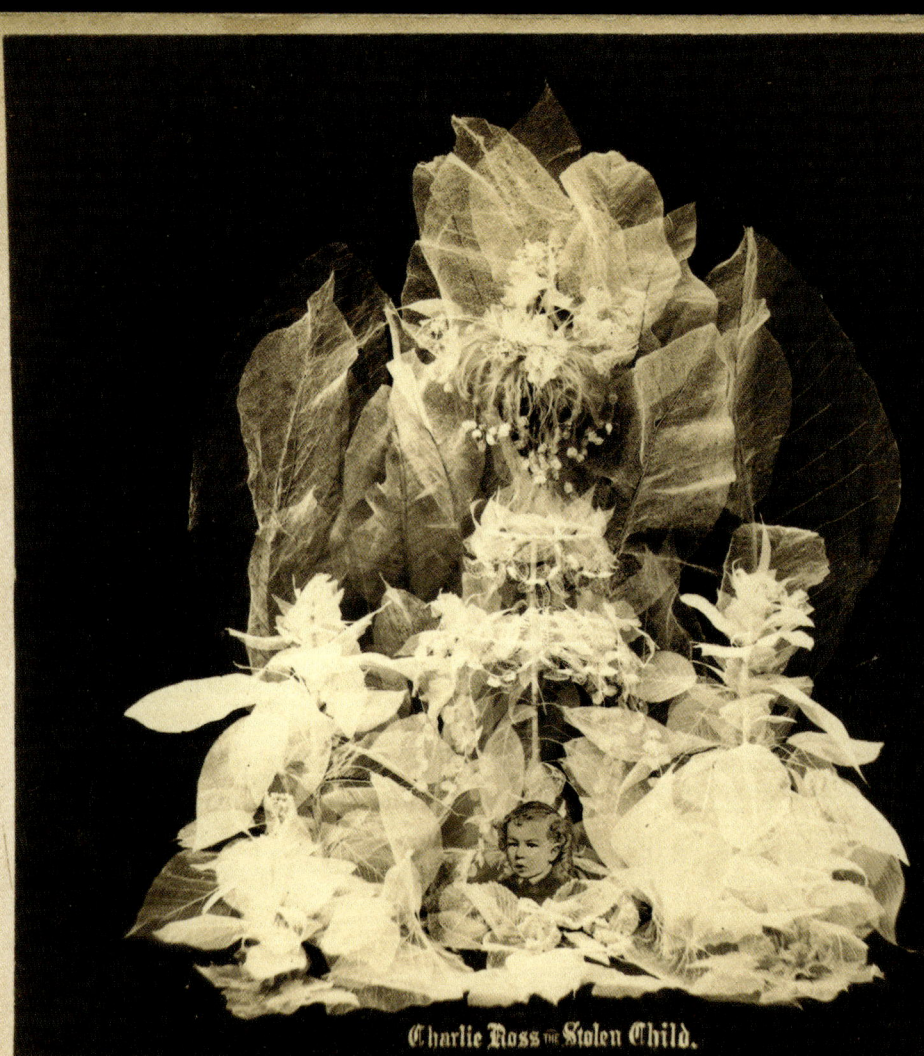

SKELETON LEAVES.

Charlie Ross the Stolen Child.

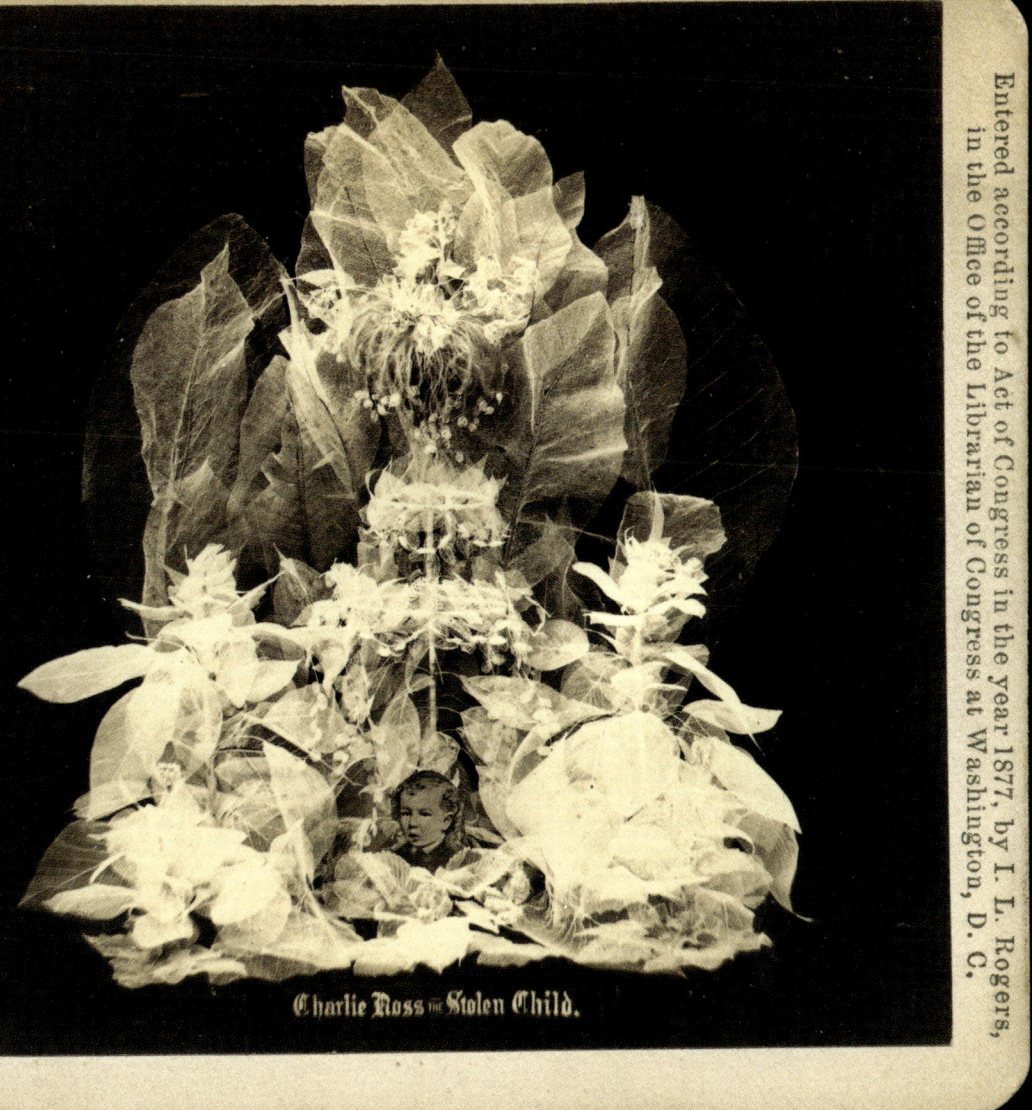

Charlie Ross the Stolen Child.

A memorial display for four-year-old Charley (or Charlie) Ross, "The Stolen Child." On July 1, 1874, Charley was abducted from in front of his home in Germantown, Pennsylvania, by two men offering him candy and fireworks. Though the family continued to search for Charley for decades, he was never heard from again. The phrase "Don't take candy from strangers" is said to have come about from this incident.

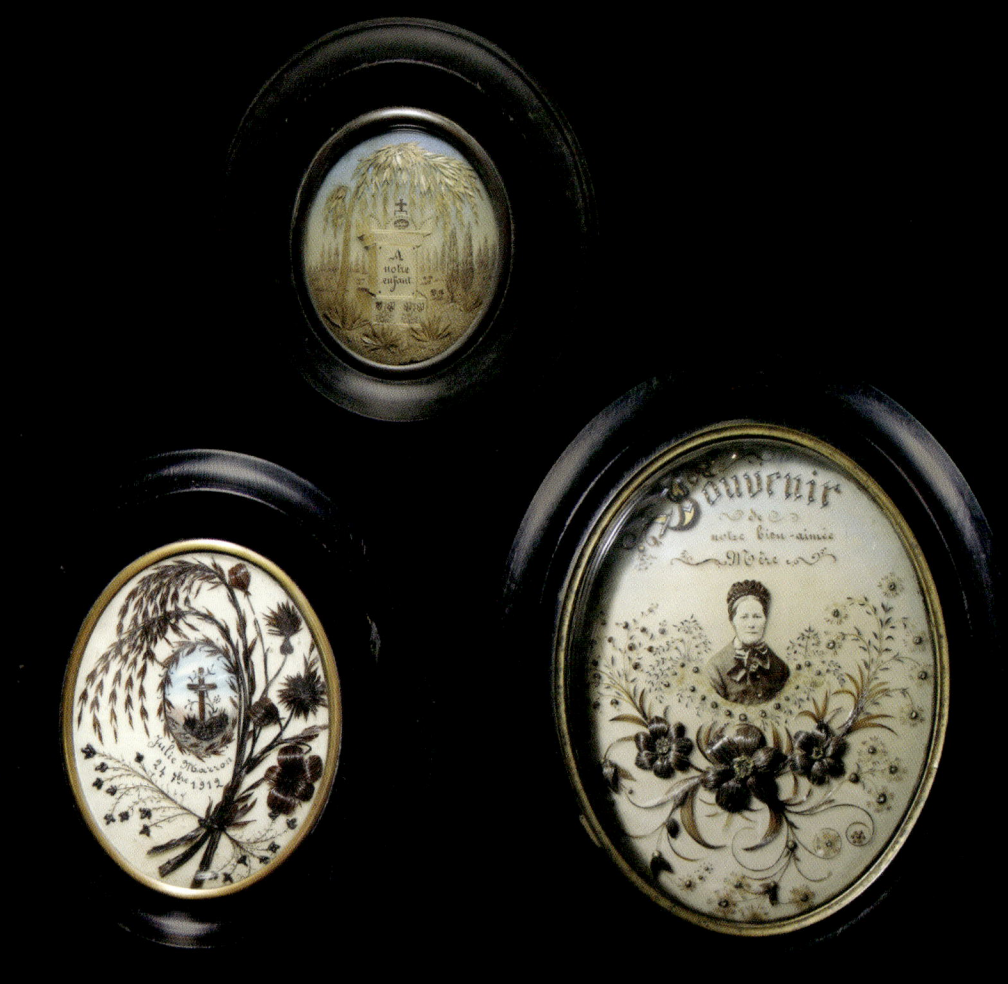

Hair Memorials

circa 1912 • mixed media • 5" x 4.5"; circa 1850s • mixed media • 7" x 6";
circa 1870 • mixed media • 12" x 10"

Three intricate memorials for a young girl, a mother, and an infant, whose memorial features a tombstone with the inscription "To our child". These amazing folk art tributes were created almost entirely from the hair of the deceased, the clipped or ground strands painstakingly formed by hand, and affixed to a backing of milk glass.

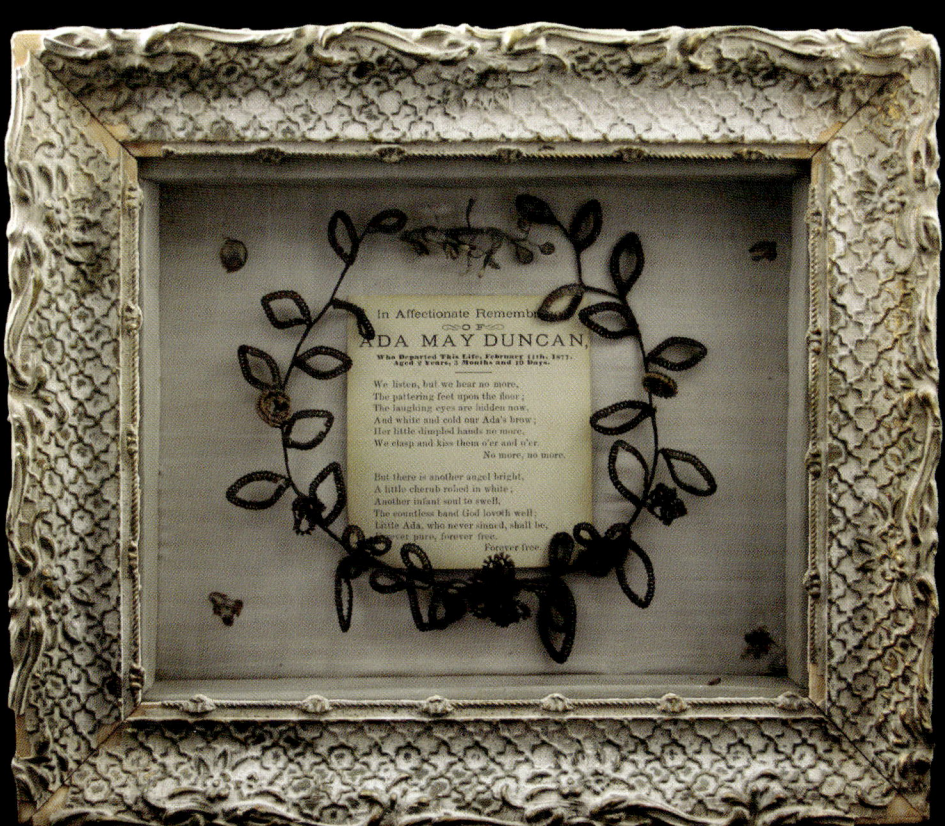

Memorial for Ada May 1877 • mixed media • 11" x 13"

A wreath memorial for a little girl made with her hair.
"In Affectionate Remembrance of Ada May Duncan Who Departed This Life, February 11th 1877.
Aged 2 Years, 3 Months, and 10 Days." On the back is a note stating her cause of death, laryngeal diphtheria,
an infection of the tonsils that quickly spreads, often leading to death by blood poisoning.

STILLED LIVES

JOANNA ROCHE

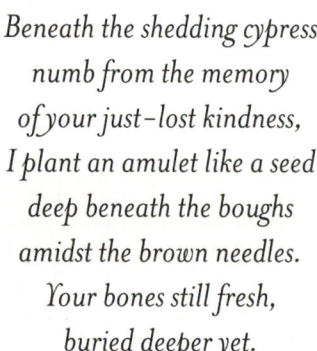

Beneath the shedding cypress
numb from the memory
of your just-lost kindness,
I plant an amulet like a seed
deep beneath the boughs
amidst the brown needles.
Your bones still fresh,
buried deeper yet.

Did those frozen moments
of post-mortem equipoise
preserved in silver, beneath glass
transmit for them—the loved ones,
the rememberers—that smell of death?
I inhale deep to learn again
the body's passage is not the same
as soul's escape,
fragrant with eternity
and grief.

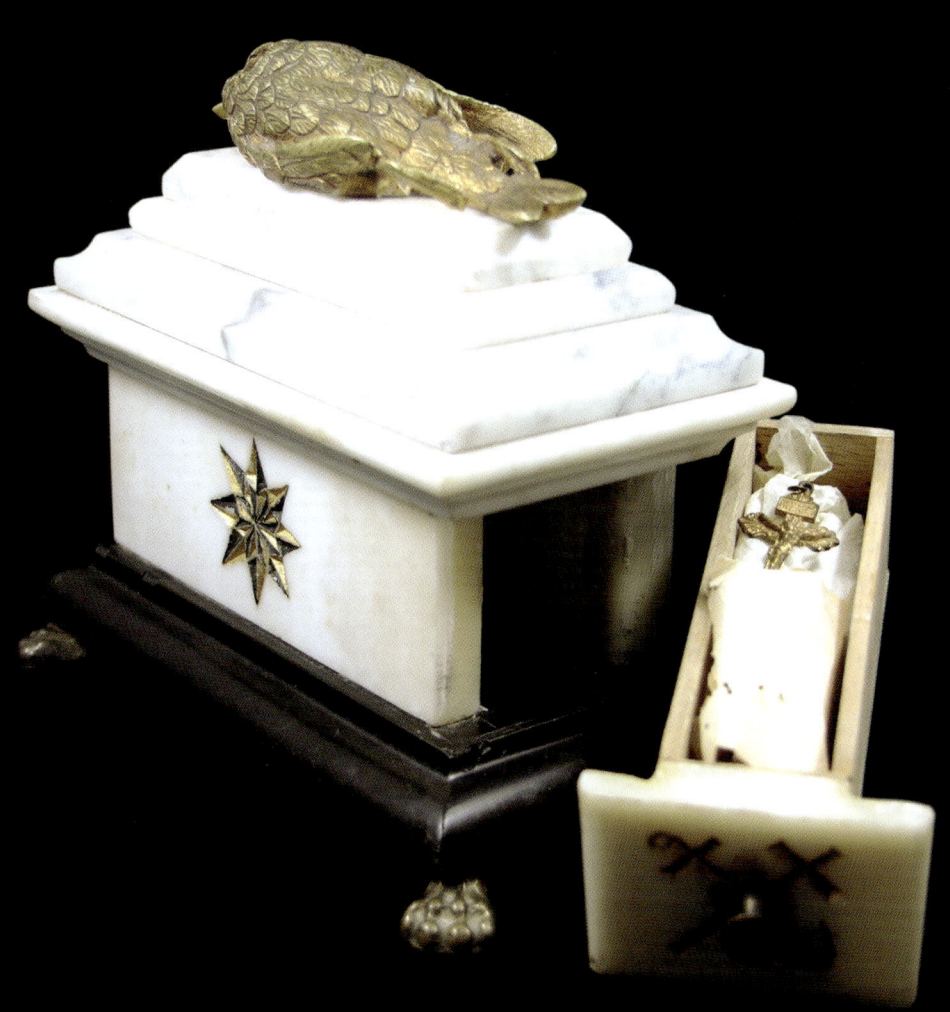

Victorian Bird Sarcophagus   1874 • brass and marble • 6.5" x 5" x 8"

An elaborate, custom-made brass and marble sarcophagus for a pet bird.
Inside is the shrouded bluebird with a small cross and a handwritten note:
"Our pet Wee-Wee, Died Monday 18 June 1874 at 7:55 o'clock."

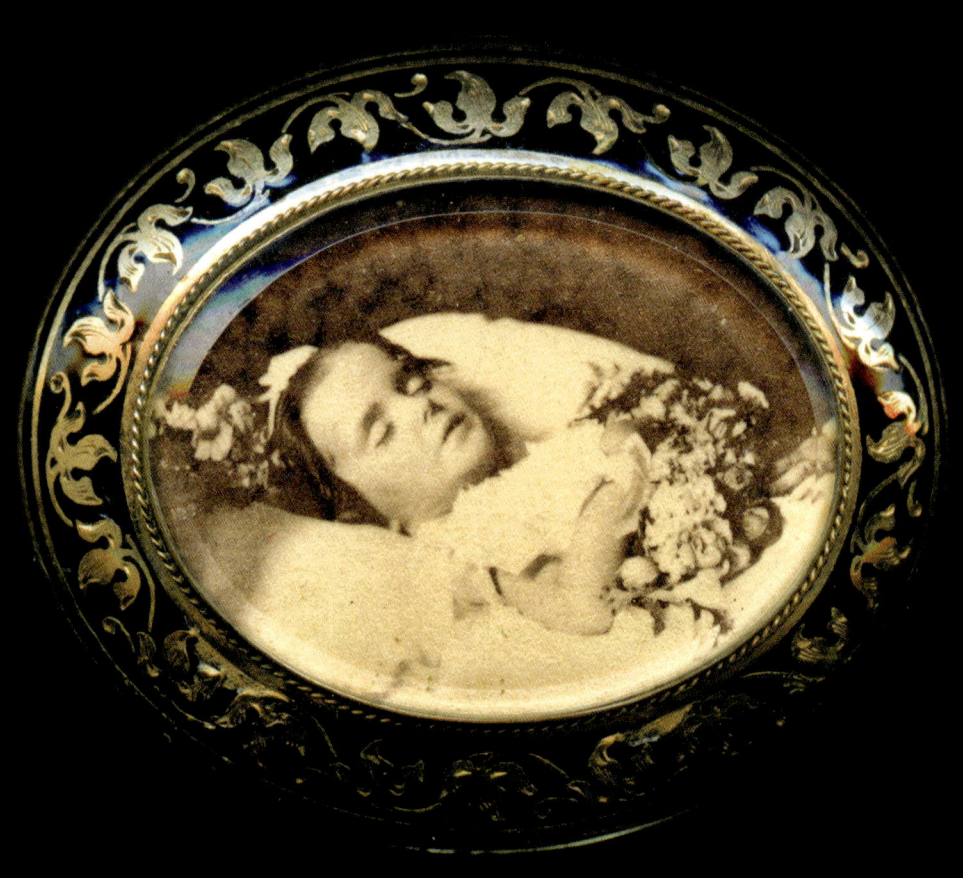

Photographic Brooch circa 1880 • jewelry • 1" x 1.5"

A tiny albumen portrait of a young girl, set into an enameled brooch.

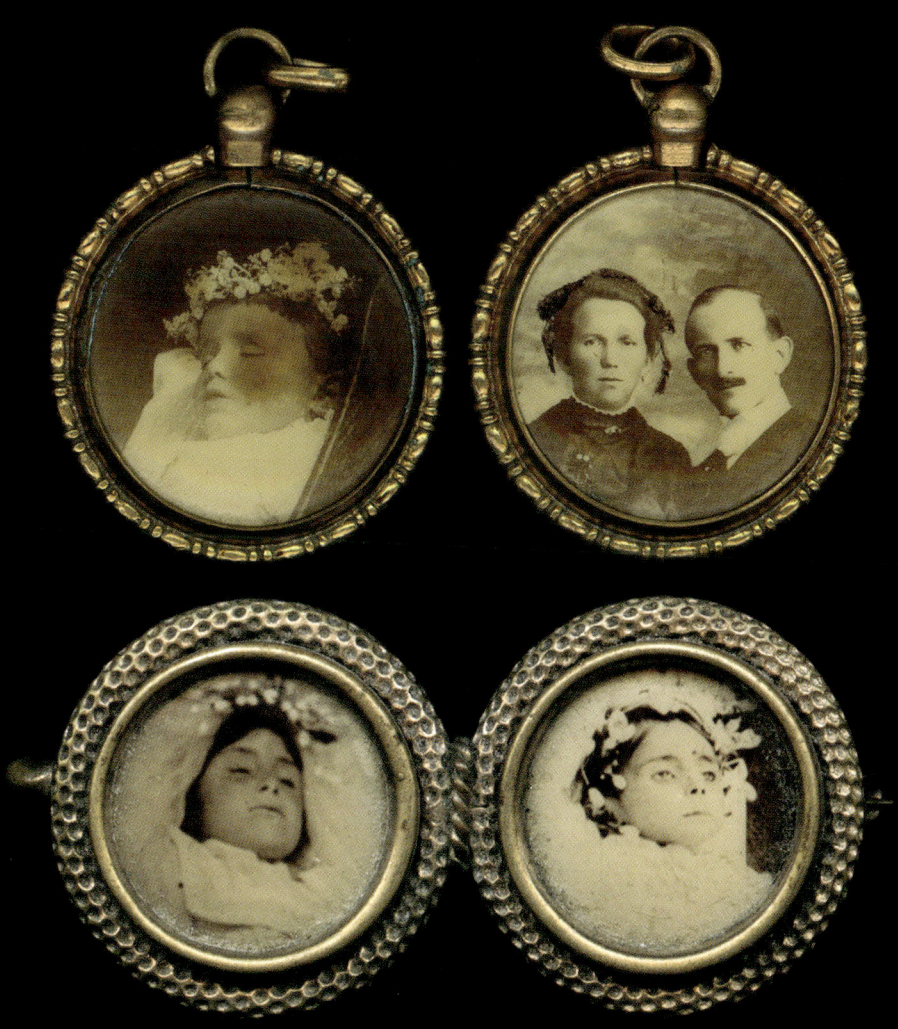

Photo Locket   circa 1900 • jewelry • 1.25" x 1"

Double-sided celluloid photo locket with a child's post-mortem photo on the front.
On the reverse is a photo of the boy's parents.

- - - - - - - - - - - - - - - - -

Double Photo Pin   circa 1900 • jewelry • 1.5" x .75"

A double photographic pin with miniature post-mortem portraits of little girls, most likely sisters.
This pin would have been worn by the girls' mother, in a public expression of grief.

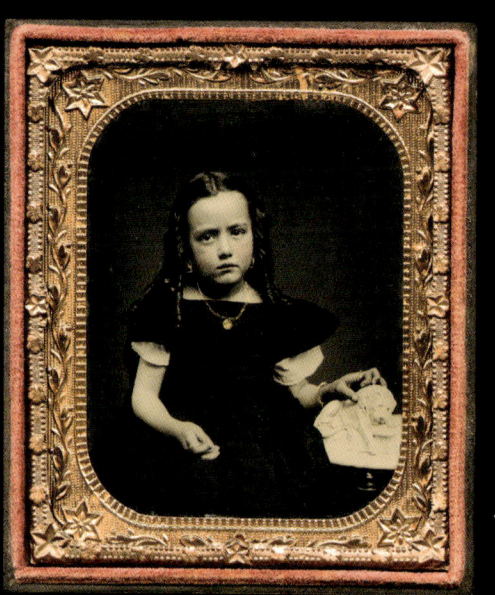
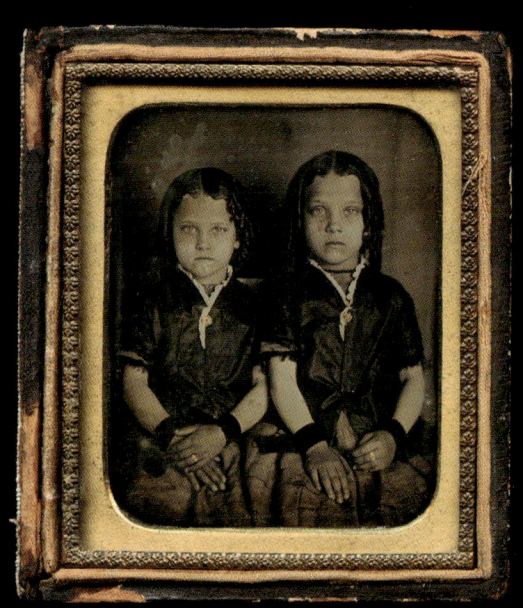

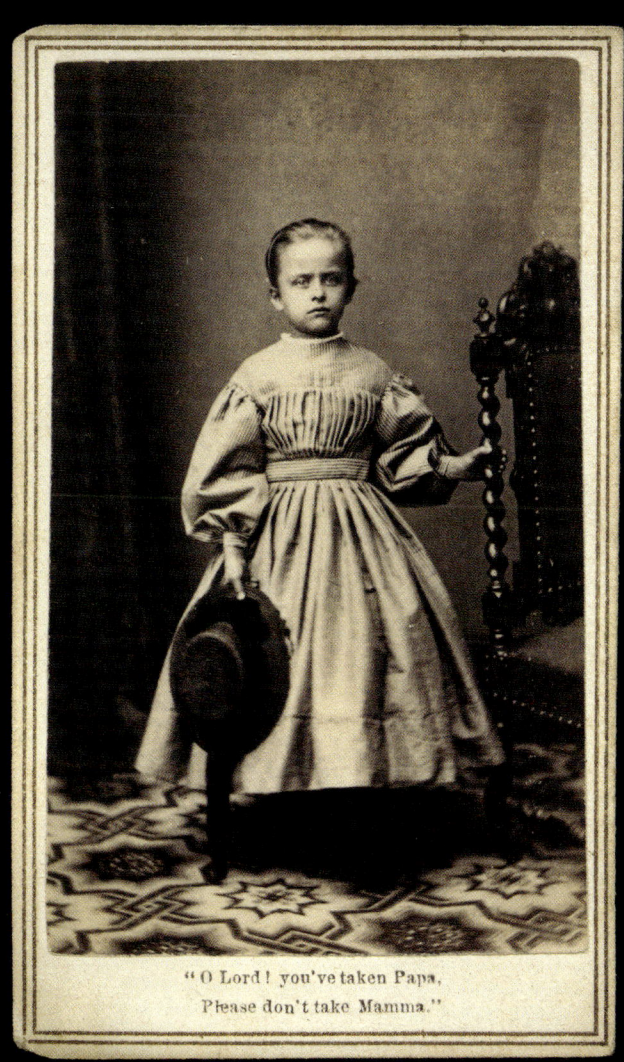

"O Lord! you've taken Papa,
Please don't take Mamma."

Don't Take Mama   circa 1864 • carte de visite • 4" x 2.5"

*A sad little girl holds her hat with a black mourning band and ribbon attached. It is likely, given the time period,
as well as the unusual addition of her quoted words to the mount, that this girl had lost her father in the American Civil War.
An image such as this may have been used to draw attention to the plight of the many orphans created by the war.*

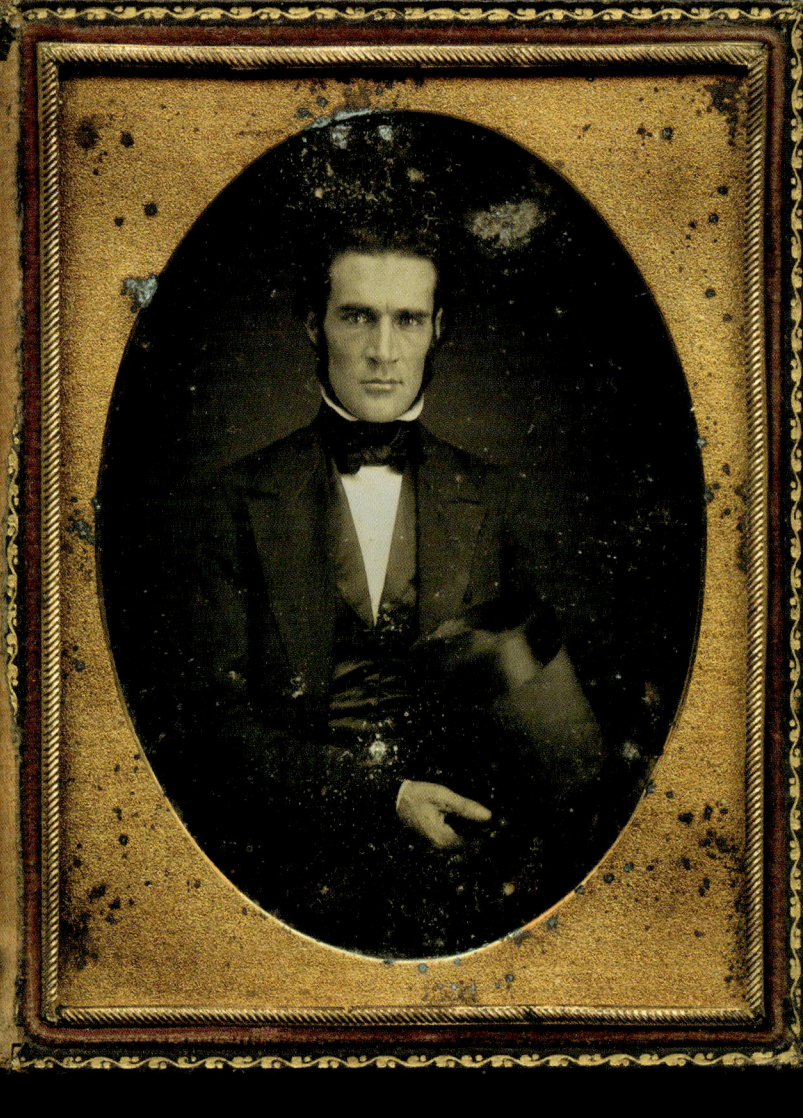

Man in Mourning Attire   circa 1850 • quarter-plate daguerreotype • 4.75" x 3.75"

A man in mourning attire, displaying his silk top hat with its wide crepe mourning band.

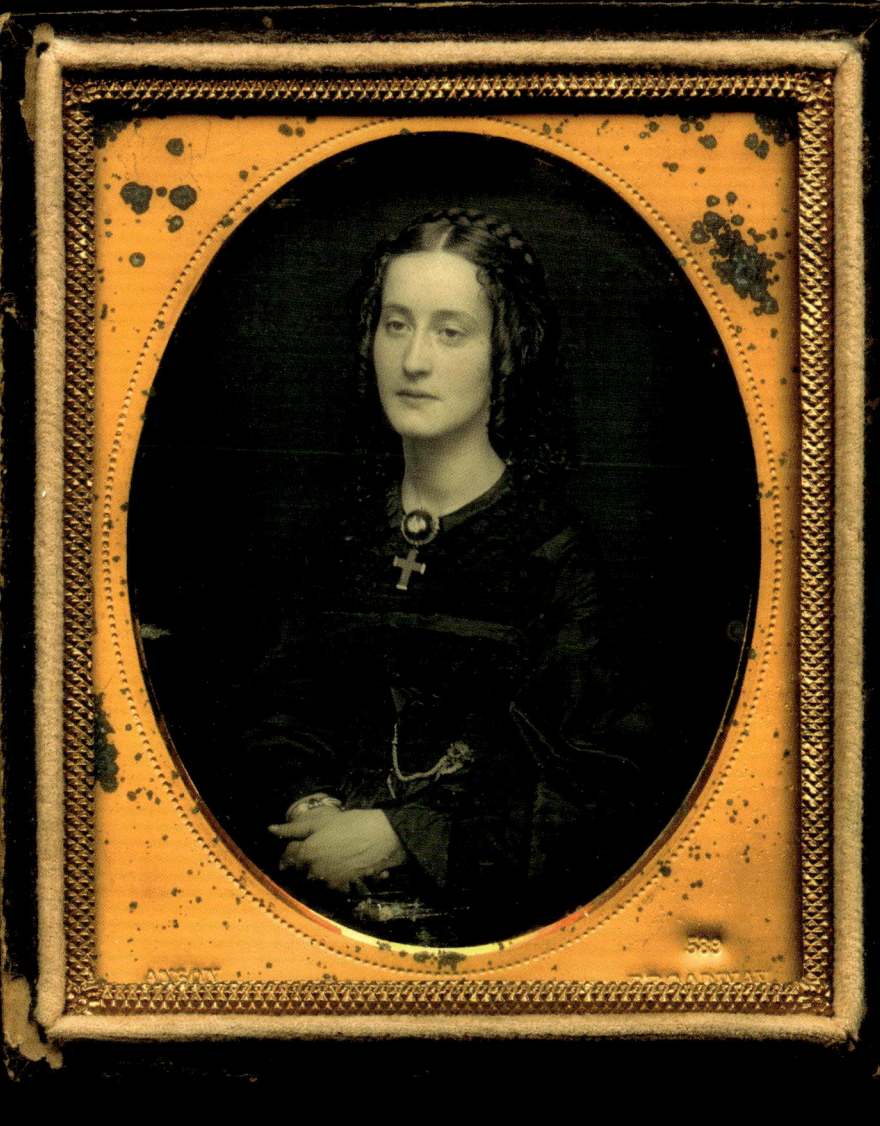

Mrs. Maxwell in Mourning   circa 1856 • sixth-plate daguerreotype • 3.75″ x 3.25″

The beautiful Mrs. Catherine Maxwell of New York City, dressed in half-mourning.

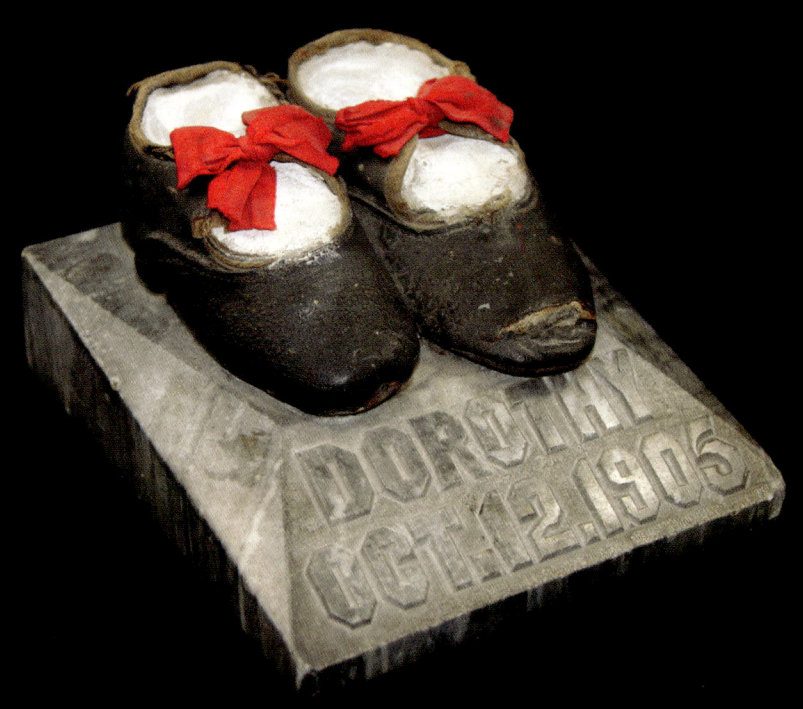

Empty Shoes 1905 • shoes, plaster, & marble • 3" x 5.5" x 6"

A unique memorial piece for a little girl named Dorothy, whose shoes have been filled with plaster
and mounted onto a marble base, showing her name and date of death.

Spirit Photo circa 1871 • carte de visite • 4" x 2.5"

A woman poses with the "spirit" of a female relative, likely representing her deceased daughter.
Spirit photography, a technique employing double exposure, was created in the early 1860s by the infamous
William H. Mumler, who photographed the image seen here. Mumler's most famous spirit photo is of First Lady
Mary Todd Lincoln, pictured with the ghost of Abraham Lincoln, approximately four years after his assassination.

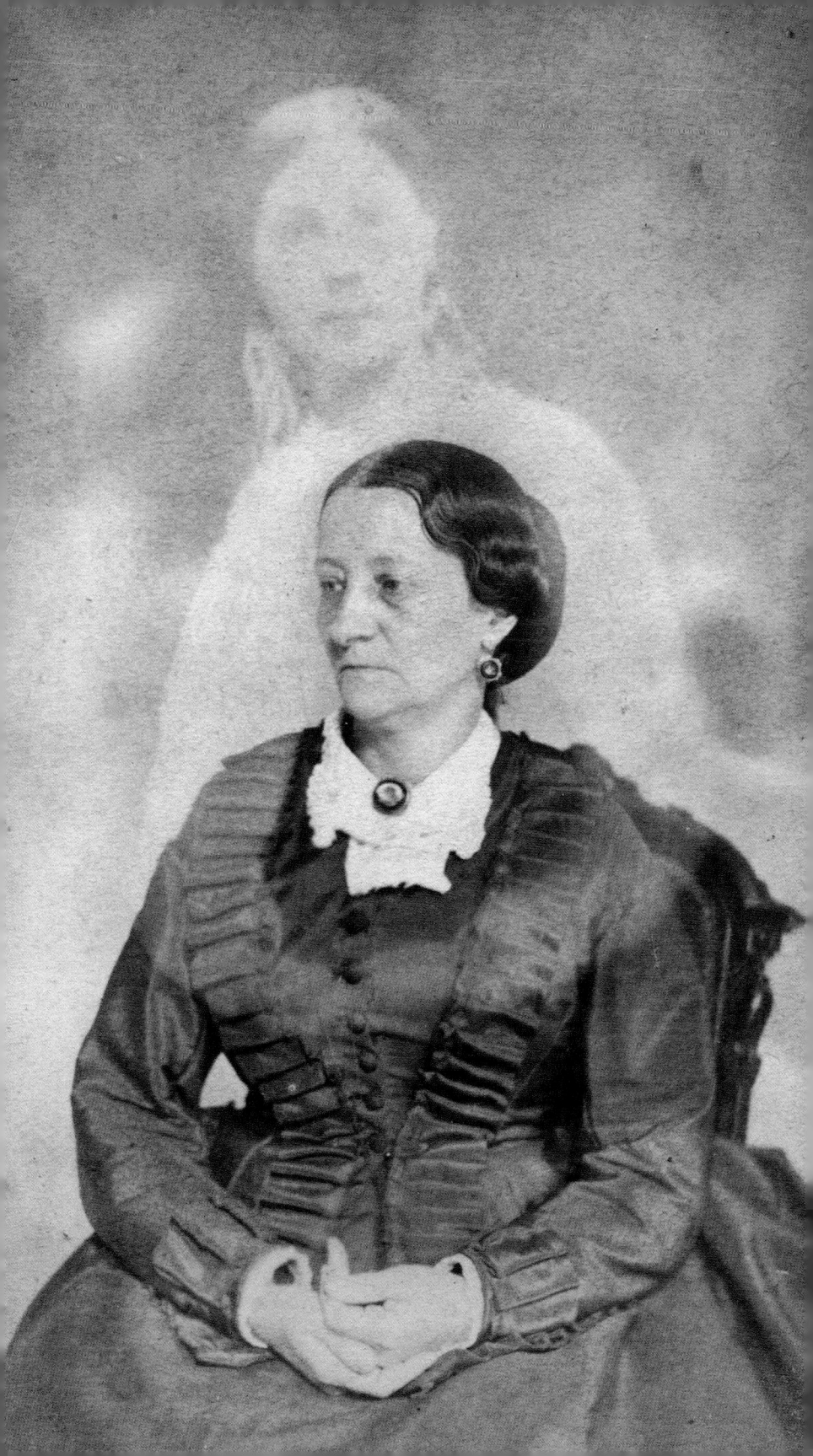

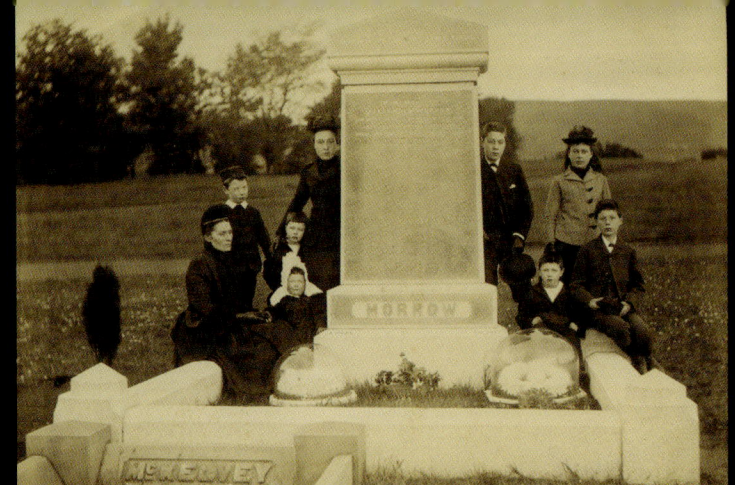

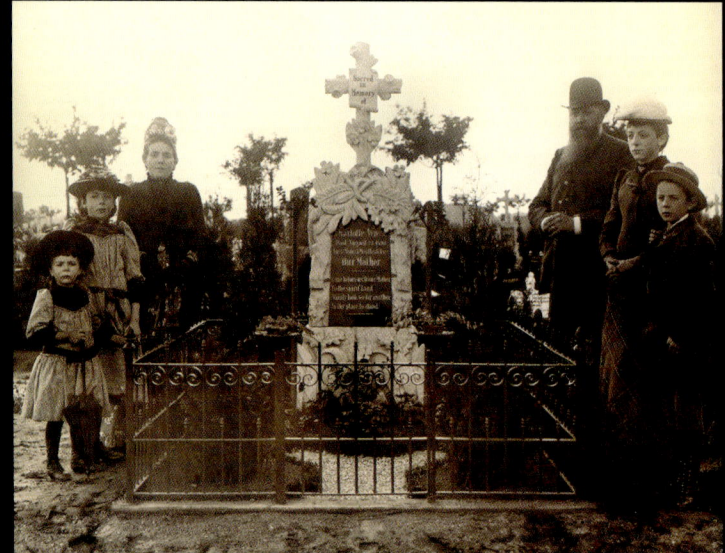

The Morrows   circa 1898 • cabinet card • 4.25" x 6.5"

The widow and children of Alexander Morrow at his grave, in Belfast, Ireland.
Mr. Morrow died on June 3, 1898, at the age of 51. Funeral flowers in the foreground are protected by glass domes.

Charlotte's Grave   circa 1891 • gelatin silver print • 11" x 14"

The family of a woman at her graveside. The inscription on the stone reads, in part,
"Sacred in memory of Charlotte Wiese. Died August 29, 1890. Age 57 months. 5 years, 15 days. Our Mother."

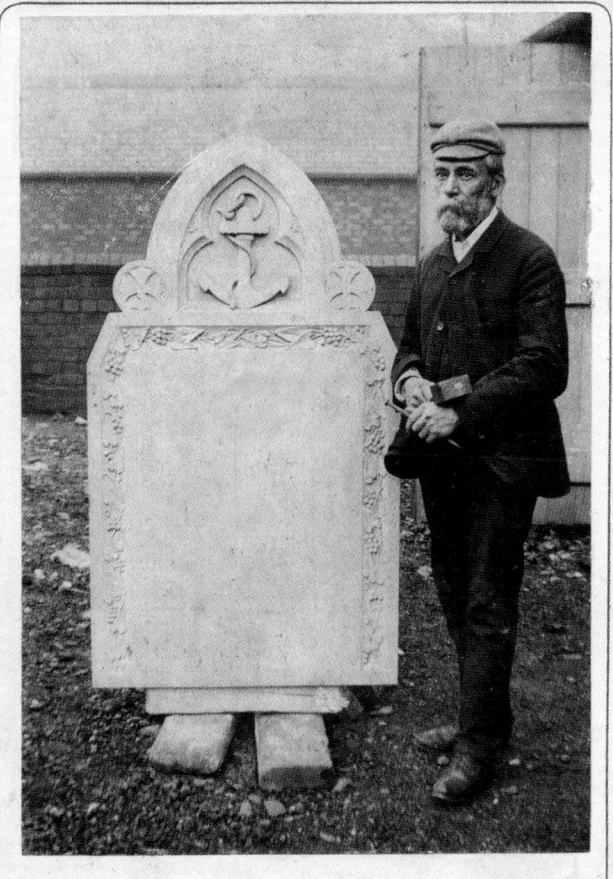

J. C. W. Atter, 465, PENISTONE, ROAD,
SHEFFIELD

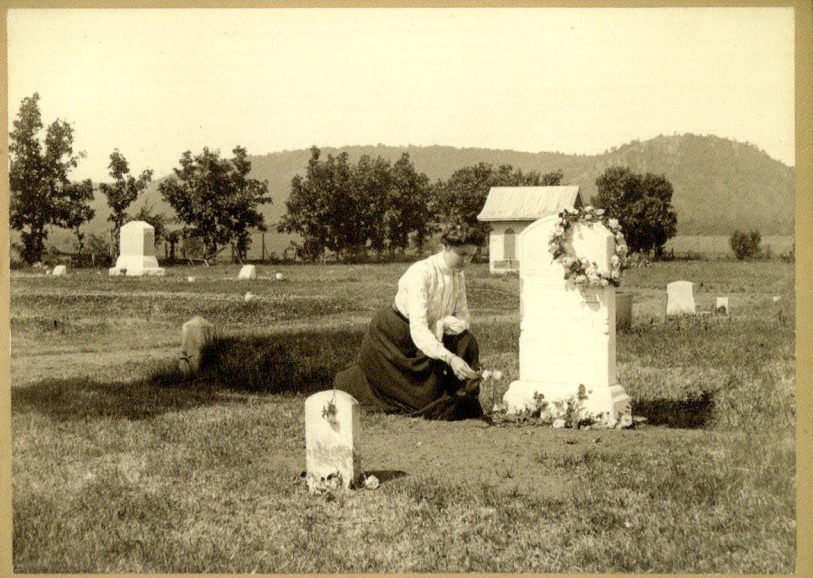

Our Mother's Grave.

Mother's Grave circa 1899 • cabinet card • 4.25" x 6.5"

Lake City, Minnesota: "Sister Dot at Mother's grave." The headstone reads:
"Jane B. Russell, Wife of Morris C. Russell. Died Aug. 2, 1878. Aged 35 years, 5 months, and 2 days."

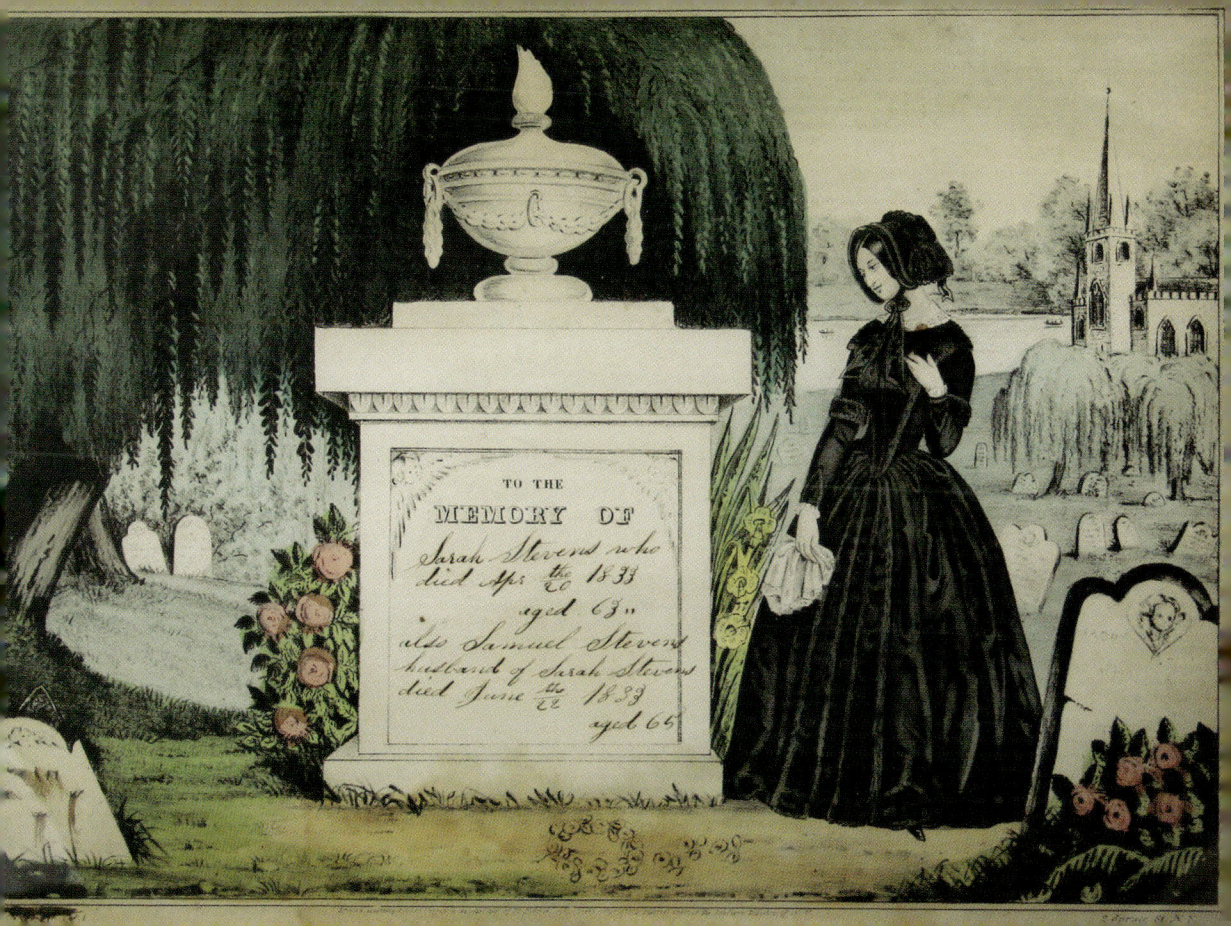

TO THE
MEMORY OF
Sarah Stevens who
died Apr. the 20 1833
aged 63"
also Samuel Stevens
husband of Sarah Stevens
died June the 22 1833
aged 65

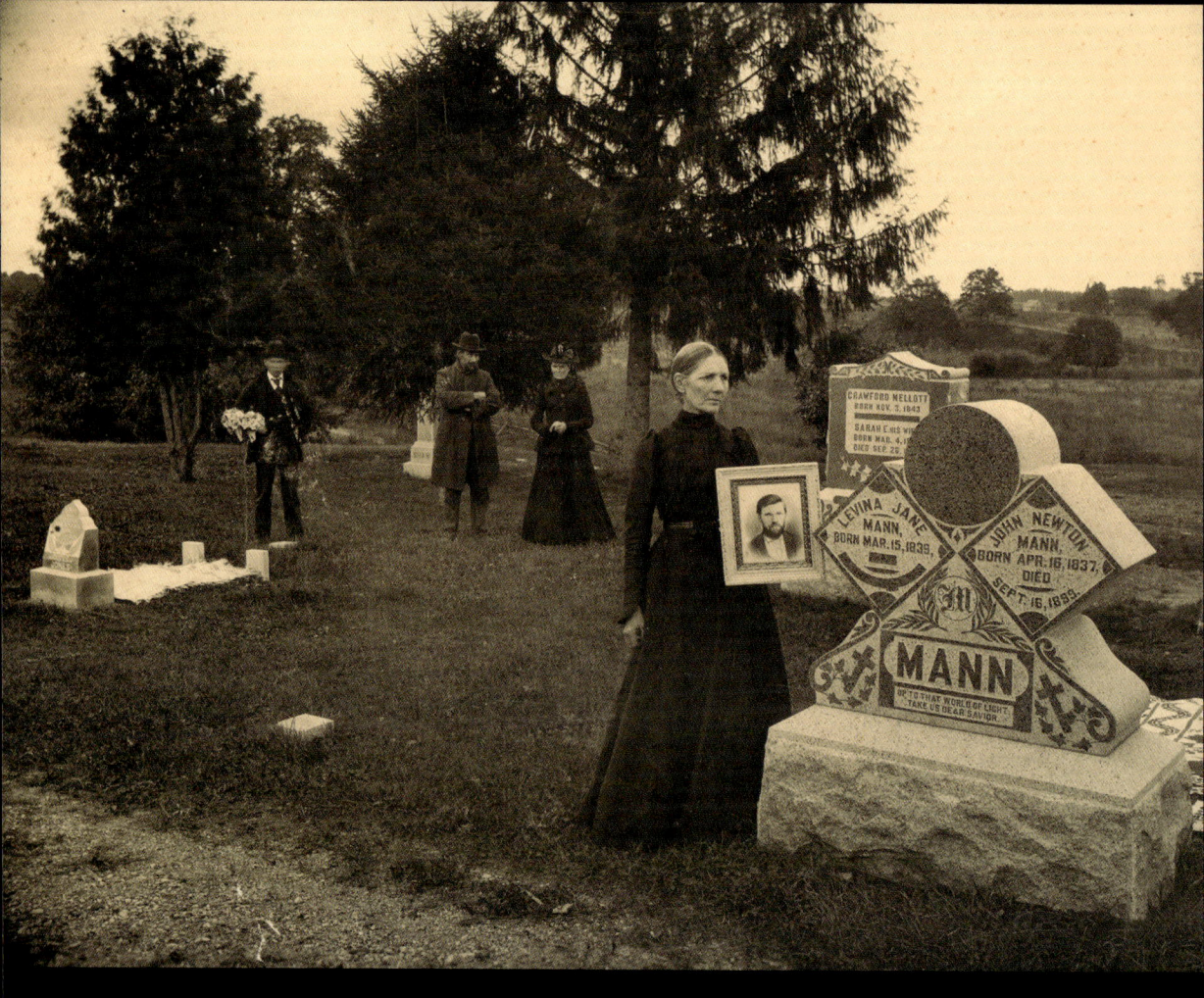

Levina Mann at Husband's Grave   circa 1900 • gelatin silver print • 10" x 12"

*Levina Jane Mann displays a memorial portrait of her husband, John Newton Mann, next to their shared grave
at Bryn Zion Cemetery in Mount Gilead, Ohio. Levina lived another 22 years before being laid to rest next to John.*

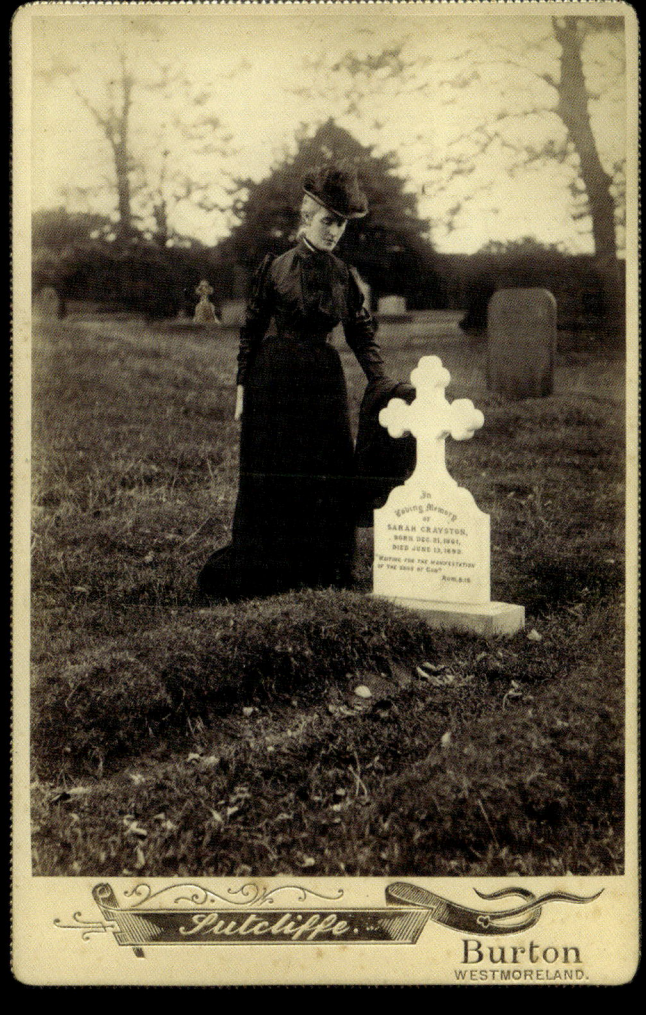

Jane and Sarah   circa 1893 • cabinet card • 6.5" x 4.25"

at her sister Sarah's grave. The marker reads, "In memory of Sarah Crayston, Born D
Died June 13, 1892. Waiting for the manifestation of the Sons of God, Rom. 8.19."

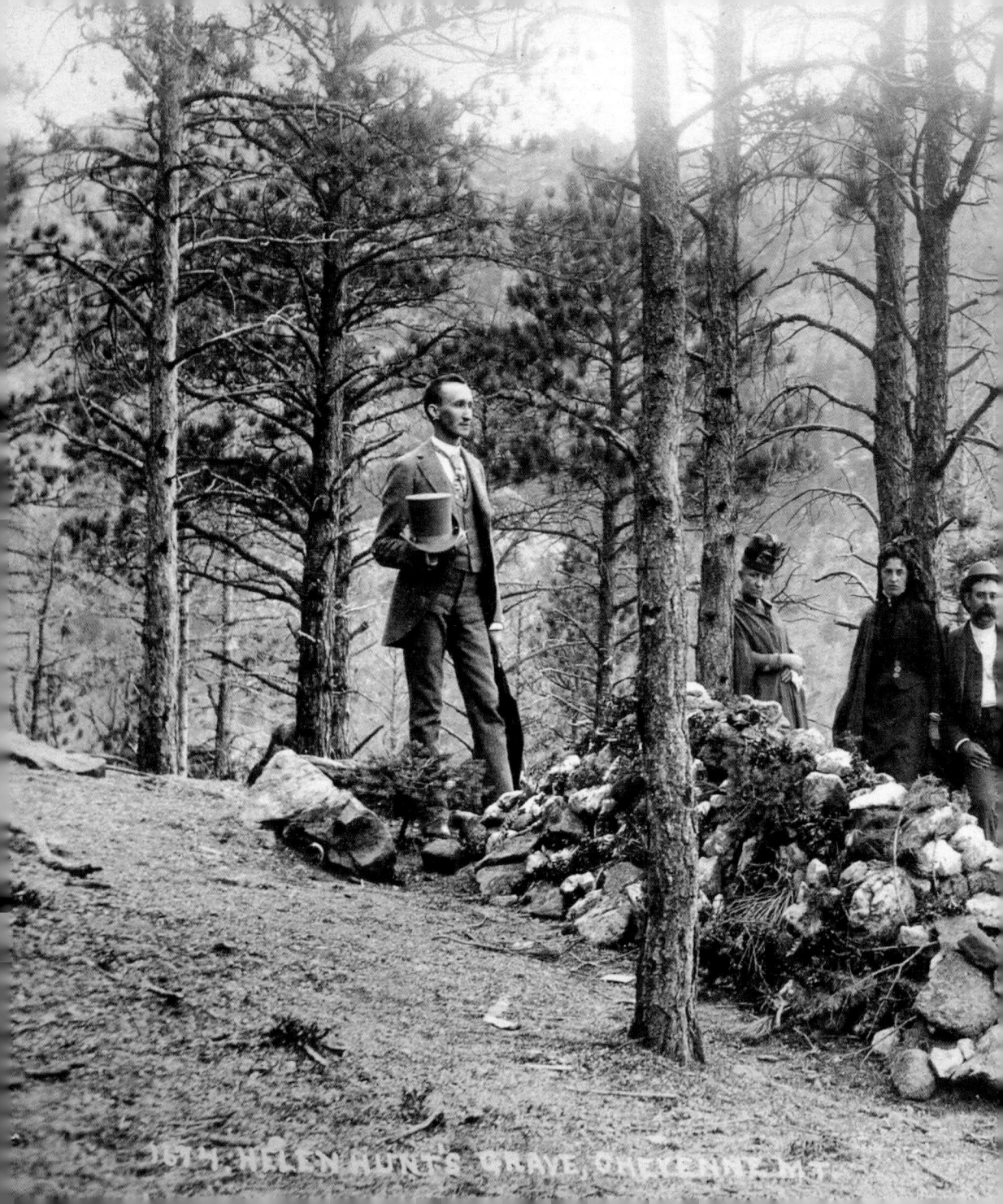

HELEN HUNT'S GRAVE. CHEYENNE. M.T.

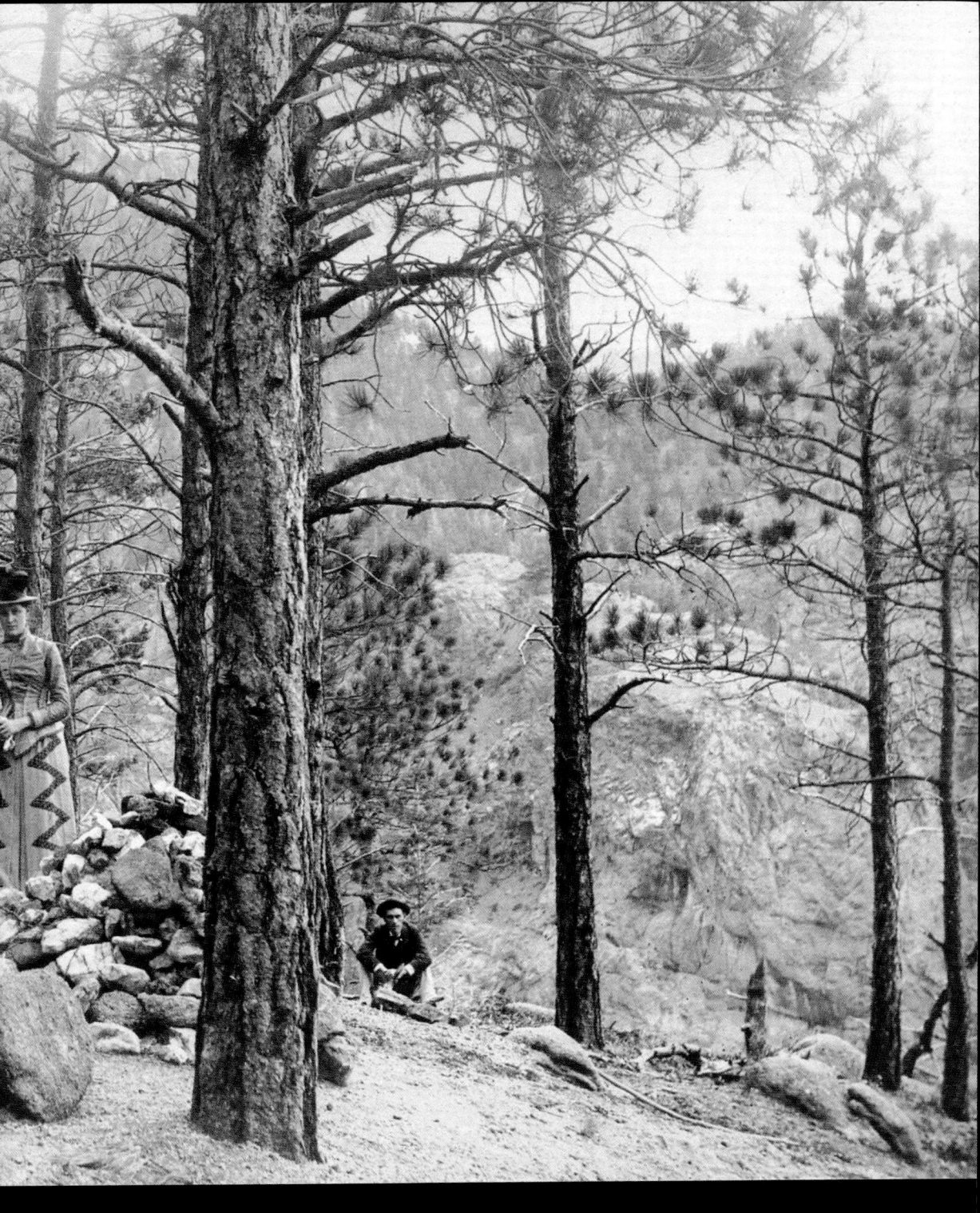

*Visitors at the original mountain gravesite of the American writer and activist
Helen Hunt Jackson, on Cheyenne Mountain, Colorado.*

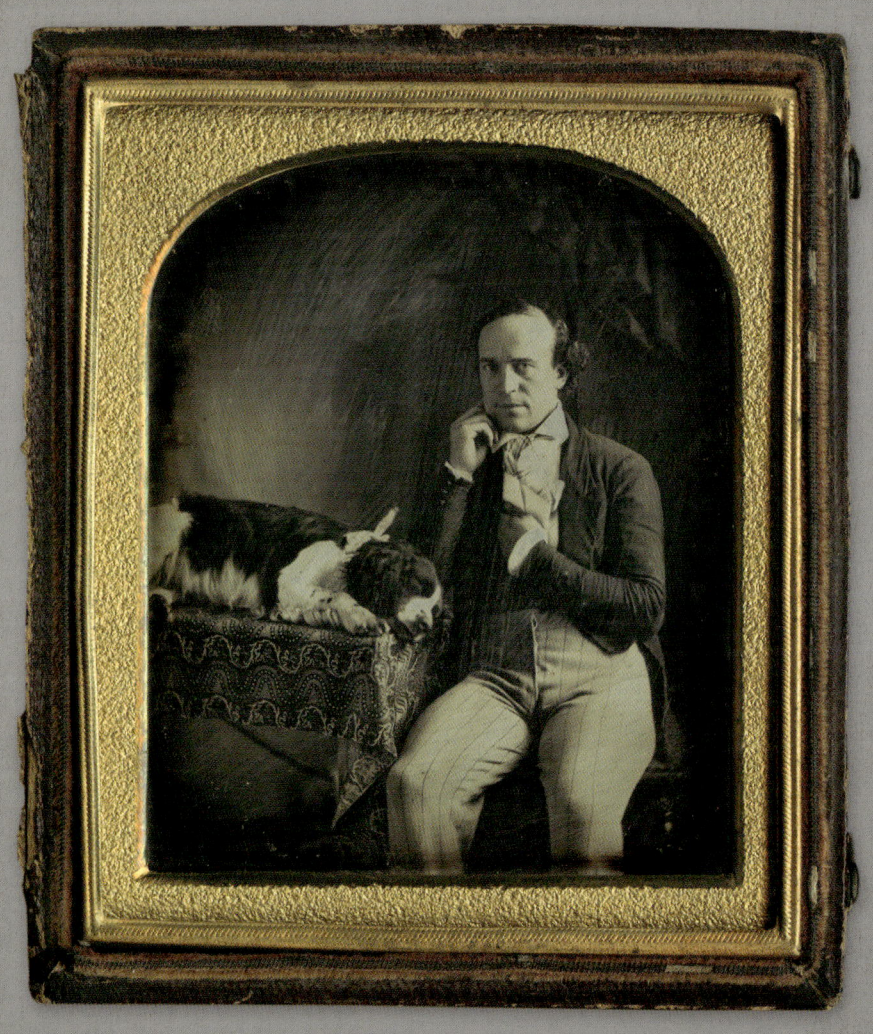

Lost Companion   circa 1846 • sixth-plate daguerreotype • 3.75" x 3.25"

Amos R. Monroe with his deceased spaniel.
Daguerreotypes are mirror images; Amos's hand was actually placed over his heart in a gesture of mourning.

PETS

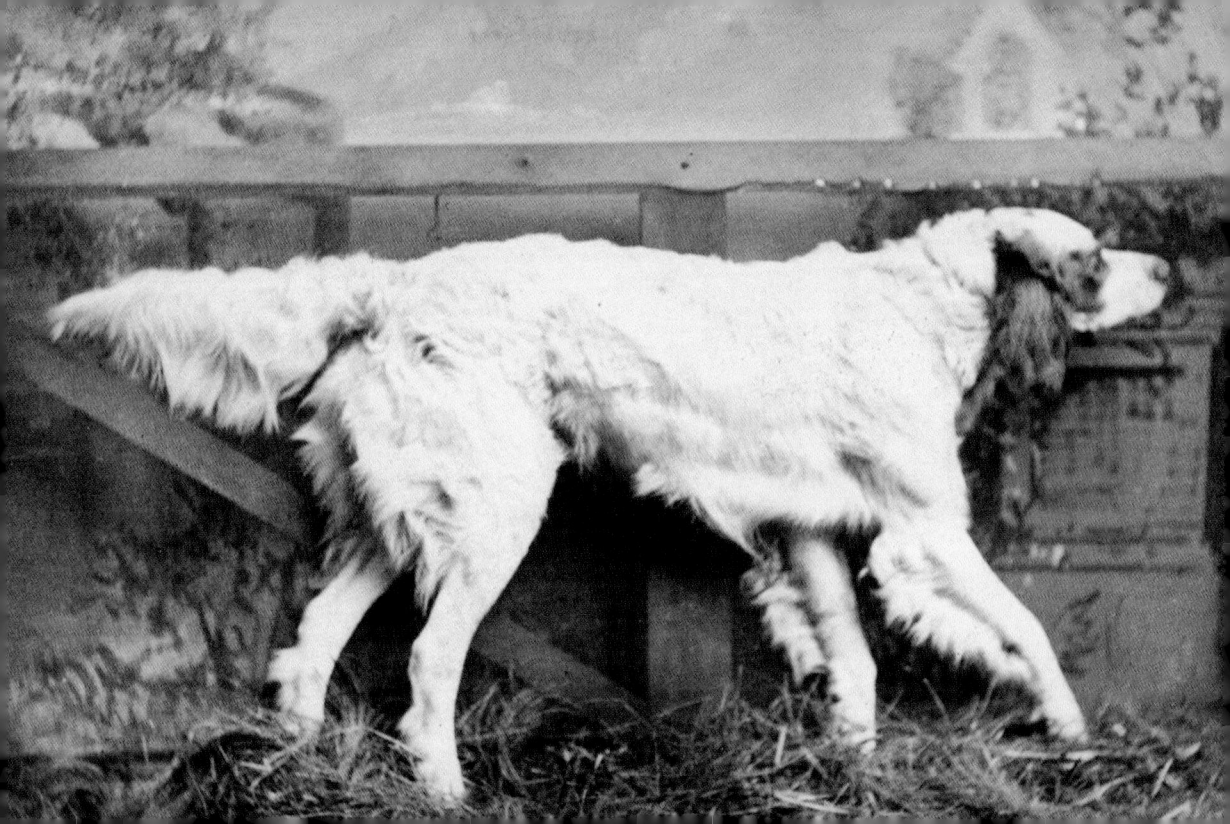

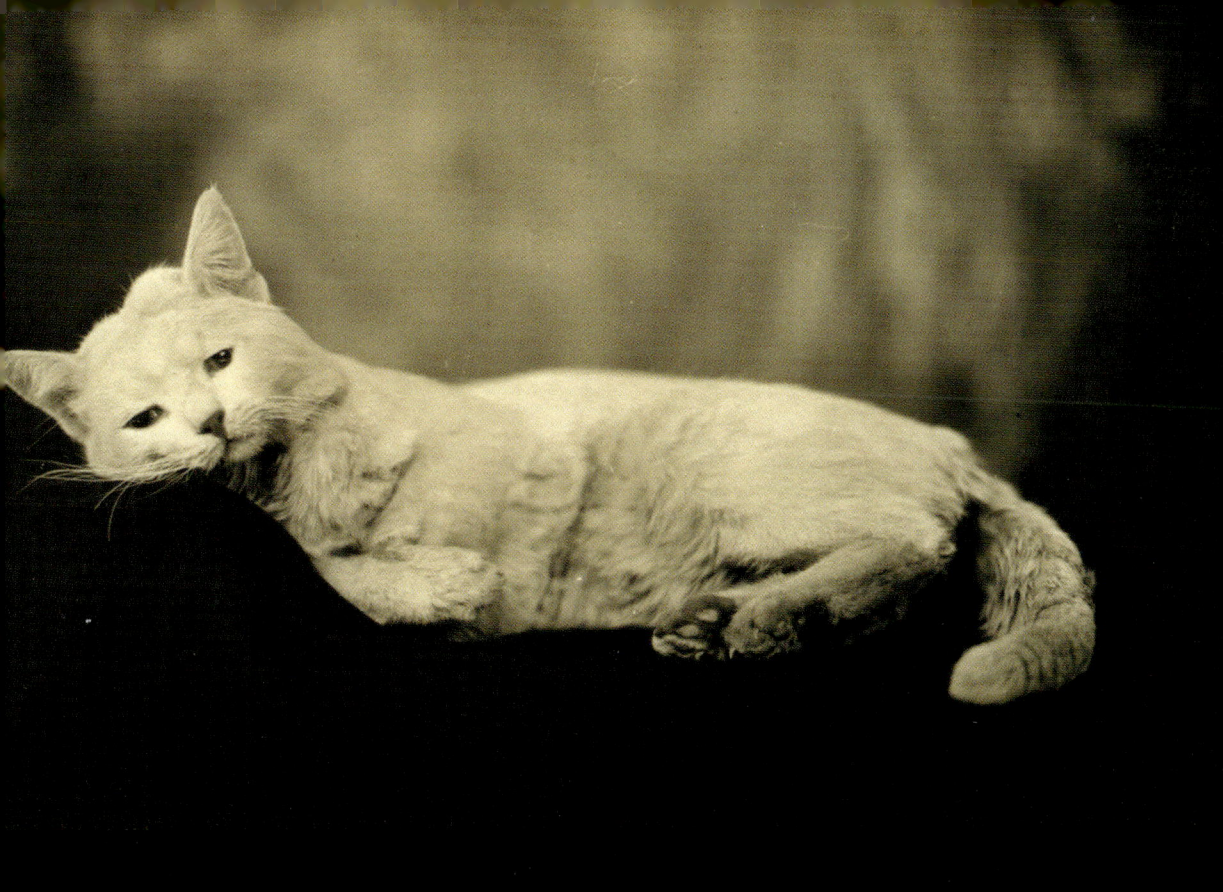

Beautiful in Death circa 1915 • real photo postcard • 3.5" x 5.5"

An amateur photo of Pippo the cat. On the back is written, in Italian:
"Pippo, bello morto." Loosely translated as "Pippo, beautiful in death."

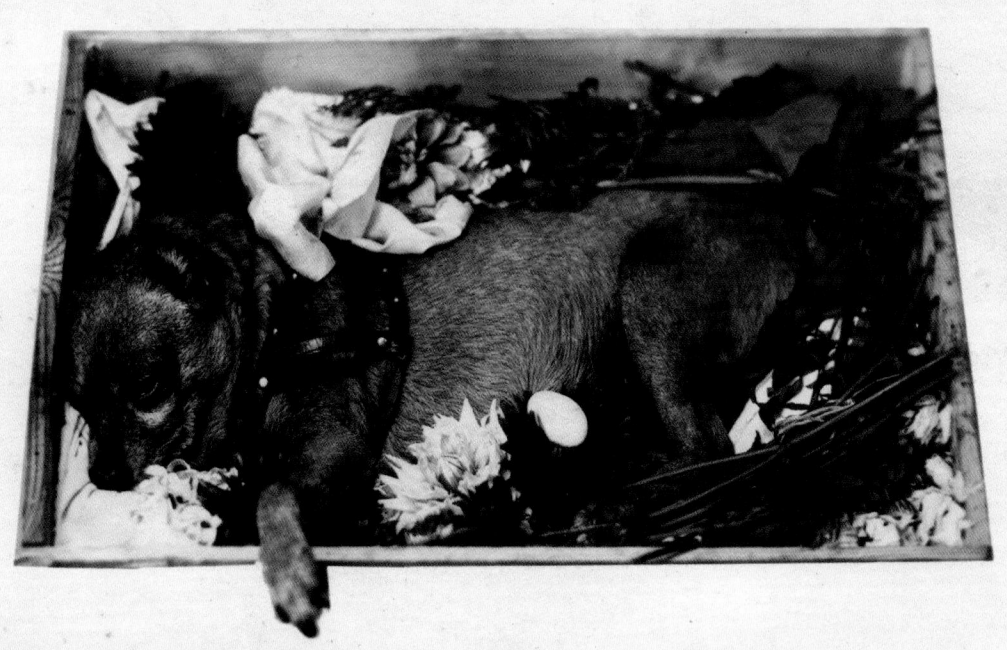

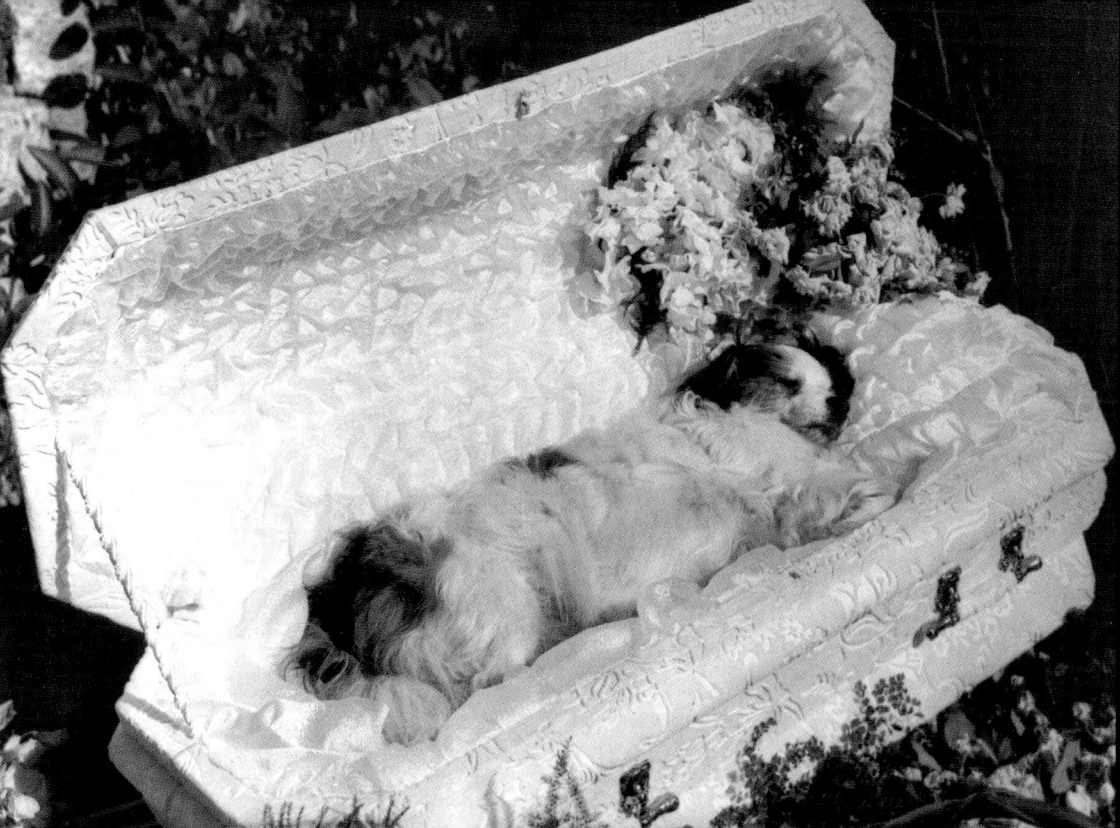

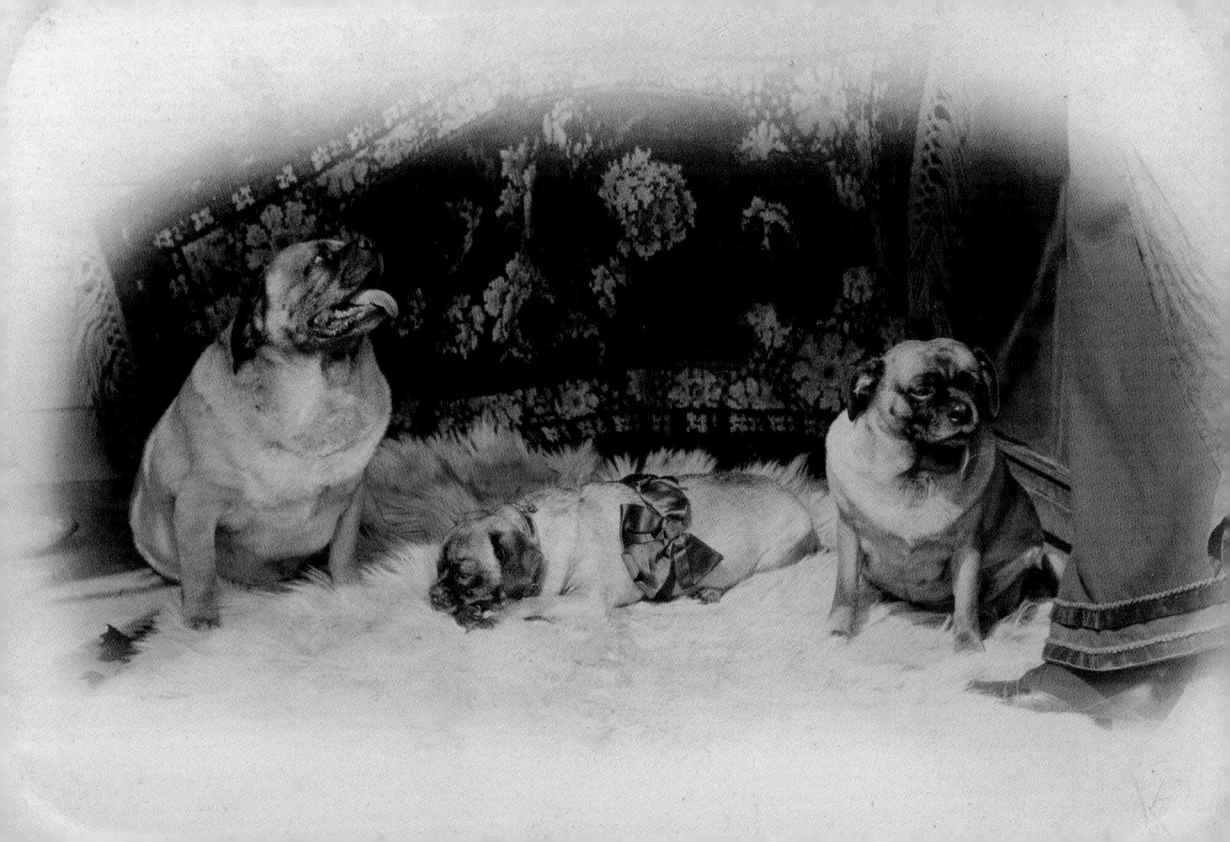

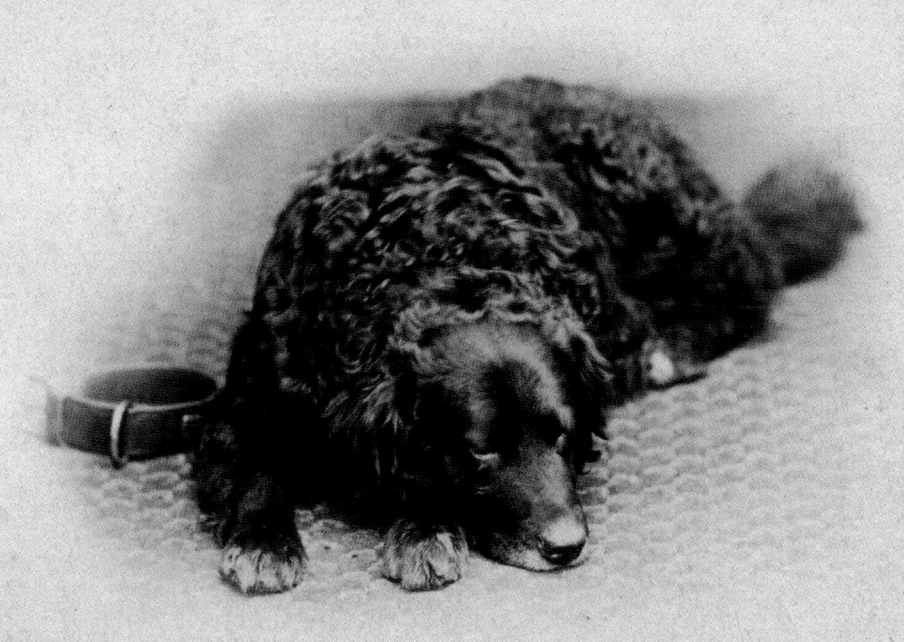

W. R. Stephenson, Lebanon, O.

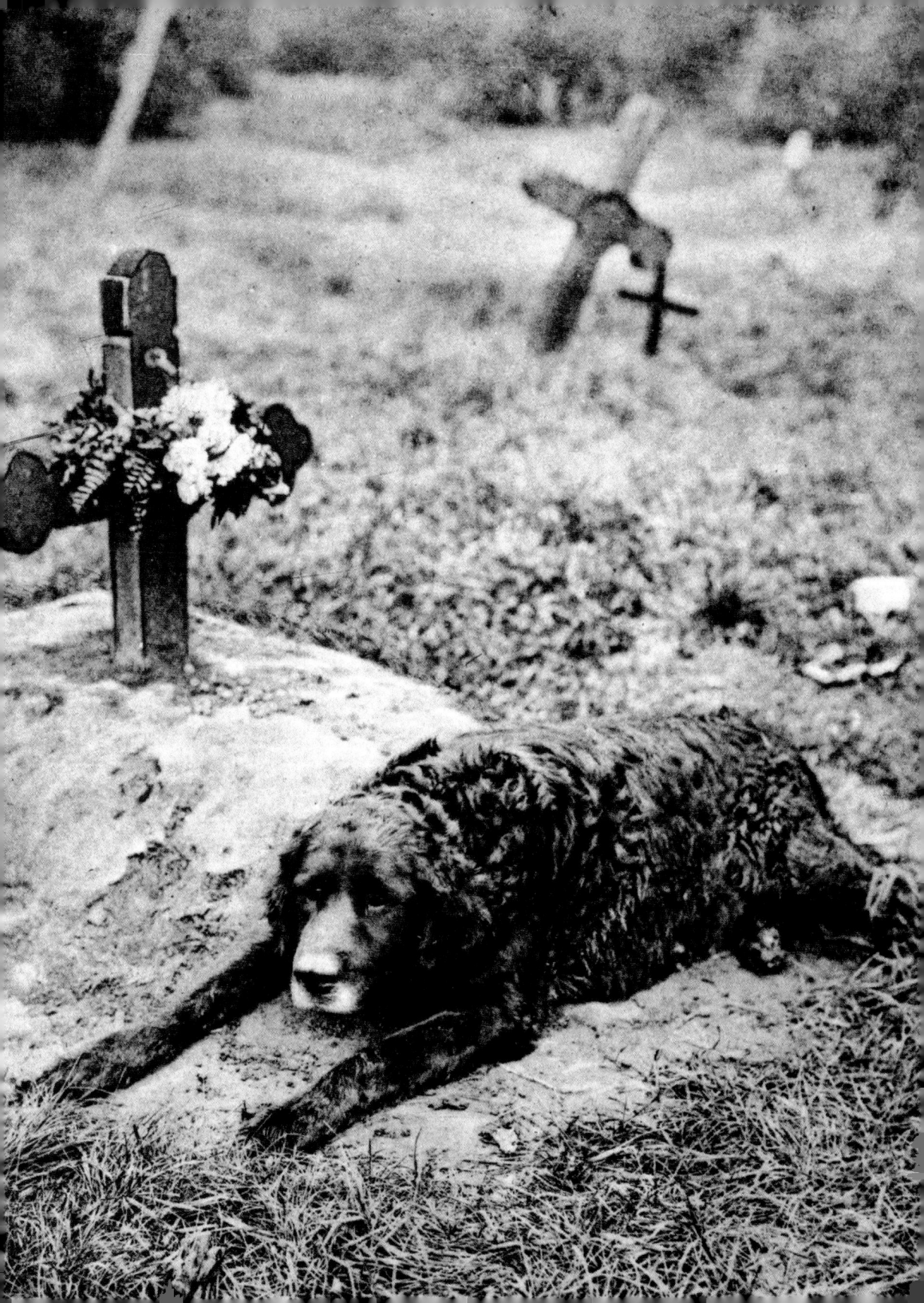

GLOSSARY *of* TERMS

ALBUMEN PRINT

Albumen printing, invented in 1850, practically defined Victorian photography; it is estimated that four out of five photographs made during the nineteenth century were albumen prints.

To produce an albumen print, paper would be precoated with a solution of albumen (strained egg white) and sodium chloride (table salt) and then dipped into a solution of silver nitrate, creating a photographically sensitive surface. After drying, light was transmitted through a glass negative onto the prepared paper, creating the image. For preservation, albumen prints would generally be adhered onto a **carte de visite** or **cabinet card.**

AMBROTYPE

An ambrotype (from the Greek *ambrotos,* meaning "immortal," and from which we get the word "ambrosia") is a photographic image made using the **wet-plate process** on a plate of glass. The finished ambrotype was actually an underexposed negative and needed to be presented on a dark surface for the image to appear (shadows are rendered transparent with this process). This was usually accomplished by backing the image with a piece of black velvet and lacquering the plate. Alternately, the ambrotype could be produced on a dark-colored glass, in which case it is known as a "ruby ambrotype."

CABINET CARD

Around 1870, advancements in technology and fashion swept the **carte de visite** away in favor of the larger cabinet card. Like its predecessor, the cabinet card was a mount for an albumen print. In comparison to the modest **carte de visite,** however, the size doubled to around 6.5 by 4.5 inches, and the cardstock became more robust. The larger format of the cabinet card gave studios an opportunity to add more decorative elements.

CARTE DE VISITE

The carte de visite (or CDV) was a small 2.5-by-4-inch card featuring a mounted albumen print on its face. These rose in popularity during the 1860s, as multiple-lens cameras came into use and as photographs became inexpensive to reproduce from negatives. Its name and size suggest the ubiquitous "calling card," which was a cornerstone of Victorian social etiquette.

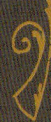

DAGUERREOTYPE

Commercially available in 1839, the daguerreotype represents the first stage of commercially available photography. It was produced by placing a copper plate faced with a layer of specially treated silver into a camera for exposure to the lighted scene or sitter. After a long exposure, the plate was next placed in a closed chamber where mercury vapors were introduced, developing the image. The signature of the daguerreotype is its reflective, metallic appearance, which demands a proper viewing angle to appear correct.

DRY-PLATE PROCESS

The major drawback of the **wet-plate process** was that all the preparation and development had to be done immediately, requiring that a darkroom/chemistry lab be set up and available wherever photography was to take place. Experiments began almost immediately after **wet-plate** photography was introduced to stabilize the chemistry; by the 1870s, "dry plates" had been perfected to a point that allowed the photographer simply to unwrap a factory-made plate and place it into a camera; development could be done at leisure. This important development of the dry-plate process opened up photography to many more amateurs and was the direct antecedent to roll film.

GELATIN SILVER PRINT

The gelatin silver print became popular in the 1880s and, with continued refinement, dominated photography well into the twentieth century. Using effectively the same concept as the simple **albumen print**, gelatin silver prints were made on prepared paper that was treated with a photo-reactive emulsion and a protective coating. Negatives were exposed directly onto this paper, creating an image. Afterward, several chemical baths were needed to halt and stabilize the image's development.

GLASS NEGATIVE

A glass negative is, as it sounds, a negative image on glass. At first, these would be created with the laborious **wet-plate process**, and by the 1880s with the **dry-plate process**. These negatives were necessary for reproducing photography with **albumen** or **gelatin silver printing**.

MAGIC LANTERN SLIDE

The magic lantern was a device used as far back as the seventeenth century to project images on walls and screens. A simple invention, it focused candlelight (and, later, electric light) behind a painted glass slide through a lens, creating a large projected image. As early as the 1840s, experimenters began replacing the painted glass with photographic plates. Magic lantern slides were produced with **albumen** on glass, as well as with the **wet-** and **dry-plate processes**.

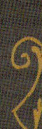

MEMENTO MORI

Latin for "remember death," the term memento mori describes a genre of art and motif
that has persisted since antiquity. Taking on different forms through time, this genre became
prominent during the European Renaissance, when artists depicted dancing skeletons and still lifes
of skulls next to earthly possessions. It can be said that all memento mori impart a simple lesson:
life is short; live a meaningful existence. The photographs contained in this book,
as literal depictions of death and artifacts of mourning, are all visceral examples of this
ancient and universal theme.

OPALTYPE

An opaltype (or opalotype) is a positive photograph that was developed on delicate
white or opalescent "milk" glass. The smooth white substrate made these images
especially suitable for embellishment with hand-coloring techniques.

PHOTOGRAPHER

Today this term refers to anyone who takes photographs, but in the middle of the nineteenth
century a practitioner was known as a photographer only if he or she was able to produce
glass negatives and then produce prints with them. This distinction explains why it was not
uncommon to see a proprietor's shingle read "Ambrotypist and Photographer," as the terms
were not considered redundant.

REAL PHOTO POSTCARD

Any sort of developed photograph on a postcard backing, or mounted
on a postcard backing, and meant to be sent through the postal service.
Postal cards, or postcards, began to be mass produced starting around the late 1880s.

R.I.P (REQUIESCAT IN PACE/REST IN PEACE)

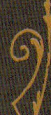
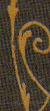

The abbreviation R.I.P. for the Latin "Requiescat in pace" (translated to English as "Rest in Peace")
is a common inscription on grave markers and various memento mori. The phrase comes from
the Catholic requiem mass, where it is repeated frequently.

STEREOSCOPE

The stereoscope is a photographic apparatus that duplicates the act of depth vision when used to view a specially produced image compatible with the device. Originally invented in the early nineteenth century for use with illustrations, it was adapted to the different forms of photography by the midcentury. The production of a stereoscopic image requires a dual-lensed camera that photographs the subject at slightly different angles (in effect duplicating the function of human eyes), resulting in a finished image that appears as two near duplicates side by side. The photograph is placed in a stereoscope viewer (the most popular of them was invented by none other than Oliver Wendell Holmes Sr.) that holds the image at a fixed distance. When viewed by the human eyes, the images merge together, creating the illusion of depth. This technique was especially popular for viewing landscapes of exotic locales, for which large "tour" sets were widely sold.

TINTYPE

A tintype (or ferrotype) is the result of the same exact **wet-plate process** used for **ambrotypes** but developed on black metal instead of glass. The "tin" was actually iron that was "japanned": coated with black enamel and baked to a glossy black in an oven. Tintyping was a relatively cheap process, and since the result was flat and durable, a print made in this manner could be kept on one's person as a beloved keepsake. With the proper lenses (on a multiple-lens camera), a photograph could be duplicated cost effectively by the tintype method.

WET-PLATE PROCESS

The wet-plate process was used to produce **tintypes**, **ambrotypes**, **magic lantern slides**, and **glass negatives**. Cumbersome and finicky, the wet-plate process was nevertheless such a magnitude of improvement over what came before it that it dominated photography from the 1850s to the 1880s.

To produce a photograph with this process, first a plate of glass or japanned iron was hand coated in a mixture of various chemical salts and collodion (nitrocellulose dissolved in ether). Then, in a darkroom, the plate was submerged in a solution of silver nitrate. Next the plate was loaded into the camera, still wet (hence the name). After exposure, the wet plate was taken back into the darkroom and developed in a solution of potassium cyanide, washed, and varnished. It is important to note that the plate was photographically sensitive only while wet, and development had to take place immediately after exposure. This meant that all preparation and development had to be done at the scene, confining most picture taking to a studio setting for all but the most intrepid photographer.

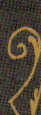

BIOGRAPHIES *of* AUTHORS

8
JACK MORD

Jack Mord is a collector of rare vintage photography and the owner and operator of The Thanatos Archive. He lives in the Pacific Northwest.
www.thanatos.net

164
JOANNA ROCHE

Joanna Roche is a poet and art historian working in Southern California. Her first book of poetry, *Tyrannical Angels and Other Love Poems*, was published in 2011.

124
ADAM ARENSON I

Adam Arenson I is assistant professor of history at the University of Texas at El Paso. He is the author of the award-winning book *The Great Heart of the Republic: St. Louis and the Cultural Civil War* (Harvard University Press, 2011) and coeditor (with Jay Gitlin and Barbara Berglund) of *Frontier Cities: Encounters at the Crossroads of Empire* (University of Pennsylvania Press, 2012). He has published several scholarly articles and has written for the *New York Times'* "Disunion" series, *The Atlantic*, the *Washington Post*, and the History News Network. He advised the Cal State Fullerton students who curated the Grand Central Art Center exhibition *Millard Sheets: The Art of Home Savings and Loan*, which was highlighted in the *OC Weekly* "Best of 2012" issue, and he appeared on a panel for their opening. He holds an A.B. in History and Literature from Harvard and a Ph.D. in History from Yale.

23
JOE SMOKE

Joe Smoke is an arts executive with the City of Los Angeles Department of Cultural Affairs. He has been teaching at colleges and universities in the Los Angeles region for more than twenty years. He is the author of numerous exhibition/catalog introductions, biographical essays, and research studies about contemporary performing, media, and visual arts in Southern California. He currently teaches courses on the history of photography and visual literacy, both of which emphasize sociological understanding of creative communications. He received a bachelor degree in art and archaeology, with a dual emphasis on American studies and the world history of photography, from Princeton University. While completing his master's degree and doctoral studies in media arts theory and practice at UCLA, Smoke became recognized in Los Angeles as a freelance graphic designer, healthcare activist, nonprofit photography center director, and social service organization fundraiser.

143
BESS LOVEJOY

Bess Lovejoy is a writer, researcher, and editor based in Seattle. She writes about death, obscure history, and sometimes art, literature, and science. She is the author of *Rest in Pieces: The Curious Fates of Famous Corpses* (Simon & Schuster, 2013).

Her writing has appeared in the *New York Times*, the *Wall Street Journal*, *Time*, *The Believer*, the *Boston Globe*, *The Stranger*, and other publications.

8
JACQUELINE ANN BUNGE

Jacqueline Ann Bunge is a curator and former museum educator currently working with the Nicholas & Lee Begovich Gallery at Cal State Fullerton, where she received her MA in Exhibition Design and Certificate in Museum Studies and completed a graduate thesis on the topic of post-mortem photography and Victorian mourning practice. She has curated exhibitions in the Orange County area, including *OsCene 2006: Contemporary Art and Culture in OC* at Laguna Art Museum, and was cocurator of the exhibition *Domestic Departures* at CSUF Nicholas & Lee Begovich Gallery. Recently, she was a contributing writer for the publications *Best Kept Secret: UCI and the Development of Contemporary Art in Southern California 1964-1971* and *Collecting California: Selections from Laguna Art Museum.*

192
ALEX JACKSON

Alex Jackson is a Southern California-born and Kansas-raised wet-plate photographer, printmaker, phenomenalist, and professional remembrancer. In 2008 he received his BFA at Cal State Fullerton. Since then he has studied the myriad forms of printmaking under several acclaimed masters of the medium, chief among them the late Patrick Merrill. Alex's prints and photographs, collected on five continents, are primarily concerned with the metaphysics and *zugzwang* of communication technology.

As a lecturer and teacher, Jackson has been invited to venerable institutions and galleries across the region, including the Bowers Museum and the Palm Springs Art Museum. An aficionado of all that is antediluvian, he prefers books over blogs and Baroque over Bauhaus, but Mahler over Mozart.

6
MARION PECK

Marion Peck is a pop surrealist painter. She was born in Manila, the Philippines, and grew up in Seattle, Washington. She received a BFA from the Rhode Island School of Design in 1985. Subsequently she studied in two different MFA programs, Syracuse University in New York and Temple University in Rome. She currently lives and works in Los Angeles with her husband, the painter Mark Ryden.

EXHIBITION AND PROGRAMMING SPONSORS
CAL STATE UNIVERSITY, FULLERTON, ART ALLIANCE,
CAL STATE UNIVERSITY, FULLERTON, DEPARTMENT OF VISUAL ARTS,
AND ASSOCIATED STUDENTS, INC.

DEAN, COLLEGE OF THE ARTS
DR. JOSEPH H. ARNOLD JR.

CHAIR, DEPARTMENT OF VISUAL ARTS
JADE JEWETT

DIRECTOR, NICHOLAS & LEE BEGOVICH GALLERY
MIKE MCGEE

GALLERY TECHNICIAN
MARTIN LORIGAN

EXHIBITION CURATOR
JACQUELINE ANN BUNGE

EXHIBITION CURATORIAL ASSISTANT
KELLY CHIDESTER

NICHOLAS & LEE BEGOVICH GALLERY OFFICE, GRADUATE ASSISTANT
WENDY SHERMAN

NICHOLAS & LEE BEGOVICH GALLERY ASSISTANTS
GABRIELA CASTILLO, MARK UPSON, & MARTHA LOURDES ROCHA

CATALOG DESIGN
WENDY PENG

PHOTOGRAPHY
COURTESY OF THE THANATOS ARCHIVE & JACK MORD

EDITOR
SUE HENGER

TYPEFACE
MRS EAVES & FF DAX COMPACT

ACKNOWLEDGMENTS

JACQUELINE ANN BUNGE AND JACK MORD
WOULD LIKE TO EXTEND A SPECIAL THANK-YOU
TO THE CONTRIBUTING WRITERS, ADAM ARENSON I,
ALEX JACKSON, BESS LOVEJOY, MARION PECK,
JOANNA ROCHE, AND JOE SMOKE.
THIS BOOK WOULD NOT HAVE BEEN POSSIBLE WITHOUT
THE HELP OF FABULOUS DESIGNER WENDY PENG,
EDITOR SUE HENGER, AND CURATORIAL ASSISTANT
KELLY CHIDESTER, WHO WORKED COUNTLESS HOURS
MAKING THIS PROJECT A SUCCESS.
LAST, BUT NOT LEAST, A SPECIAL THANK-YOU TO
MIKE MCGEE, DIRECTOR OF THE CAL STATE UNIVERSITY,
FULLERTON, NICHOLAS & LEE BEGOVICH GALLERY, AND
DANA LAMB, FORMER CHAIR OF THE CAL STATE UNIVERSITY,
FULLERTON, DEPARTMENT OF VISUAL ARTS,
WHO SUPPORTED THIS PROJECT FROM
THE VERY BEGINNING AND EVERY STEP OF THE WAY.

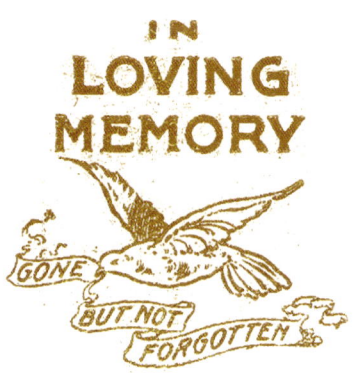